GOD'S PROVINCE

God's Province

*Evangelical Christianity, Political Thought,
and Conservatism in Alberta*

CLARK BANACK

McGill-Queen's University Press
Montreal & Kingston • London • Chicago

© McGill-Queen's University Press 2016

ISBN 978-0-7735-4714-8 (cloth)
ISBN 978-0-7735-9930-7 (ePDF)
ISBN 978-0-7735-9931-4 (ePUB)

Legal deposit second quarter 2016
Bibliothèque nationale du Québec

Printed in Canada on acid-free paper that is 100% ancient forest free (100% post-consumer recycled), processed chlorine free

This book has been published with the help of a grant from the Canadian Federation for the Humanities and Social Sciences, through the Awards to Scholarly Publications Program, using funds provided by the Social Sciences and Humanities Research Council of Canada.

McGill-Queen's University Press acknowledges the support of the Canada Council for the Arts for our publishing program. We also acknowledge the financial support of the Government of Canada through the Canada Book Fund for our publishing activities.

Library and Archives Canada Cataloguing in Publication

Banack, Clark, 1981–, author
   God's province : evangelical Christianity, political thought, and conservatism in Alberta / Clark Banack.

Includes bibliographical references and index.
Issued in print and electronic formats.
ISBN 978-0-7735-4714-8 (hardback). – ISBN 978-0-7735-9930-7 (ePDF). – ISBN 978-0-7735-9931-4 (ePUB)

   1. Christian conservatism – Alberta – History – 20th century.
2. Conservatism – Religious aspects – Christianity – History – 20th century.
3. Politicians – Religious life – Alberta – History – 20th century.
4. Christianity – Alberta – History – 20th century. 5. Religion and politics – Alberta – History – 20th century. 6. Alberta – Religion – 20th century.
7. Alberta – Intellectual life – 20th century. 8. Alberta – Politics and government – 20th century. I. Title.

FC3674.2.B35 2016   320.5209712309'045   C2016-900336-1
                                                         C2016-900337-X

This book was set by True to Type in 10.5/13 Sabon

For Kendell and Brynn. Thank you.

Contents

Tables   ix

Acknowledgments   xi

1 Introduction   3

2 Democracy and Millennialism in American Evangelical
Protestantism: The Context of Religious Interpretation in
Alberta   31

3 Religion and the Political Thought of Henry Wise Wood:
Liberal Postmillennialism and the Initial Rejection of Prairie
Socialism in Alberta   63

4 Religion and the Political Thought of William Aberhart and
Ernest Manning: Fundamentalist Premillennialism and
Anti-Socialist Sentiment in Alberta   103

5 Religion, Political Thought, and Public Policy in Contemporary
Alberta: Social Conservatism vs the Anti-Statist Religious
Perspective of Preston Manning   158

6 Conclusion   211

Appendix: Interview Participants   219

Notes   221

Bibliography   249

Index   273

Tables

2.1 Total population and American-born by province, 1911   57

2.2 Total population and American-born by province, 1931   57

2.3 Religious affiliation by percentage of population across Canada, 1911   59

2.4 Religious affiliation by percentage of population in Alberta and Saskatchewan, 1921   59

3.1 Alberta population, urban and rural, 1911–1941   94

3.2 UFA male membership, 1912–1935   94

5.1 Religiosity in Canada, by province and region, as percentage of population   171

5.2 Religious identification across Canada as percentage of population, 2001   172

Acknowledgments

This project began as a PhD dissertation at the University of British Columbia (UBC), and I would like to thank those individuals who assisted me in these early stages. My supervisor, Philip Resnick, and committee members Allan Tupper and Barbara Arneil were especially helpful in this regard, continually pushing me on a number of fronts to make this study better. Paul Burns, Gerald Baier, and external examiner Trevor Harrison also took the time to participate in the final stages and made several critical suggestions that helped mould this manuscript into its current form. I also owe thanks to those who read and commented on different sections of the dissertation, sat through my many conference presentations, or engaged in helpful conversations with me along the way. This list includes, but is not limited to, Roger Epp, Jim Farney, David Rayside, Jared Wesley, and David Goa and the broader community associated with the Chester Ronning Centre for the Study of Religion and Public Life housed at the University of Alberta's Augustana Campus. Finally, to my former professors at UBC and the good friends I made while working through graduate school: you ensured that my time at UBC was intellectually fulfilling and immensely enjoyable and that my dissertation was made better because of this.

I would also like to express my gratitude to the many librarians and archivists who were patient and helpful with the requests I made at each of the archives visited over the course of this study. The current and recently retired politicians from Alberta who took the time to speak with me, many of whom requested anonymity because of the personal nature of the topic, were also supremely open and accommodating. Preston Manning, in particular, patiently sat through two lengthy interviews and allowed me access to a number of helpful documents.

I would also like to thank those who supported the completion of this project financially. They include UBC's graduate fellowship program, the

Department of Political Science at UBC, the Department of Political Science at York University, SSHRC's Awards to Scholarly Publications Program, and Rod Kay, "Blue" Lefebvre, and the boys from the SGS Imperial Oil Rail Yard who provided an unlikely but much appreciated source of funding, as well as camaraderie, over the course of my stay in Edmonton.

This work was significantly revised while I was a member of the Department of Political Science at York University, and I would like to acknowledge the opportunity department members gave me to continue working in this field while completing this project. Dennis Pilon and Gabrielle Slowey stand out as two very helpful colleagues from York whose support over the past years is much appreciated.

I must also acknowledge the fine work of the many contributors from McGill-Queen's University Press who added so much to this project. Kyla Madden, in particular, was a consistent source of both positive energy and critical advice while shepherding me through this process with great skill and efficiency. And a significant debt of gratitude is also owed to the three individuals who reviewed this manuscript and pushed me on several fronts to make this a much better work. Of course, all errors in fact and interpretation are mine alone.

My thanks as well to the University of Toronto Press and the *Journal of Canadian Studies* for allowing me to reprint aspects of my work that initially appeared in

- Banack, Clark, "American Protestantism and the Roots of 'Populist Conservatism' in Alberta," in J. Farney and D. Rayside, eds, *Conservatism in Canada* (University of Toronto Press, 2013), 231–48.
- Banack, Clark, "Conservative Christianity, Anti-Statism and Alberta's Public Sphere: The Curious Case of Bill 44," in S. Lefebvre and L. Beaman, eds, *Religion in the Public Sphere: Canadian Case Studies* (University of Toronto Press, 2014), 257–74.
- Banack, Clark, "Evangelical Christianity and Political Thought in Alberta," *Journal of Canadian Studies* 48, no. 2 (Spring 2014): 70–99.

Finally, I offer deeply felt thanks to my parents Larry (whose incessant newspaper reading generated my interest in politics while I was still a boy) and Linda, my sister Candace, my grandmothers Luella and Olga, and my in-laws Robert and Carrie, who have consistently offered support and encouragement over the course of many years while I have chipped away at this project. To Kendell, words cannot capture the debt I have incurred for the love and patience you have demonstrated while being asked to shoulder such a heavy burden while I pursued this career. And to Brynn, thank you for bringing a smile to my face so many times each and every day.

GOD'S PROVINCE

Introduction

The political history of the Canadian Prairies is one of vigorous regional protest, non-traditional party formation, unprecedented policy experimentation, and a more general populist culture that has repeatedly emphasized the moral and intellectual capacity of the "common man." Of course, much scholarly ink has been spilled by social scientists in an attempt to analyse this unique tradition of thought and protest that saw the growth of a number of diverse political movements, each seeking to rectify real (and sometimes imagined) economic and political injustices.[1] Although such studies have added much to our understanding of the region's identity and political culture by focusing on the political and economic factors that motivated such action, there has been surprisingly little sustained attention paid to the role that religious interpretation and discourse have played within this tradition of protest and experimentation. This is so despite the fact that a large number of Prairie political leaders and their supporters were, from the earliest days of the agrarian revolt, through the periods of Co-operative Commonwealth Federation (CCF) and Social Credit dominance, and into the relatively recent appearance of the Reform Party, devout practitioners of a Protestant Christian faith. Moreover, many were quite comfortable clothing their political discourse in blatant religious language. Indeed, historian R. Douglas Francis has noted that, within the Prairies, "religious aspirations and beliefs have always formed a backdrop to revolt."[2] Yet this backdrop remains largely unexamined by students of Canadian Prairie politics and populism.

This is especially so for the province of Alberta, which has received considerable academic attention over several decades from those eager to explain the long-running dominance of political parties that emphasize an anti-statist sentiment that has consistently encouraged both a populist and decidedly anti-socialist approach to its politics. Although many of these studies have been quite insightful, they have been near-ly unanimous with respect to their silence on the influence of religion. Surely the impact of political and economic conditions related to the province's initial quasi-colonial status within Confederation, its distinct immigration patterns, and its economic reliance on particular natural resources (and the immense wealth these resources have generated) are critical to understanding Alberta's political development. However, as this book will demonstrate, religious interpretation remains an influ-ential underlying factor that also helps to explain the long-running emphasis on populist democracy and the consistent aversion to redis-tributive economics that one finds in the policies and rhetoric of the province's dominant political parties.

Of course, there is nothing novel in the suggestion that religion and politics have intermingled throughout Alberta's history. From the early days of "social gospel" influence on the agrarian movement, through the period of Social Credit rule dominated by fundamentalist Christian radio evangelists William "Bible Bill" Aberhart and Ernest Manning, and into the more contemporary era that witnessed the emergence of high-ranking evangelical Protestant politicians from Al-berta such as Preston Manning and Stockwell Day, it is clear that vocal Christians have played an important role in the province's politics. Yet the influence of religion upon Alberta's political development has been treated, in the best of cases, superficially. There exists a general aware-ness of the liberal and conservative forms of Christianity that operated within the confines of the United Farmers of Alberta (UFA) and Social Credit respectively, and much has been made, especially by journalists, of the connection between religion and contemporary social conser-vatism in Alberta. However, the precise nature of the relationship be-tween religion and the province's long-term political trajectory has not been probed with much persistence. This has resulted in a picture of Al-berta's political development that is not entirely accurate. Not only has this impeded our ability to better understand the early ideological roots of the province, it also interferes with our attempts to better understand the nature of Alberta conservatism, which, given the obvious links between long-time Alberta premier Ernest Manning, Alberta-based founder of the federal Reform Party Preston Manning, and the current incarnation of the federal Conservative Party of Canada, is now influ-encing policy debates well beyond its provincial borders.

This book seeks to rectify aspects of this blind spot by exploring the influence of religion on the political thought and action of four influ-

Introduction

ential political figures from Alberta whose contributions to the province's political development span nearly a century. In approaching the question of religion's influence in this manner, I admit to being sympathetic to Prairie historian Nelson Wiseman's lament regarding the ascendancy of a science of politics that significantly downplays the importance of history.[3] Thus, the political actors studied in this book include Henry Wise Wood, president of the UFA from 1916 until 1931; William Aberhart, founder of the Alberta Social Credit Party and premier from 1935 until 1943; Aberhart's protegé Ernest Manning, premier from 1943 until 1968; and Manning's son Preston, founder and leader of the Alberta-based federal Reform Party of Canada from 1987 until 2000. By focusing almost exclusively on the thought of these four formidable leaders as opposed to the broader population, this study is, first and foremost, a work in the area of Canadian Political Thought. Indeed, a full accounting of religion's influence on the political development of Alberta would require a careful investigation of the manner by which various faiths have interacted at the societal level. Although the focus of this study is more modest, the findings that emerge reveal something quite important concerning the general political development of Alberta as well, especially with respect to the influence of Wood, Aberhart, and the elder Manning. In fact, I follow Jared Wesley in arguing that political parties, and especially their leaders, possess a significant degree of agency with respect to shaping the political trajectories of their communities, a notion that will be expanded upon below.[4]

This is not to say that Alberta is the only province to have been influenced by religion in different and significant ways. Nor is Alberta unique in that some of its most formative leaders were religiously motivated. One needs only to glance eastward to Alberta's neighbouring Prairie provinces to find examples of key figures who made significant contributions to their respective provinces while working from a clear religious foundation. The most obvious in this regard would be Tommy Douglas, the Baptist minister turned social democrat politician who ruled Saskatchewan from 1944 to 1961, but there are certainly other examples from across the federation as well. No doubt a larger study aimed at illuminating and comparing religion's influence on the political development of various provinces is long overdue, but such a project is beyond the scope of this book. It is also obvious that Alberta has had influential leaders who were not religious, or at least as overtly religious as Wood, Aberhart, and the Mannings were. This should not come as a surprise given that, as various statistics will demonstrate throughout this book, Alberta was not an unusually religious place in the early twentieth century; nor is it today. Indeed, despite the prevalence of socially conservative arguments that emanated out of governing Progressive Conservative (PC) caucuses in the 1990s and early 2000s, contemporary Alberta is actually one of the most secular provinces in Canada. That fact does not, however, immediately rule out a significant role for religion in the province's political development.

Overall, by asking three broad questions, this study seeks to ascertain systematically the manner by which the religious interpretations of the leaders mentioned influenced their political thought and action and how this influence, in turn, affected the political development of Alberta. First, in what way were these key Alberta political leaders' personal conceptions of human nature, agency, justice, citizenship, democracy, and the proper role of the state in relation to the market shaped by religious belief and how, in turn, did this influence their political goals, strategies, and discourse? Second, given the well-documented influence of American political populist traditions in Alberta, to what extent can one trace these strains of political thought back to specific American religious movements? Third, and more generally, what pattern emerges with regard to the political thought and action of these leaders and Alberta's broader political development when we consider these questions over nearly a century of the province's history? In answering these questions, this book advances one central argument and two secondary arguments that emerge from the first.[5]

The central argument of this book is that religion has played a significant role in the political thought and action of the political leaders studied. Religion was not merely a curious affectation for such leaders but rather the key force influencing their thinking about human agency, the ends of politics, the role of the state, the nature of the economy, and the proper duties of citizens. Of course, it would be an exaggeration to suggest that religion was the *sole* influence at work for each of these individuals. Nor is such influence easily separable from the multiplicity of factors that shape the thinking of any human mind, no matter how "religious" an individual might claim to be. Speaking to this issue, Preston Manning admits that "very often 'reality' intrudes on your theology no matter what it is."[6] Even if one acknowledges this qualification, it would still be a significant oversight to ignore the clear, traceable connections that do exist between the religious outlook of the leaders studied and their political thought and action. In fact, by failing to identify these connections, certain aspects of the political thought of these leaders, and by extension certain aspects of the movements they led, have thus far been misunderstood by scholars.

Introduction

For Henry Wise Wood, long-time president of the UFA, it was a liberal and *postmillennial* Christian religious and political outlook that most influenced his thinking. The essence of this stream, which differed in important ways from the mainstream progressive social gospel message espoused by Prairie radicals Salem Bland, J.S. Woodsworth, and William Irvine, was a belief in the capacity of individual citizens to work towards building the kingdom of God on earth by way of intense ground-level participation and co-operation, as well as a corresponding focus on the high degree of individual responsibility such a process depended upon. Social Credit leaders William Aberhart and Ernest Manning, on the other hand, adhered to a more conservative *premillennial* fundamentalist Christian interpretation. Rather than seeking to build the kingdom of God on earth, this stream understood the coming kingdom or *millennium* to be in God's hands alone and was therefore most concerned with ensuring that individual citizens were granted the freedom necessary to build a personal relationship with God. Ernest Manning's son Preston similarly followed a premillennial Christian interpretation that characterized individual freedom as the chief political value.

The second argument advanced within this book is that each of the political leaders mentioned above drew from a Christian perspective that had important American evangelical Protestant roots that thereby gave it a more individualistic and populist flavour, as opposed to the British Tory flavour so familiar in much of the rest of Canada. Wood on the one hand, and Aberhart and the Mannings on the other, did subscribe to distinct streams of Christian interpretation that thereby ensured the important differences in political thought and action between them. However, the liberal postmillennial and the fundamentalist premillennial streams that they drew on respectively were imported (some directly, others more indirectly) from the broader American evangelical Protestant tradition. As will become more apparent as one proceeds through the chapters that follow, this shared heritage has ensured many points of continuity between these diverse political leaders over much of Alberta's history that have subsequently helped to place the province on a political trajectory much closer to the individualistic pattern one finds in the United States as opposed to the more Tory-stained and communal political culture of much of the rest of Canada. This book therefore represents a further contribution to the broader thesis that an important connection exists between the individualist and anti-socialist ethos present within the province and the broader influence of American streams of political thought.[7] Yet, rather than focusing on the impact of "waves" of American immigrants or on the influx of

American religious and political periodicals in the first three decades of the twentieth century, this book focuses exclusively on the religious-based thought of four influential leaders in order to understand more fully the direct connections between religious interpretation, political action, and the province's development.

In essence, both Wood and Aberhart initially imported individualistic and populist versions of Christian-based thought from American sources that were at odds with the more communal and hierarchical version associated with European Christianity. The result has been a consistent preoccupation in dominant strains of political thought in Alberta with the moral and intellectual capacity of common individuals and their corresponding right to be free. This in turn has helped to generate a strong anti-statist sentiment that fuels both a more populist approach to the province's politics as well as a more fervent desire for a limited state and an unregulated market economy. Yet, given the strong emphasis on the moral authority of the Bible in the American-based religious tradition that early Alberta leaders were drawing from and the corresponding importance that individual "rebirth" held within this religious tradition, a simultaneous demand that the individual behave responsibly can clearly be detected alongside this emphasis on the capacity of the common citizen. This unique combination has produced a populist conservatism that stands in opposition to the more hierarchical Tory conservatism that has played such an important role in the ideological development of much of the rest of Canada.

The third and final argument of this book is this: because each of these formative leaders, most especially Wood, Aberhart, and Ernest Manning, worked from a particular religious foundation when advancing specific policy propositions at key moments in the province's history, the distinct trajectory of Alberta's politics owes something to these particular religious foundations as well. There has been no shortage of scholarly attention paid to the nature of Alberta's politics over the past century given the province's unique penchant for supporting unorthodox, although ultimately conservative, leaders and parties for significant stretches of time while simultaneously shunning self-avowed collectivist parties of the left (at least until the unexpected victory by the Alberta New Democratic Party (NDP) in 2015, which will be addressed in due course). Although Alberta's political trajectory has been far more nuanced than most outsider observers realize, there exists a largely unnoticed yet vitally important connection between the respective religiously motivated political views these leaders held and the particular *anti-socialistic* nature of the movements they led, a connection that goes

Introduction

some way towards helping us understand the distinctiveness of Alberta politics. For Wood, who understood commerce to be a natural institution, the notion of centralizing more economic control in the state (so popular in radical social gospel circles at the time) went against both his evangelical populist impulses that stressed the problem-solving capacity of ordinary people and his more fundamental belief that the economic oppression of the farmer was due to the sinful behaviour of individuals operating within the market system, not to the system itself. Only large-scale individual spiritual regeneration, not government regulation, could lead to a society wherein trade became a more just enterprise conducted on the basis of Christ's moral laws. Such a position lay behind his opposition to, and frequent defeat of, the radical socialist factions within the UFA during his tenure. Aberhart and both Mannings would have agreed that, ultimately, economic oppression was rooted not in "the system" but in the depravity of humanity and that society's only hope to fully rectify the situation was a wide-scale religious conversion or rebirth at an individual level. Yet from their premillennial perspective, the notion that the widespread conversion required to build a perfected social system could be achieved was fantasy. Thus, the proper aim of the state was not to work towards such a system, as it had been for Wood, but rather to simply ensure that the freedom of the individual was protected. Alberta Social Credit's consistent and influential vilification of any form of economic collectivism that may jeopardize the freedom of the individual was built atop this intense, religiously motivated devotion to individual freedom. This was a belief that would similarly underpin much of Preston Manning's influential free-market/anti-statist political thought several decades later. Surely each of these leaders existed within a broader environment conditioned by unique structural factors that have ensured that Alberta is particularly fertile ground for arguments that favour individualism over collectivism, a point made by nearly every commentator on the province's political trajectory. But such factors should not blind us to the way in which the thought and action of formative leaders can also aid in the directing of that very trajectory.

"INTERPRETING" RELIGIOUS INTERPRETATION

The fact that social scientists have thus far failed to fully consider the impact of religion on the thought of these men, as well as its subsequent impact on Alberta's political development more generally, is not a simple instance of neglect by the handful of scholars who have focused solely on one region. In fact, religious historian Mark Noll once claimed that the relationship between religion and Canada's development is "the most important understudied story in the religious history of twentieth-century North America."[8] This Canada-wide reluctance to consider the influence of religion is most likely due to two interrelated factors. First, the strong devotion to explanations related to political economy within Canadian academia seems to have suppressed the inclination to consider religious influence as a significant motivator. Second, and more fundamentally, the overarching acceptance of the broader secularization thesis in academic circles, which predicted a decline in religious belief generally and the decoupling of religion from political allegiance specifically, has no doubt encouraged this general tendency to overlook or downplay religious influence on historical and contemporary political thought and action. Yet, as many of the central tenets of the secularization thesis begin to crumble in the face of evidence that suggests religious traditions are not in fact withering away in the face of modernity, the question of religious influence on political realities re-emerges. However, Canadian political scientists, alongside the bulk of their contemporary North American counterparts, have not pursued the question of religion's influence with much persistence.[9]

Canadian philosopher Charles Taylor has written about this phenomenon, arguing that the reluctance of contemporary academics to take religion seriously is part of an unnoticed background of social science. It is not that academics, whose penchant for atheism is far stronger than that of the average citizen, take an overt ideological stance in claiming that religion and its political influence must be in decline because religious belief is "wrong." Rather, Taylor suggests, religion tends to be overlooked as a serious factor because of "the more subtle way that one's own framework beliefs and values can constrict one's theoretical imagination."[10] Susan Harding's discussion on the general treatment of Christian fundamentalism by academics speaks well to this tendency. In short, Harding suggests that Christian fundamentalists are largely constituted by a modern academic discourse that subconsciously treats them as a cultural "other," a backward and bigoted collection of individuals subscribing to a dated system of beliefs that can only be explained by broader social, political, or economic factors. Furthermore, any researcher who seeks to challenge this modern representation of fundamentalism risks the charge of "consorting with 'them,' the opponents of modernity, progress, enlightenment, truth, and reason."[11] Such an attitude, however, grossly underestimates the signifi-

Introduction

cant explanatory power available to those who are willing to take the beliefs of the religious seriously. As religious historian George Marsden has noted, American fundamentalists

> were convinced that sincere acceptance of [the Gospel of Christ] was the key to virtue in this life and to eternal life in heaven; its rejection meant following the broad path that ended with the tortures of hell. Unless we appreciate the immense implications of a deep religious commitment to such beliefs – implications for one's own life and for attitudes towards others – we cannot appreciate the dynamics of fundamentalist thought and action.[12]

Given these "immense implications," the challenge for the modern academic, whether or not one is a believer, is therefore to resist the urge to explain "why" someone happens to be religious and instead attempt to work through the uncritical modernist presuppositions that halt meaningful inquiry towards a genuine understanding of the meaning such belief has for the religious other. It is only by moving in this direction that one can fully embrace the implications that the religious interpretations of believers have for their thought and action.

Speaking to efforts aimed at understanding such implications, the esteemed anthropologist Clifford Geertz made a vital distinction between *religion pure*, the religious individual's encounter with the supernatural or sacred, and *religion applied*, "a viewing of ordinary experience in light of what that encounter seems to reveal."[13] The experience of the supernatural or the sacred is of immense importance, but the parameters of this study are built around the notion of religion applied. That is, this book explores how certain subjects' experience of the sacred has influenced the manner by which they understood the universe, their society, and their own place and role within each. Not only did this influence provide the individual in question with a certain moral orientation and overall purpose, it further provided a conception of proper communal life. To seek to grasp the manner by which religious interpretation influences an individual's thinking about politics is simply another way of asking how the individual's experience of the sacred colours his or her thinking with respect to the appropriate way to structure life in common and how this, in turn, influences the specific public policy choices they make when engaged in the process of law-making. Clearly, to be convinced that God prefers this action to that means that indifference on the part of the true believer with respect to the action in question is impossible. And this obviously has immense implications for the believer's approach to politics.

Yet, committing to take religion seriously does not, on its own, allow the researcher to escape the rather significant methodological question related to one's quest to unearth an accurate connection between a subject's particular religious beliefs and his or her broader political thought and action. Indeed, how do researchers know they are "getting it right," so to speak, when they attempt to find a coherence between the religious beliefs and the thought and action of this other, especially when the subject exists in a different cultural or historical period than that of the researcher? Speaking to this question, Charles Taylor has famously argued that we make sense of the action of the subject in question "when there is a coherence between the actions of the agent and the meaning of his situation for him. We find his action puzzling until we find such a coherence."[14] This reference to grasping "the meaning of his situation" in this quest for coherence refers to Taylor's groundbreaking argument that the human subject is a "self-interpreting animal" that exists within in a "field of meaning" or a moral framework, and it is the continual interpretation of this field or framework that provides the individual in question with a particular moral orientation.[15] Working from this starting point, we must therefore take the self-understanding or "self-interpretation" of this moral framework of this religious other seriously and attempt to bring this understanding into our own language and understanding as an observer outside the subject's field of meaning. But, Taylor continues, the act of acquiring, grasping, and communicating these "fields of meaning" or moral frameworks on the part of the subject in question is dependent upon our linguistic capacities as humans. Thus, one's behaviour is necessarily related in an intimate way to language, something that "only exists and is maintained by a language community."[16] This, in turn, points to the importance of the communal or *intersubjective* meanings of linguistically expressed concepts in order to make sense of the verbal or written description of the reasons or meaning behind the particular action of a particular subject. Thus, our efforts to understand the actions of some individual within a particular culture "cannot escape an ultimate appeal to a common understanding of the expressions, of the 'language' involved."[17]

In other words, any attempt on the part of a researcher to grasp the meaning of a religious expression uttered by the subject in question, for example, requires a broader contextual understanding of the linguistic, cultural, and historical community from which the subject in

Introduction

question comes. Yet even this acknowledgment, as obvious as it may seem, is further complicated by the admission that the researcher's quest to unearth and subsequently depict such meaning is also bound up in the imperfect act of human interpretation. That is, researchers are also self-interpreting animals and all efforts on their part to understand the thoughts and actions of the agent is inescapably shaped to a certain degree by their own grasp of particular concepts or prejudgments or expectations with respect to the subject. Once they admit such realities, it becomes clear that any interpretation of the thought or action of another can never approach the levels of precision demanded by the natural sciences. Rather, one is forever trapped, notes Taylor, within the hermeneutic circle wherein "what we are trying to establish is a certain reading of text or expression, and what we appeal to as our grounds for this reading can only be other readings [or interpretations]."[18] Yet such a realization should not prevent efforts in this direction. Rather, we need to approach such attempts in the most appropriate manner, ensuring that the interpretation offered is as convincing as possible given such complexities.

Quentin Skinner, who wrote much on the problems associated with contemporary researchers offering interpretations of historical texts, has formulated a helpful approach towards this end. Skinner maintains that the goal of historical interpretation should be the identification of the *illocutionary meaning* of the textual passage in question, the intended force or purpose the subject or author had when making the particular utterance under investigation. Because the contemporary researcher is necessarily situated in a particular historical, cultural, and linguistic context that is different from that of the subject in question, specific techniques must be followed to ensure an accurate interpretation of the intended meaning of a written or recorded utterance by a historical other. The essential question in studying any given historical passage, Skinner notes, "is what its author, in writing at the time he did write for the audience he intended to address, could in practice have been intending to communicate by the utterance of this given utterance."[19] To grasp this intention, modern scholars must do as much as possible to bracket their own expectations and conceptual understandings throughout the process of interpretation. Thus, modern scholars must take great care to properly explicate the intellectual and social context in which the subject found him- or herself. This is necessary to ensure that the scholar's interpretation of what the subject intended to mean with his or her words is, in fact, something the subject *could have* meant given the historical and cultural period in which the subject was situated. Andrew Davison has since summarized three particular aspects of the context Skinner identifies as being crucial to grasping the potential intention of the author in question as follows:

1. Intersubjective Context: The prevailing linguistic, ideological or intellectual assumptions, conventions or vocabulary that help to make the "best sense" of the speech act of the subject.
2. Social Context: The social and political context that the subject finds him or herself in.
3. Personal Biography: The subject's personal history that reveals the potential framework of meaning they operate within and its relation to the intersubjective context.[20]

It is by way of careful attention to each of these three aspects of the context that the subject operates within that the scholar builds a "framework for helping to decide what conventionally recognizable meanings, in a society of *that* kind, it might in principle have been possible for someone to have intended to communicate."[21] In this way, the context is treated as vitally important but not wholly determinant. The author in question retains an agency that must be respected, but any hope to grasp the author's intentions requires rigorous contextual study.

The philosophical ruminations on the nature of the human subject by Taylor and the specific method of interpreting the meaning of the utterances issued by the subject identified by Skinner seem particularly appropriate for this research project. Not only does an understanding of the relationship between the religious beliefs and the political thought of Henry Wise Wood, William Aberhart, and Ernest Manning require the interpretation of historical documents, but the focus on religious belief presents a unique challenge given what R. Scott Appleby has called the "ambivalence of the sacred," the notion that the religious understanding of the subject is filtered through his or her faculties of perception and then interpreted though his or her own culturally and historically bound conceptions of the sacred. To acknowledge such a notion is to acknowledge that understanding the behaviour of religiously motivated individuals is rather difficult without significant understanding of both their personal biography and the wider contextual setting from which they emerge.[22] Similarly, the relatively high levels of disdain within the academy for the version of Christian fundamentalism adhered to by Aberhart and Ernest Manning pose a problem related to scholarly interpretation. In fact, much

Introduction

of the contemporary misunderstanding of the relationship between the religious belief and political thought of Aberhart in particular may be due to the tinge of anti-fundamentalism sentiment at work (consciously or otherwise) in the minds of scholars who have studied the Alberta Social Credit movement.

Rather than offering an implicit judgment on the "correctness" of the religious belief of these historical figures, this study approaches this belief with a seriousness that is not often granted by academics. Because this project comprises both a historical and a more contemporary focus, the data upon which its conclusions are based have been generated in two distinct ways. The historical section considers the religious beliefs of Wood, Aberhart, and Ernest Manning and the manner by which these beliefs informed their political thought and, subsequently, their political actions. The primary research conducted for this section involved a careful examination of a significant collection of historical documents that recorded each of these individuals' thoughts on their religious beliefs and their broader political implications. These documents included a wide variety of writings, speeches, letters, personal notebooks, radio addresses, government documents, and interviews by the leaders in question housed in a variety of archives throughout Alberta. In addition, I explored popular periodicals such as the *Grain Growers' Guide*, the *Nutcracker*, the *Alberta Non-Partisan*, the *Western Independent*, the *UFA*, and the *Social Credit Chronicle*, as well as publications produced by the Calgary Prophetic Bible Institute, not only for writings by the authors in question (of which there were many) but also so I might gather as much historical and linguistic context as possible. Indeed, given Skinner's contention that we must "surround the particular statement of belief in which we are interested with an intellectual context that serves to lend adequate support to it," significant contextual research was undertaken. In addition to reading such periodicals, archived letters, speeches, and commentaries authored by the colleagues or family members of these leaders, I also thoroughly explored the relevant secondary literature that focused on these men, the movements they led, and the religious and political environments from which they emerged. This last point proved to be especially important. Although many scholars have rightly alluded to the political or economic context surrounding the UFA and Social Credit governments in addition to the personal biographies of the political leaders in question in their attempts to make sense of their political thought, there has been a significant gap in our grasp of the broader intellectual and religious context within which such leaders found themselves. Thus, in an effort to provide an appropriate intellectual framework by which one can judge the nature of the religious belief of these leaders and make sense of their recorded pronouncements on such, this project includes an important prefatory chapter (Chapter 2) that chronicles the relevant intellectual development of various religious strands within American evangelical Protestantism. It is in understanding the conceptual meanings present in this historical movement that one is best positioned to interpret and understand the utterances of the Alberta political leaders under study.

The contemporary dimension of this project, which explores the influence of religion on the political thought of Preston Manning and other, lesser-known, religiously motivated social conservatives such as Ted Byfield, similarly relies upon various speeches, writings, and journals authored by the subjects in question. Manning's personal journals, housed at the University of Calgary Archives and thus far largely unavailable to researchers, were of significant importance to this study. In addition, however, this section relies much more heavily on one-on-one, in-depth, semi-structured interviews. Just as great care must be taken to ensure that researchers approach the meaning of concepts and descriptions of a different historical period with the proper contextual awareness, researchers must also seek to avoid substituting their own expectations and conceptual understandings for the responses of the interview subject. Therefore, the interviews conducted for this study were flexible, slightly directed conversations wherein the subjects were permitted space to explore and further reflect upon their ideas and responses. The specific nature of the questions posed during the interviews was also informed by a careful study of the intellectual and cultural context of the subjects and their religious background. Finally, an explicit reflexivity on the part of the researcher was consistently adhered to during the interviews as well as throughout the data-analysis stage. As someone familiar with a version of the Christianity that is often more progressive and flexible than that of many of the key participants in this study, it was a challenge at times to ensure that my personal response to certain religious-based social views offered by participants within historical texts or contemporary interviews did not impede my ability to grasp the meaning that their religious interpretation had for them. But the goal remained to overcome the potential for ascribing incorrect meaning to the thought or action of the subject.

Introduction

ALBERTA'S POLITICAL DEVELOPMENT
AND THE ROLE PLAYED BY STRONG LEADERS

Alberta is often depicted as a clear anomaly among Canadian provinces, yet the politics of the province are more nuanced than often assumed, a fact highlighted by the unexpected victory of the NDP in 2015. Of course, on the surface, the province's political track record seems to leave little doubt that it is Canada's most conservative province. Until 2015, Alberta citizens elected an unbroken string of conservative-leaning provincial administrations since 1935 (if not before, depending on how one qualifies the UFA). The province's federal constituencies have also been consistently dominated by conservative parties, including a period in the 1990s wherein it served as the unofficial home base for the hard-right federal Reform Party. In addition, the province's PC government, which ruled the province from 1971 to 2015, displayed blatant hesitation around progressive social issues, especially those pertaining to homosexual rights, in the 1990s and 2000s, which was unparalleled in Canada. Finally, the first legitimate challenge in decades to the governing PCs' grip on power (prior to the aforementioned surprising NDP victory) was found in the Wildrose, a party that lived even further to the right. No doubt, Alberta's conservatism appears to run deep.

Yet, with only a little digging, a more complex picture of Alberta's politics emerges. As Peter McCormick long ago demonstrated, the single-member plurality electoral system has severely distorted the legislative seat counts relative to the popular vote in Alberta. For instance, between 1905 and 1979, the party that won office received, on average, 51 per cent of the vote, a proportion that places Alberta side by side other Canadian provinces.[23] Social Credit, which seemingly ruled nearly uncontested for thirty-six years, received at least 85 per cent of the seats in the legislature in seven of nine elections while averaging only 52 per cent of the popular vote.[24] More recently, the PCs won 87 per cent of the seats with roughly 53 per cent of the popular vote in 2008 and 70 per cent of the seats with only 44 per cent of the popular vote in 2012. In other words, although specific seat counts give the impression of a single-minded electorate, nearly half of Albertans have consistently voted *against* the governing party. In addition, pundits who bemoan long stretches of one-party rule often fail to note the significant differences in approach and policy between the somewhat interventionist Aberhart and the firmly free-market approach of his Social

Credit successor Manning, or the wide gulf between the activist administrations of PC leader Peter Lougheed (1971–85) and the neo-liberal approach of Ralph Klein's PCs (1992–2006). Recent research that highlights the high per capita spending record of both Social Credit and PC provincial governments – or the relatively moderate political views on both moral and fiscal issues held by the majority of contemporary Albertans – further complicates the notion of Alberta being an unabashedly conservative province. Work by David Stewart and Anthony Sayers has been especially illustrative on this point. Building on previous studies that have noted the contemporary population's general support for high levels of government spending, maintaining the public health-care system, and increasing royalty rates on oil and gas companies, they conducted a 2008 survey that revealed that a majority of Albertans support a variety of government actions to address issues related to poverty and the environment.[25] Given such data, the NDP's 2015 victory should perhaps not have been as surprising after all.

However, despite these qualifications, it remains undeniable that, for at least eighty years, political parties on the left in the province utterly failed to gain traction. Indeed, prior to 2015, the CCF and its successor the NDP have averaged only 13.9 per cent of the popular vote since 1940, a remarkably poor showing given that the CCF/NDP won twelve of sixteen elections in neighbouring Saskatchewan between 1944 and 2003, nearly mirroring the dominance enjoyed by conservative parties in Alberta.[26] Of course, there have certainly been unique points in Alberta's history prior to 2015 wherein support for the CCF or NDP spiked (24.9 per cent of the popular vote in 1944, 29.2 in 1986, and 26.3 in 1989, for example), but on the whole, Albertans consistently rejected the state-led economic collectivism or redistributive politics espoused by the CCF or NDP in favour of the largely pro-market economic rhetoric of centrist or right-leaning administrations. Indeed, as Jared Wesley has clearly demonstrated, both Alberta Social Credit and the Alberta PCs consistently preached a "freedom-based narrative" structured around populist or anti-establishment themes, western alienation, and a conservative individualism that emphasizes "personal responsibility, free enterprise, private-sector development, entrepreneurship, a strong work ethic, the evils of socialism, and the protection of individual rights and liberties."[27] It is the eighty years of dominance by parties that utilized this rhetoric and, perhaps more importantly, the corresponding rejection of self-avowed collectivist parties during that near century that sets Alberta apart not only from Saskatchewan but from all of the remaining Canadian provinces.

Introduction

Classic explanations of this phenomenon tend to point to the initial socio-economic conditions of the province, including its so-called homogeneous class composition and quasi-colonial status,[28] its unique inheritance of American agrarian settlers,[29] its early religious makeup,[30] and its economic reliance on specific resource staples and the conservative economic pressures such reliance placed upon governments.[31] Overall economic prosperity and the corresponding ability of conservative governments to spend generously while maintaining relatively low tax rates also impeded the growth of left-leaning parties. Speaking to the impressive electoral success enjoyed by Social Credit, Alvin Finkel introduced a helpful distinction between "rich government" and "big government" that illustrates this reality well. Premier Manning's penchant for high per capita spending on health, education, and infrastructure (made possible by impressive resource royalties) while simultaneously vilifying socialism and avoiding high tax rates in the 1950s and 1960s created a scenario, argues Finkel, in which ordinary Albertans came to expect the benefits of "rich government" while being ideologically groomed to oppose the so-called oppressive nature of a redistributive "big government" and its high levels of taxation.[32] Of course, it is not difficult to see the persistence of such sentiment in contemporary Alberta politics (at least prior to 2015) wherein per capita government expenditures consistently rank well above those of most other provinces while taxes remain low and left-leaning parties that advocate policies aimed at economic redistribution are generally unpopular.

In addition to such structural explanations, low voter turnout, especially among a largely depoliticized working class, electoral financing laws that favoured the deep-pocketed PCs, numerous follies on the part of opposition parties, as well as the PC's general capacity to adapt to changing economic circumstances and select distinct leaders who pursued objectives more appropriate to the times, further fortified the Alberta legislature against high numbers of left-leaning representatives. Speaking to the dominance of the PCs in particular, Stewart and Sayers have pointed towards specific mechanisms utilized by the party, such as leader-centred politics and especially the use of a particular brand of plebiscitary voting to select party leaders who have allowed them "to convince voters of the inevitability of its success," thereby generating something akin to "a cultural hegemony that robs voters of the capacity to imagine an alternative."[33] In other words, broad structural factors may have helped set Alberta politics on a particular path, but one cannot discount the role played by parties with respect to their ongoing success as well.

Clearly, it would be inconceivable to offer any explanation of Alberta's long-time aversion to collectivist parties without alluding to such factors, but this book argues that the political thought and action of formidable leaders within Alberta's history have also helped to shape the province's political development, most especially its penchant for populist politics and its consistent rejection of left-leaning parties. In fact, this book will make the broad argument that these two particular characteristics are actually two sides to a single "individualist" coin and are related in an intimate way to the strong individualist ethos associated with the versions of Christianity that motivated the political leaders included in this study. Of course, suggesting that political leaders, especially strong leaders, can influence the trajectory of a society's political development raises the long-running debate between human agency and societal structure. Ever since Herbert Spencer authored his influential rebuttal of Thomas Carlyle's "Great Man Theory," suggesting that great leaders were not the drivers of history but rather the products of society, most theories of societal development have tended to favour structural explanations rather than the influence of leaders. Recently, however, a more nuanced understanding of the "agency vs structure" debate has emerged that does allows for a more active and influential role for leaders. Alan Cairns's provocative thesis with respect to provincial governments' "capacity to mould their environment in accordance with their own governmental purposes" was an important initial shot across the bow of those solely focused on societal factors in the late 1970s.[34] Leslie Pal, noting the dearth of focus on the role played by leaders in the policy process, followed Cairns with the rather intuitive argument that leaders "are not merely amusing themselves with empty rituals; they are trying to shape events. While the results vary, their efforts must invariably have some effect." At an epistemological level, Pal continues, "it seems highly implausible that the entire policy process can be explained without recourse to human agency."[35] Wiseman, an early proponent of utilizing various structural factors to explain political outcomes on the Canadian Prairies, has softened his stance in this direction. Noting the "interconnected and interwoven circular relationship between agency – what people and parties say and do – and structure," he writes:

> [P]rovincial governments and the parties and leaders who command them are not merely epiphenomena of their societies or echoes of their cultures. Once formed, governments use their jurisdictional supremacy and their institutional infrastructures ... to

affirm their autonomy, assert their authority, and embed their status in the minds of the populace. At the same time, to be successful, political parties must advantageously lever the distinctive symbols and characteristic vocabularies of their provinces.[36]

Laycock's classic study of Canadian Prairie populism similarly stressed that "[a]utonomy must be granted to cultural factors and social actors in explanations of ideologies developing and interacting in particular settings."[37]

Given the "interwoven circular relationships" between agency and structure, it is not possible to demonstrate the influence of political leaders upon a society's political development with the precision of certain quantitative models and neither are the causal arrows between the actions of leaders and the broader political culture of a society always perfectly clear. Yet this ambiguity around the potential influence of leaders is no reason to avoid exploring the potential connection between their political thought and action and the broader development of their society. Indeed, leadership scholars Joseph Masciulli, Mikhail A. Molchanov, and W. Andy Knight suggest that it is possible to draw a distinction between successful or "strong" leaders, "those who have demonstrated their ability to move their society tangibly in the direction that seemed clearly supportive of their suggested 'grand design,'" and unsuccessful leaders, "those whose efforts to move their society in the direction of their choosing have backfired or brought about results clearly destructive of their propagated strategic vision." In making this distinction, however, they are also careful to note that "leadership is a part of multicausal social processes that bring about concrete political outcomes."[38] In fact, they continue, "the actual 'supply' of leadership is driven by a pre-existing societal 'demand' which the political entrepreneurship of a would-be leader seeks to satisfy," a situation that clearly speaks to the importance of structure. Often, however, "there is more than one way to satisfy that demand, or to create an impression that the problem can be resolved."[39] This is a crucial point when considering the influence possessed by leaders. Clearly context matters (and it often goes a long way in explaining why a certain leader has emerged in any given period), but there are moments when the decisions made by such leaders can and do influence the social and political trajectory of the community they are a part of. The challenge is to identify such moments and demonstrate how and why a particular leader helped lead his or her community along path X rather than path Y. After demonstrating the manner by which each of the leaders in this study was strongly motivated by a particular religious interpretation, this book, as its secondary goal, identifies those points where the leaders in question chose path X and therefore helped to steer Alberta's political development in a particular direction.

Daring to suggest that leaders matter when one considers the political trajectory of a community seems especially important within the context of Alberta where, as McCormick has argued, the provincial electorate's lack of a stable, deep-seated partisan affiliation has meant that the leader rather than the party or ideology often becomes the focal point of the province's politics.[40] Indeed, when seeking to understand the success of certain parties at particular moments in Alberta's history, a whole host of scholars have commented on the significant role played by leaders. Henry Wise Wood's biographer wrote at length about the popularity and influence of the president of the UFA, dubbing him the "uncrowned king of Alberta."[41] John Irving's classic investigation into the rise of Social Credit in Alberta took pains to stress the role played by William Aberhart, concluding that "it is doubtful if the movement would have won political power in Alberta without his leadership."[42] John Barr's chronicle of the Social Credit years under the leadership of Ernest Manning notes that the premier "stood over the public life of Alberta like a colossus." In fact, "that anyone else could or should be premier ... was, for many voters, unthinkable."[43] Leslie Pal, Edward Bell, and David Steward and Keith Archer have similarly stressed the vital role played by leaders, especially Peter Lougheed and Ralph Klein, in their explorations of the long-running success of the PC party in Alberta.[44] Wesley has gone even further, demonstrating the role leaders play not simply in popularizing their respective parties amongst the electorate but, more importantly, in shaping and perpetuating their communities' political culture through the ongoing use of "political codes" within party manifestos and campaign literature, a notion I return to when discussing the influence of Aberhart and Manning in Chapter 4.[45]

Such work has undoubtedly gone a long way towards explaining the success of the Social Credit and PC parties throughout Alberta's history, in addition to the persistence of a particular populist and anti-socialistic political culture in the province. This book seeks to build on this line of scholarship and demonstrate the manner by which Wood, Aberhart, and Ernest Manning, strongly motivated by a religious interpretation, helped to steer the province in this populist and anti-socialistic direction. Surely these leaders existed within a broader culture conditioned by structural factors, and the ongoing public support they enjoyed says

Introduction

something important about Alberta's pre-existing political culture, including the pervasive influence of what Goa has labelled a "Great Plains evangelicalism" that blossomed in the province in the early and mid-1900s.[46] Yet there remains a vitally important connection between the respective religious views these leaders held and both their populist approach to politics and the particular anti-socialistic public policies they favoured that has thus far gone largely unacknowledged.

Despite the existence of a strong left-leaning contingent in Alberta between the world wars, both Wood and Aberhart were successful in convincing the bulk of citizens to reject traditional state-led collectivism in times of economic uncertainty. Instead, Wood initially succeeded in encouraging Albertans to embrace voluntary rather than mandatory co-operatives, while Aberhart eventually persuaded a large segment of the population' to support his plan for a government-initiated credit provision program as opposed to the more radical overhaul of the economic system demanded by Prairie socialists. The distinction between these particular solutions and more traditional state-led collectivist schemes was somewhat subtle, resulting in many left-leaning Albertans avidly supporting first the UFA and eventually Social Credit rather than the CCF.[47] Indeed, Myron Johnson has argued that the failure of the CCF in Alberta was not wholly the result of structural factors but was rather more "an accident of history" owing to the large swath of potential CCF supporters who embraced the promises of Aberhart in the throes of the Depression, thereby impeding the growth of a traditional left-wing party at a crucial time.[48] Yet the respective religious interpretations that motivated both Wood and Aberhart in this regard have not yet been clearly explicated.

For Wood, it was a liberal and postmillennial Christian outlook that helped to encourage both the optimistic and intensely deliberative approach to politics found within the UFA, as well as the group's initial preference for the use of voluntary co-operatives and other "self-help" mechanisms rather than government-sanctioned socialist schemes when attempting to enhance its economic well-being. For Aberhart, as well as his protegé Manning, it was the conservative premillennial Christian interpretation and the intense dedication to individual freedom that it inspired that sat at the foundation of their stridently anti-socialist and non-deliberative populist party that soundly defeated the UFA in 1935 and would help to mould Alberta's unique political culture in opposition to redistributive economics over a remarkable thirty-six-year stretch in power. In fact, Manning's twenty-five-year reign as premier delivered a significant blow to the development of a successful left-leaning alternative in the province. Obviously, general societal wealth and high per capita government spending with relatively low taxes undercut potential support for left-leaning alternatives, but Manning's decades-long blatant vilification of the socialism associated with the CCF, in both government speeches and publications, as well as over the air of his popular Christian radio program, influenced the political sentiments of large swaths of the Alberta citizenry as well.[49] Indeed, it seems plausible that a good deal of contemporary disdain for left-wing parties in Alberta, despite the personal economic views among the citizenry that are less individualistic and anti-statist than often assumed, can be traced back to the impact this process of vilification, led by Manning, had on Alberta's general anti-socialist political culture, at least until very recently.

Although he was not nearly as influential on the overall trajectory of Alberta politics as Wood, Aberhart, and Manning, it was Alberta-based federal Reform Party leader Preston Manning (the fourth central figure in this study), with his call to significantly rein in government spending in the late 1980s and early 1990, who helped to shift the public mood in the province. This change in mood ultimately led to the drastic cuts in the size and scope of Alberta's provincial government unleashed by Ralph Klein's PCs in the mid-1990s. In a testament to the sudden popularity of this fiscally conservative approach in contemporary Alberta on the heels of many years of more interventionist government on the part of Lougheed's PCs, Klein's government was able to maintain, and perhaps even enhance, its support among the electorate after instituting this neo-liberal attack on public expenditures.[50] Importantly, Preston Manning's motivation in this regard was – like Wood's interest in voluntary co-operatives, Aberhart's in social credit economics, and Ernest Manning's vilification of socialism – derived squarely from his particular religious perspective. Thus, there emerges a clear link between the religiously inspired political thought of these leaders, the political rhetoric and public policy decisions they favoured, and the more general trajectory of Alberta politics.

Of course, Wood, Aberhart, and the Mannings were surely not the only influential leaders in the province's history. Indeed, any study aimed at providing a full accounting of Alberta's political trajectory would make a grave error in overlooking the contributions of two more secular leaders: Peter Lougheed, recently voted Canada's greatest premier of the past forty years, and Ralph Klein.[51] Yet this book does not attempt to provide such an account. Rather, the goal is to demonstrate, first, how religion influenced the political thinking of the four indi-

Introduction

viduals under study and, second, the manner by which the religiously motivated political thought and action of these leaders helped to shape Alberta's trajectory in unique ways. Clearly, this is not the only factor that has contributed to this trajectory, and neither is Alberta alone as a province that has been influenced by religiously motivated political thought. However, a deeper engagement with the additional factors that have shaped Alberta's trajectory, outside what has been stated above, is beyond the scope of this book. Similarly, although comparative points emerge throughout the analysis, especially with respect to the differences between traditional Ontario-based Tory Protestantism and that which emerged on the Prairies or the differing religious strains that motivated political leaders in Saskatchewan and Manitoba as opposed to Alberta, a more detailed and systematic comparison is beyond the scope of this study.

OVERVIEW OF THE BOOK

While the arguments listed in the opening paragraphs of this book promise to reveal an important aspect of Alberta's unique political trajectory, it is also useful to briefly explain what this project is not. In short, this is not a history of Alberta, or of its politics, or even of its religious practices. Much good work on these topics already exists, and instead the precise focus of this particular study is solely the political thought of a handful of key political figures from Alberta's history and their broader influence on the province's political development. Beyond providing a bit of historical context to properly situate each of these political figures and their political actions, I have dedicated little room to expanding on the vast number of important events that have influenced Alberta in important ways. Nor do I expand on the influence of other key leaders such as Lougheed or Klein, two individuals who, working from a decidedly less overt religious position, undoubtedly left their mark on the province. Furthermore, this study is neither a systematic dissection of the composition of each political party mentioned nor a detailed analysis of their respective rise and fall. Again, much good academic work has already been completed on such themes. Finally, this study is not intended to be a complete explication of Alberta's particular political culture.[52] Although the study refers to important foundations of the province's political culture (as well as to certain polls and studies that reveal aspects of this political culture), it is not meant to be read as a comprehensive account of Alberta's political culture. Similarly, because the study focuses on the political thought of only a few key political figures, it does not directly attempt to identify any precise patterns with respect to the role of religion in the general public's political preferences, although elements of this phenomenon emerge at points in the book, especially within sections of Chapters 2 and 5.

Now that I have outlined what this project is not, it is surely appropriate that I offer a brief outline of the study itself, which proceeds as follows. Given the importance of communal or *intersubjective* meanings and intellectual developments within the communities relevant to the subjects in question, Chapter 2 provides the appropriate religious and intellectual context one needs to properly interpret the religious-based political thought of Wood and Aberhart, two historical figures who were strongly influenced by the American evangelical Protestant tradition. Thus, this chapter provides a significantly abridged history of this religious tradition, with a particular focus on its democratic and populist tendencies as well as its persistent fascination with Christian *millennial* ideas, two elements that would play hugely influential roles in the political thought of both Wood and Aberhart and subsequently would help to place Alberta on a particular political path. Chapter 2 also offers a brief comparison between this American religious tradition and the more British religious tradition that played such a significant role in the cultural and political development of much of central and eastern Canada, outside Quebec. The chapter concludes with some general comments on the migratory and ideological connections between America and Alberta as well as on the general religious and cultural landscape of the province in the early and mid-twentieth century and the manner by which this context influenced its early politics and leaders.

Having established the necessary intellectual and religious context, Chapter 3 explores the political thought of Wood, the long-time president and unofficial philosopher of the UFA. It is here one finds the liberal, post-millennial stream of religious-based political thought mentioned above. Although Wood drew from his American evangelical Protestant background by lamenting the "fallen" nature of man and the need for individuals to seek "regeneration," he harnessed this focus on individual piety to a belief in "social regeneration" wherein "reborn" citizens could build a perfectly democratic and just society, a true "Kingdom of Heaven on earth," through meaningful political participation and co-operation. After considering the implications of this religious-based strain of political thought in detail, the chapter highlights the differences between the

Introduction   27

thought of Wood and the broader social gospel movement present
within the Prairies before concluding with an exploration of the concrete
connections between the thought of Wood and the political direction
embarked upon by the UFA both under Wood's watch and upon his retirement, at which point the organization swung sharply to the left before quickly fading from the political landscape.

Chapter 4 turns to the Alberta Social Credit League, which governed
Alberta from 1935 until 1971, and the political thought of its two most
important leaders, William Aberhart and Ernest Manning. It is within
the thought of these two men that one finds the fundamentalist, premillennial stream of religious-based political thought that largely overtook the postmillennial strand espoused by Wood in Alberta. In
rejecting the notion of building a "Kingdom of Heaven" on earth, Aberhart and Manning presented a dramatically different understanding of
the state, one that focused on the importance of ensuring individual
freedom, a focus that ultimately produced an intense vilification of socialism on the part of Social Credit. In addition, the intense pressure on
citizens to participate politically in a meaningful and deliberative way
that had been stressed by the UFA was abandoned by Social Credit and
replaced by a call for citizens to state their "preferences" and allow
benevolent politicians and their "experts" to install programs that
would ensure that individual freedom would be protected as far as possible. This shift, which grew in part out of the distinction between
"post-" and "pre-" millennial religious interpretations, represented both
the beginning of a blatant anti-statism and the end of a more radical
and participatory politics in Alberta.

Chapter 5, which leaps ahead to the politics of contemporary Alberta, is substantially different in style and content than the previous two
chapters. Although the focus of the book thus far has been a comparison of the postmillennial and premillennial streams present within the
UFA and Social Credit respectfully, this chapter first pauses to consider
the influence of a third stream of religious thought that has surfaced in
contemporary Alberta politics: a socially conservative sentiment most
concerned with the declining influence of Christian morality in society. This exploration begins with a brief consideration of the religiously
motivated thought of Ted Byfield, a hugely influential socially conservative journalist in Alberta in the 1980s and 1990s. The chapter then
considers the role played by this sentiment within the contemporary Alberta PC party, which essentially waged a fifteen-year battle against the
advancement of homosexual rights in the 1990s and early 2000s. Al-

though this particular stream tends to receive the most attention from contemporary observers (and is often assumed to be the product of the long reign of fundamentalist Christians Aberhart and Manning[53]), an important underlying argument that runs through this book is that religious-based social conservatism has not influenced the overall direction of Alberta politics anywhere near to the extent that postmillennial or premillennial religious streams of thought have. As this chapter demonstrates, neither Alberta in general nor the PC party in particular was dominated by religious conservatives. Rather, a set of unique electoral factors, mostly related to the overrepresentation of rural Alberta in the PC caucus, led to a situation wherein socially conservative views were amplified in an exaggerated manner.

Chapter 5 then shifts its focus to a second strand of religiously motivated political thought, one that has been largely overlooked by commentators but one, I argue, that has been far more influential than social conservatism with respect to the direction of contemporary Alberta politics. This is the thought of Preston Manning, founder and long-time leader of the federal Reform Party of Canada. Obviously, Manning was a federal rather than provincial politician and the bulk of his legacy can be connected to the ideology of the current Conservative Party of Canada. That is not to say, however, that he did not indirectly influence Alberta politics as well. In fact, several scholars have noted the significant pressure placed on the provincial PCs in the late 1980s and early 1990s with respect to the importance of deficit reduction by the strong anti-statist message articulated by Manning in his stump speeches throughout Alberta.[54] What scholars have largely overlooked, however, was the way in which this anti-statism was connected to his religious outlook. Largely adhering to the religious interpretation espoused by his father, Ernest, Preston Manning understood the ills of contemporary society as having grown because of our distance from God and that only an individual effort on the part of the citizen, perhaps aided by the church, to re-establish a relationship with God could make things better. The divine role of the state in this process was simply to guarantee the individual the personal freedom necessary to allow this relationship with God to flourish; it was not the state's role to "legislate righteousness," as was often the perception of emboldened social conservatives such as Byfield. As was the case for his father, this focus on individual freedom encouraged in Preston a certain anti-statism that, in turn, generated an aversion to any state-led efforts to impose an economic collectivism on an un-

Introduction 29

willing public. Hence, the result was a clear preference for an unregulated market economy and a simultaneous reduction in the size and scope of the state. The dissemination of this message across the province in the late 1980s encouraged the Alberta PCs to embark on a program of cutbacks aimed at substantially reducing the size and scope of the provincial government under the leadership of Ralph Klein in the early 1990s. Thus, it is in this point of agreement between Ernest and Preston Manning that we find a vital, religious-based continuity with respect to the pro-market leanings that have defined Alberta politics for decades and remain more influential than the social conservative strain that, while no doubt influential in the mid-1990s and 2000s, has today been largely pushed to the sidelines.

At the conclusion of each of these substantive chapters, a broad analysis is provided that points to the specific political implications of the religiously inspired political thought of the individuals in question and the manner by which a good deal of continuity is found across Alberta's political history with respect to these implications.

Chapter 6, the final chapter of the book, recaps the central arguments of this study. In general, I conclude that the influence of religion on the development of Alberta politics goes well beyond the oft-mentioned presence of social conservatism in the province. It is found, rather, in the continued persistence of the broader populist conservative sentiment within Alberta's political discourse. It is this sentiment, which both celebrates the capacities of individuals and places clear limits on their behaviour, that helps to explain the individualistic, populist, anti-statist, and pro-market elements of the province's unique political culture. And, as I argue throughout, this sentiment is rooted largely in religious arguments that emerged out of the American evangelical Protestant tradition and were initially imported into Alberta provincial politics by Wood and Aberhart, later to be taken up by Ernest and Preston Manning. Despite this common heritage, however, it is worth reiterating how important the defeat of Wood's postmillennial religious interpretation by Aberhart's premillennial version was to the precise direction of Alberta politics. Although Wood helped to lay the foundation for a distinct aversion to state-led collectivism in the province, since 1935 Alberta politics have been defined by an emphasis on individual freedom that both encourages an anti-statist and pro-market sentiment and questions the need for traditional deliberative politics. Surely this particular freedom-infused sentiment in Alberta has largely disassociated itself from its initial religious mooring, but to miss the fact that this religious foundation did exist is to miss a good deal of the story of Alberta's political development. Of course, the legacy of this populist conservatism has perhaps been thrown into question by the left-leaning NDP's unexpected victory in the 2015 election. I address this issue as well, concluding that it is far too early to assume that such an occurrence represents a dramatic shift in the overall trajectory of Alberta's politics.

2

Democracy and Millennialism in American Evangelical Protestantism

The Context of Religious Interpretation in Alberta

Seymour Martin Lipset, in his influential comparison of the institutions and values of America and Canada, begins with a simple yet compelling thesis:

> Americans do not know but Canadians cannot forget that two nations, not one, came out of the American Revolution. The United States is the country of the revolution, Canada of the counter-revolution. These very different formative events set indelible marks on the two nations.[1]

It is this revolution/counter-revolution dichotomy that, he argues, essentially explains the fundamental divergence in social and political values one finds in the neighbouring countries. One of the most significant differences that Lipset notes relates to the influence of religion. Following independence, American religion embarked on a more sectarian path, embracing a congregational and voluntary style that encouraged a participatory and egalitarian populist spirit prone to protest when encountering hierarchy. Canadians, on the other hand, remained loyal to the motherland and thus maintained stronger links with the European-based Catholic or Anglican churches and their hierarchical structures that encouraged an attitude of deference to traditional sources of authority among adherents. The Protestant Canadians who did break away from the Anglican Church tended to gravitate towards the homegrown United Church, whose ecumenical and communitarian leanings clearly distinguished it from the dominant "individualistic" spirit of American Protestantism.

Although the revolution/counter-revolution thesis, together with the impact this difference has had on the nature of religious practice in

Canada and America, remains a rather helpful starting point for general comparison, there is little doubt that any attempt to generalize on a scale this grand is bound to overlook examples of diversity that do not quite fit with this simple interpretation. This is especially true with respect to Canada, whose Tory or "Loyalist" tradition is much stronger in eastern and central Canada (with the obvious exception of Quebec) than in the Prairie provinces, most especially Alberta. In other words, Lipset's interpretation of Canadian religious development as essentially counter-revolutionary and therefore more oriented towards hierarchy and stability is much more applicable to the Protestant sections of Ontario and Atlantic Canada and to Roman Catholic Quebec (although the situation here has obviously changed since the Quiet Revolution) than it is to Alberta. In fact, this book will make the broad argument over the next three chapters that the particular religious perspectives that most influenced the streams of political thought in Alberta within both the United Farmers of Alberta (UFA) and the Social Credit movements respectively have much more in common with the American tradition of religious development identified by Lipset than with the Canadian Tory one that I associate more accurately with the Protestantism of eastern and central Canada or the Roman Catholicism of historical Quebec.

That is not to say that the UFA and Alberta Social Credit leaders interpreted Christianity in precisely the same way, for they did not and their political ideologies differed accordingly, a claim that will be substantiated in far more detail in the following two chapters. However, two broad yet fundamental aspects of the American Protestant tradition became significant cornerstones underlying the religious perspectives that most influenced the UFA and Social Credit. In particular, a radically democratic ethos and a strong tendency towards Christian millennial thinking, two central dimensions of American more so than Canadian Tory Protestantism, lie at the foundation of the religious perspectives that guided political thought in both the UFA and Alberta Social Credit. Therefore, from the beginning, the interplay of religion and political ideology in the province of Alberta has had much more in common with the similar interaction that has occurred in large swaths of Protestant United States than with what has occurred in central or eastern Canada. The remainder of this chapter will provide the appropriate foundation for this argument by offering a succinct overview of the evolution of this democratic ethos and an exploration of the unique varieties of millennial thought within American Protestantism, as well as a brief comparison to Canadian Tory Protestantism. It is only by

Democracy and Millennialism in US Evangelical Protestantism 33

grasping this background that one acquires the necessary religious and intellectual context to fully understand and appreciate the unique strands of religiously infused political thought found in Alberta in the first half of the twentieth century. The chapter concludes with an overview of the migratory and ideological connections between the US and Alberta as well as the general social and religious landscape of the province in the early and mid-twentieth century.

Of course, to suggest that one can capture the whole of the long and varied history of the American Protestant religious tradition within just a few pages is ridiculous. Rather, the goal is to highlight some of the key intellectual and theological developments within this history that both capture something of the essence of this tradition and help to frame the eventual religious and political pronouncements of influential leaders in Alberta who were well versed in certain aspects of this tradition. Although Lipset begins his analysis with the American Revolution, it is important to understand that many of the seeds of the populist religious tradition he identifies as quintessentially American were actually sown well before the revolution took place. Thus, I want to drop the "revolutionary" label and instead refer to this religious tradition as that of American evangelicalism. However, such a label requires a certain qualification.

The term *evangelicalism* can mean different things to different people, so much so that some have wondered aloud about the contemporary usefulness of employing the term at all.[2] Much recent scholarship, and nearly all contemporary journalism, tends to equate evangelicalism with conservative "fundamentalist" Protestant sects that operate outside traditional mainstream Christian avenues and espouse a strict literal interpretation of the Bible, often centred around prophetic themes involving the "Second Coming" or "the Rapture." The popularity of this definition of evangelicalism has grown in step with the re-emergence of the "religious right" in the public sphere of America and, most especially, the demand from certain sectors of this movement that American domestic and foreign policy be structured around the goal of hastening this Second Coming.[3] In fact, this group of Christians have literally appropriated the term "evangelical" as their own, referring to themselves as "evangelical Christians" to distinguish themselves from more "liberal Christians." However, within this chapter I want to retrieve a much broader definition of evangelicalism of which this particular strand of conservative Christianity is only a part.

Following religious historian John G. Stackhouse, I use the term *evangelicalism* to identify a broad historical stream of Christianity that began with the Protestant Reformation and carried on though the creation of the Methodist Church in England and the popular evangelical revivals of the American "Great Awakenings" and, at all points, places special emphasis on the individual believer's personal relationship with God.[4] Importantly, no one Protestant denomination can claim ownership of this stream, for evangelicalism has infiltrated a number of churches, both mainstream and unorthodox, and has influenced, and been influenced by, the specific theological commitments and cultural traditions of various churches for a very long time. In fact, the particular patterns of thought and practice of evangelicals often differ substantially from one denomination to another, as this stream of Christian practice has shown itself to be flexible in terms of intermingling with distinct traditions.[5] However, it is still possible to identify certain foundational characteristics that bind these various denominational groups together under the banner of "evangelical" and distinguish them from other currents within Christianity.

Stackhouse, who follows David Bebbington's influential work, suggests that these basic characteristics are fourfold. First, evangelicals affirm the good news of God's salvation in Jesus. Second, they believe this good news is expressed most authoritatively in scripture. Third, evangelicals believe personal salvation requires an individual transformation or conversion. Fourth, they are active in proclaiming this good news.[6] Mark A. Noll has condensed this core down further by suggesting that the central characteristics of evangelicalism include both an acknowledgment of the Bible as a fundamental bedrock of authority and the conviction that true religion requires the active personal experience of God.[7] It is the broad, trans-denominational grouping of Protestant Christians who practise their faith within this "biblical experientialist" tradition that I deem evangelical. Such practice often takes place in a "low church" congregational structure that parallels the evangelical emphasis on egalitarianism and anti-elitism, for it is clearly understood that all members stand as equals under God and must approach and experience His saving power directly as individuals. The active pursuit of this personal experience is often encouraged within a mass revival led by pastors who deliver unsophisticated sermons in a manner that excites the emotions rather than the intellect of participants. No doubt such a loose definition of evangelicalism ensures significant theological and organizational deviation between evangelical practitioners within divergent denominations, but this shared emphasis on the need for a personal experience of God is, overall, what holds evangelicals together as a useful historical category. Any use of the term *evangelical* in this book, unless otherwise noted, refers to this broad definition as opposed to the more contemporary "conservative Protestant" definition often employed by present-day journalists and scholars. In fact, I will follow the lead of most religious historians by referring to these contemporary conservative Protestants as *fundamentalists*, a particular subset of the broader evangelical Protestant community defined by a "militantly antimodernist" sentiment that encompasses a belief in strict biblical literalism.[8] As will be discussed in more detail below, fundamentalist Christian belief has evolved into one of the most prevalent forms of American Protestant evangelicalism, a fact that helps differentiate both the character of that country's dominant religion's traditions and its broader cultural and political milieu from those found in Britain and Canada.

THE DEMOCRATIC THEOLOGY OF AMERICAN EVANGELICAL PROTESTANTISM

Implicit within Lipset's comparison of mainstream religious practice in Canada and the United States is the influence that social conditions have had on religious development. For Lipset, it was the act of political revolution, not a theological breakthrough on the part of a secluded monk, that set American religion on its distinct path. Although I will argue shortly that the seeds of American Protestantism were sown well before the American Revolution, it is worth remembering that Christianity has never been a pure set of doctrines operating in a vacuum, untouched by historical happenings. Theological breakthroughs such as those by Paul or Augustine or Luther have influenced the course of world events, but the progression of history and the broad social changes that accompany it have similarly influenced the direction of Christian theology. Indeed, the story of American religious development that this chapter will briefly tell is one of a constant interplay between traditional religious ideas and broader social developments. And the initial social conditions that most affected the direction of American Christianity were not simply those related to the late eighteenth-century revolution but rather those that stretch back to the conditions of colonial settlement. The United States (the colonies) was perceived to be a New World, a blank slate, *tabula rasa*, a stretch of land open to those eager to pursue the power or wealth available on a new continent but also to those who took issue with the conditions of life in the Old World. The Old World religion surely accompanied the settlers but so too did a spirit of freedom from Old World conventions and constraints. The vast spaces free of traditional denominational control offered the opportunity to those with such a spirit to propose and develop new interpretations of the Christian religion.[9]

This desire for a new start was encapsulated most clearly by the Puritans, a group of religious dissenters who arrived from England in the 1630s eager to build an authentic Christian nation free of the corruption they sensed in the Church of England. It was the influence of this group that planted the first seeds of a religion that would grow to be a distinctly American version of what historian George Marsden has labelled a "dissenter Protestantism."[10] The archetype of Christian dissent is obviously encapsulated within Martin Luther's initial challenge to the Church of Rome, an act that set off the Protestant Reformation and undoubtedly shaped all Christian denominations in some form. Yet a proper understanding of American religious development requires an acknowledgment of the importance of the early American Protestants' belief that they were "completing" the Reformation on American soil, something the Europeans, stuck in their hierarchical class structures and traditions, had left unfinished.[11] Central to this act of completion was the Puritans' rededication to two key Protestant tenets: first, the sole authority of the Bible as a guide to proper Christian living and, second, the principle of justification by faith rather than works – that is, the idea that God's righteousness, and thus the individual's salvation, is not earned by humans but given freely by God. The two foundational theologians of the Reformation, Luther and John Calvin, agreed on these basic ideas but only Calvin envisioned justification (becoming righteous before God) as predestined and a permanent feature of being connected to Christ following a spiritual rebirth. Importantly, the dissenting Puritans were Calvinist and thus popularized a strong emphasis on the authority of the Bible and a personal relationship with God built upon a "once in a lifetime" personal conversion or rebirth. It was upon these two tenets that American evangelicalism would thereafter grow.

Although the origins of American "dissenter" Protestantism stretch back to the Puritans, it was the revivalism associated with the First Great Awakening in the first half of the eighteenth century that was the central stimulant in the shift from an English-based Puritanism to an indigenous American evangelicalism.[12] An important consequence of Calvin's doctrine of predestination was the presence of anxiety among followers who were eager to assure themselves that they were "predestined" to receive God's salvation. According to Calvin, only those called by God to experience a spiritual rebirth or personal conversion would be saved. Believers thus went through life anxiously awaiting their own personal conversion. The introduction of the evangelical mass-revival meeting in the first half of the eighteenth century encouraged a permanent shift in the style of religious worship in America because of its ability to assist in easing this angst. Revivals were often led by talented orators, gifted in biblical knowledge, able to speak in an unsophisticated yet emotional manner to common people, and generally understood to be an instrument of the Holy Spirit. By promising to assist with the "conversion experience," and thus with the salvation that anxious believers were seeking, revivals exploded in popularity. The result was a sudden upsurge in religious activity. Such activity built upon the Puritan/Calvin premise that emphasized the ultimate authority of the Bible and the need for personal conversion, but it moved in a new direction by encouraging a more active and emotional Protestantism. Local and national preachers took to the open-air pulpits and delivered the Word of God in plain language to the plain people of colonial America. Implicit within this popular religious movement was a rejection of the Puritan desire for an established national church, complete with formally trained ministers and a new emphasis on the layman's ability to interpret scripture and experience a personal conversion in an emotional revival setting rather than in the formal church. This line of thought opened the door to a variety of non-Puritan denominations, and the religious pluralism that blossomed has been a feature of American life ever since.

It was the Congregationalist, Presbyterian, and Baptist denominations, the latter being the most numerous and thus influential in eighteenth-century America, that gained the most adherents from this sudden upsurge in religious activity.[13] Each of these denominations embraced the tradition of religious dissent introduced to America by the Puritans, but it was the Baptists who further popularized the Calvinist doctrine of personal conversion. However, they did so in a manner that explicitly emphasized the spiritual equality of all individuals who committed themselves to a Christian life. Such a notion implied that a church was not meant to be a hierarchical organization but rather a gathering of individuals who stood equally before God. It is difficult to overstate the significance of such a class-levelling notion for a society that was still familiar with the hierarchical structures of both traditional religious organizations and the general societal order of the Old World. In fact, Marsden suggests that the popularization of ideas such as these – related to individual equality and capacity and the right to challenge established forms of power within popular religious circles – intensified the sentiment of dissent in America to such a degree that the First Great Awakening can be understood as a significant factor in the eventual revolution that took place in the second half of the eighteenth century.[14]

If the development of an American-based Protestant theology before the American Revolution assisted in laying the necessary groundwork for the broader acceptance of basic democratic principles such as individualism, egalitarianism, and the right to challenge authority, it was the explosion of ground-level religious activity in the period immediately following the revolution that not only fortified the righteousness of democracy in the minds of practitioners but further and permanently legitimated a populist dimension in religious practice. This was essentially the completion of the shift towards an indigenous American evangelical Christianity initiated by the revivalism of the First Great Awakening. In the course of documenting religiosity in post-revolution America, Nathan Hatch has demonstrated that it was ordinary people, "aided by a powerful new vocabulary, a rhetoric of liberty that would not have occurred to them were it not for the Revolution," who turned their sights on the church and effectively reshaped the practice of Christianity in America.[15] Building upon this rhetoric of liberty and the accompanying sense of individual capacity, American "populist" evangelicalism took off, driven by "increasingly assertive common people [who] wanted their leaders unpretentious, their doctrines self-evident and down-to-earth, their music lively and sing-able, and their churches in local hands."[16] The result was the emergence of a wildly popular evangelical movement in the early nineteenth century (the Second Great Awakening), complete with the formation of many new religious sects led by "folksy" pastors who relied on unsophisticated sermons and urged much congregational participation. As Donald Matthews has argued, by encouraging the multiplication of religious units, or sects, the revivalism of the Second Great Awakening facilitated American democracy by encouraging the creation of local religious organizations that provided important avenues for lay participation.[17]

Such ground-level action was supported by similar shifts within theological and intellectual circles in America. Although the promise of "conversion experiences" made by revivalists during the First Great Awakening seemed to imply a degree of human agency in the quest for Christian salvation, it was not until Charles Finney, a leading post-revolution revivalist from 1825 to 1835, began to promote the notion of conversion as an act of choice by a free individual rather than one initiated by God that American evangelical theology shifted from a purely Calvinist foundation to one fused with the Methodism of John Wesley. This Arminian notion that conversion, and thus salvation, was in fact an act of free individual choice had little trouble gaining support, for it coalesced rather neatly with the broader republican ideals that were prominent in post-revolution America.[18] Indeed, William McLoughlin has argued that the revivalism of the Second Great Awakening provided American Protestants with the reassurance that God approved of the principles espoused by the revolution.[19] This fusion of republican and religious ideals even extended towards the approval of commercialism according to Noll, who points to a correlation between early American evangelicals and their preference for a free market.[20]

The religious and political empowerment of the "plain people" during this period was also aided by the popularity, in American post-revolutionary intellectual and theological circles, of the Scottish Philosophy of Common Sense. This was a severely democratic and anti-elitist outlook that emphasized the capabilities of the "common man" to interpret reality by way of his "common sense" and thus think and act in an intellectually and morally sound manner, regardless of social classification and without assistance from a mediator.[21] This emphasis on individual capacity was essential, as it provided a philosophical foundation for the evangelical Christian to experience God personally and freely choose to accept His grace by way of conversion, thus fulfilling a fundamental requirement for salvation. Of course, the flip side of this coin has been a tendency towards anti-intellectualism, "a resentment and suspicion of the life of the mind and those who are considered to represent it" in American life, in the words of Richard Hofstader, an idea that would continue to reverberate within the halls of American evangelical Protestantism and American populist movements more generally.[22] Indeed, the popularity of this common sense philosophy goes a long way towards explaining the significant growth of Protestant fundamentalism in America when compared to both Britain and Canada. Nevertheless, the Baptists, and now the growing contingent of Methodists, stormed the American frontier, carrying with them this personal and emotional form of worship, and its inherent sense of individual capacity and American Protestantism has maintained this tendency towards individualistic, emotional, and participatory behaviour ever since. Scholars have even demonstrated a strong link between this democratic evangelical spirit and the populist political movements that spread across America in the late nineteenth century.[23]

Certainly a great deal more could be said about the long and varied development of Protestant theology and practice in America, but this very brief overview should be enough to give the reader a sense of its intensely democratic nature. We can best grasp the revolutionary aspect of this American evangelical spirit, according to Michael Gauvreau, by contrasting it with medieval or early modern religious practices "which subsumed the individual in a web of divinely sanctioned hierarchies ... buttressed by established churches, which claimed ... to mediate between the individual and God."[24] American evangelicalism radically challenged such hierarchical relationships by interpreting the condition of the individual as one of impressive moral and intellectual capacity. Because a personal and unmediated experience of the divine was necessary for salvation (and made possible by the moral and intellectual capacities of the individual), evangelicals placed extreme importance on the notion of freedom of individual conscience. Unsurprisingly, such an outlook produced a strong democratic ethic among followers who, by way of their quest for personal religious experience, sought political structures that allowed for the individual freedom required to live their faith. Indeed, the social consequences of a faith that empowered the individual at the expense of the elite within religious establishments were such that traditional hierarchies of a non-religious nature eventually met with the same dissenting spirit.

That said, it is not my intention to trace the history of the secularization of this spirit of dissent. Rather, I simply want to reiterate that a radically democratic theology that emphasized the freedom and capacity of the common individual to shape society according to the dictates of God as they, rather than established clergy, understood Him is a central component of American evangelical Protestantism and its individualistic conception of faith. Of course, the connection between theological interpretation and religious practice in America and America's distinct form of democracy has been a topic of study ever since Alexis de Tocqueville wrote of the intermingling of religion and liberty in the first half of the nineteenth century.[25] Yet, as McLoughlin has argued, this religious tradition contains an inherent tension, often overlooked, between a radically democratic and anti-establishment sentiment and a broader conservatism associated with the belief in a universal moral code established by God that governs the conduct of individuals.[26]

From the Puritans, through the denominations and sects that emerged out of the First and Second Great Awakenings, to the fundamentalist sects of the late 1800s and early 1900s, the absolute authority of the Christian Bible has remained paramount. This continuity has obviously ensured a long-running adherence to a particular moral code derived from the Word of God that places divine restrictions on the conduct of individuals. Beyond specific biblical commandments, American Protestantism emphasized the need for an "orderly life" built upon a foundation of sobriety, discipline, and hard work upon which a proper family could be raised.[27] Given the fallen nature of humanity described in scripture, the societal stability and order necessary for the further spreading of God's Word required the constant protection and maintenance of institutions that could both educate and police individuals with respect to God's laws. It is in this spirit that one finds religious groups from nearly any period of American history, through their function as moral/religious educators, praising the church and family as the central pillars of society while occasionally demanding that the state enact legislation that can assist with such guidance. To recognize this internal tension between these conservative and radical tendencies is to see the significant gulf that exists between the radically individualistic and democratic ethos of American Protestantism and the individualism of secular liberalism or even post-modernism. As Phillip Hammond has argued, American evangelicalism "saturated America with the idea that people should be free to do pretty much as they like, as long as they look out for themselves ... and, of course, behave."[28] Exuding both radical and conservative tendencies such as those identified by McLoughlin, this American evangelical tradition helps to explain the parallel tensions that exist in American public life. In fact, these same tensions between radicalism and conservatism will appear again as a major theme within the examination of political thought in Alberta and its relation to this broad American evangelical perspective that appears in the following chapters.

Although the presence of these characteristics within American evangelical Protestantism seems readily apparent, their uniqueness becomes even more visible when compared to the development of Protestantism in Canada. Yet Lipset's dichotomy between the Protestantism of the United States and that of Canada fails to account for an early streak of radicalism in the northern neighbour. Indeed, historians now agree that a similar strain of democratic evangelicalism was an important cultural/religious force in late eighteenth- and early nineteenth-century English-speaking Canada as well, counteracting the conservative tendencies present within traditional Anglican circles. In fact, the strong evangelical current in Atlantic Canada in the late eighteenth century may have been even more radical than its counterpart in America.[29]

Central to this movement was the preaching of Henry Alline, a largely self-taught Christian who was born in New England but spent most of his adult life in rural Nova Scotia. It was here, in the 1770s, that Alline did much to bring the unique revivalism of the American First Great Awakening northward; the result was a popular movement built atop a message of evangelical pietism catching fire in the Maritimes. Evangelicals in Upper Canada, primarily Methodists associated with the American Methodist movement, were also embracing the same radical democratic ethos that swept through post-revolution America. Nancy Christie has convincingly demonstrated that this strand of evangelicalism was one of the central mechanisms responsible for implanting antiestablishment and reformist notions in the minds of the common people of Upper Canada who stood outside the Tory Anglican elite. This anti-elitism was shared by Upper Canadian Baptists who, with the Methodists, offered a critique of traditional and hierarchical religious and political institutions by way of their emphasis on spiritual egalitarianism and the necessity for individuals to develop an unmediated connection with God.[30]

This radicalism came to a sudden halt, however, in the wake of the War of 1812 and the anti-Americanism that followed; Upper Canadian evangelicalism became much more British in character and would, over the next century, adopt a Victorian world view that stressed order and theology over the popular emotionalism of "republican" evangelicalism.[31] The notion of personal conversion so critical to American evangelicalism was present within this strand of evangelicalism, but as Noll has argued, "that conversion had to be joined to public responsibility in the construction of a civilization." In other words, Ontario Tory Protestantism was infused with a particular evangelicalism, but it was not as populist or individualistic as American evangelicalism. In fact, Noll continues, "Canada's dominant Protestant theology ... was uniquely Canadian in balancing an American openness to innovation, optimism, and personal liberty with a British commitment to order, stability, and tradition."[32] This is not to suggest that a more democratic or populist radicalism was not present in Canada, for surely one could be found, especially if one investigated aspects of Canadian Methodism following Confederation, but this strand was never as central to Canadian Protestantism as it was for the Protestantism south of the border.

Although these few paragraphs represent a rather abrupt and pithy overview of eastern and central Canadian Protestant evangelicalism, the differences between it and the broader American tradition described above are easily identifiable. As Lipset correctly noted, there is a distinct democratic and individualistic essence within the American evangelical tradition that is not as prominent in its (central and eastern) Tory Canadian counterpart, at least after the War of 1812. Yet it is wrong to simply assume that the more conservative Canadian Protestantism is equally applicable to all parts of Protestant Canada. But before I expand upon this assertion, I must elaborate upon a second unique characteristic of American evangelical Protestantism, one not mentioned in Lipset's comparison but just as important if one hopes to grasp the entirety of the logic operating within the streams of political thought explored in the following two chapters. This is the strong tendency towards Christian millennialism.

MILLENNIALISM AND AMERICAN EVANGELICAL PROTESTANTISM

The notion that America was God's chosen nation, a new land comprised of especially devout followers who were destined to escape the corruption of Old World Christianity and develop a proper relationship with God by building *the* authentic Christian nation in accordance with His will, has been one of the most important elements of America's broad self-understanding. This belief stretches back to the Puritans, was prominent in the revivals of both Great Awakenings, and remains close to the heart of a number of contemporary American Christians. A central consequence of this belief is the parallel notion that America has a special responsibility to ensure the coming of the kingdom of God promised by Christ in the New Testament. In fact, prominent American theologian Richard Niebuhr has argued that American Christianity "is a movement that finds its center in the faith in the kingdom of God ... indeed [it has] been the dominant idea in American Christianity."[33] Although the concept of the kingdom of God has been interpreted differently at various points in American religious history, it is the distinct eschatological interpretations related to versions of Christian millennialism that are most applicable to this book.

Christian millennialism is generally understood to refer to a belief in a long period of unprecedented peace and righteousness closely associated with the Second Coming of Christ. This "long period" is usually interpreted as a reference to a one thousand–year period, or millennium, that either is, or is the preface to, the establishment of the kingdom of God on earth. This is a Christian notion that originates in Chapter 20 of the Book of Revelation wherein an angel is witnessed locking Satan into the Abyss for one thousand years while the souls of those who resisted the temptations of Satan during their lifetime return to life to reign with Christ for the same thousand-year period. American religious historian Timothy Weber notes that Christians have tended to interpret this biblical verse in one of three general ways. *Amillennialists* understand this reference in a symbolic manner and contend that Christ's reign will occur in the hearts of His followers. *Postmillennialists* believe that Christ's Second Coming will occur on earth *after* the Millennium has been established by the work of the church. *Premillennialists* contend that Christ will return to earth *before* the thousand-year period begins and will use His powers to establish it.[34] It is the latter two of these eschatological views that have been most influential in the American evangelical Protestant tradition.[35] On the surface, post- and premillennialism are distinguished from each other simply by the question of timing: will Christ return before or after the thousand-year period of peace and righteousness? At a deeper level, however, they presuppose very different conceptions of divine and human agency with respect to the establishment of the kingdom of God on earth. Thus, the implications of each of these distinct eschatological viewpoints have generated divergent political world views on the part of various Christian groups in America. A similar influence (and divergence) will reappear when the relationship between religious interpretation and political thought in Alberta is explored in the next two chapters.

Christian millennial thought in America stretches back to the Puritans, who held to a premillennial outlook, and into the thought of Jonathan Edwards, a theologian of the First Great Awakening and America's first prominent postmillennialist.[36] Since the time of Edwards, through the American Revolution and Second Great Awakening and up until the American Civil War, the revivalism that dominated American Protestantism was full of an optimistic spirit that tended towards a postmillennial world view and the implicit understanding that the church must do its part to usher in the kingdom of God. There was certainly a brief period in the 1830s and 1840s wherein the premillennial view of Baptist lay preacher William Miller became quite popular in America, but Christ's failure to return in the window predicted by Miller ultimately led to its decline in popularity. For American postmillennialists, history was understood to be shaped by a cosmic struggle between the forces of God and Satan. The upsurge in outward and emotional religious activity in the mid-eighteenth century, together with the success of the revolution, convinced Christians that things were getting progressively better and it was their own piety, undertaken by their own free will, in combination with God's grace, that was moving them towards God's final victory. Indeed, early nineteenth-century postmillennialists were convinced that the spiritual and cultural progress of America had grown so substantially that the defeat of Satan and the beginning of the Millennium was imminent.[37]

This optimism, combined with the belief that both individual humans and the collective church possessed significant efficacy with respect to establishing the Millennium, encouraged a whole host of social reform movements.[38] In fact, certain elements of this postmillennial stream of Protestant thought underlie the emergence of the American "social gospel" movement that formed largely in the urban centres of the American northeast in the late nineteenth and early twentieth centuries. Responding to the social problems associated with rapid industrial expansion in American cities, a collection of progressive pastors and academics sought to apply Christ's "golden rule" to industrial organization in the hope of constructing a literal "kingdom of God" on earth. Although policy prescriptions meant to hasten the building of this kingdom varied from a call for a more co-operative approach to economics to the more radical demand that capitalism be abolished and replaced with socialism, the overall progressive influence of the movement was strongly felt in both the political and religious circles of America.[39] However, the degree to which America's evangelical Protestant tradition influenced this particular strand of Christian theology is a point of contention.

Richard Goode and Paul Harvey have both argued that a more authentic evangelical version of a social gospel message is to be found in the agrarian populist movement of the American South and Midwest in the late nineteenth century. This was a "rural social gospel" distinct from and less sophisticated than the northern, urban, and largely academic social gospel espoused by the likes of Washington Gladden and Walter Rauschenbusch. This rural social gospel drew heavily from the evangelical values of individual autonomy and piety but shared with the northern social gospel a social condemnation, based on the golden rule of Christ, of the political and economic conditions imposed upon the plain people by an ever-industrializing economy.[40] Joe Creech also distinguishes the evangelical "social Christianity" that motivated the American populist agrarians from the more sophisticated combination of theological liberalism and progressive economic theories that emerged from the oft-cited northern social gospel movement. This "common folk" social Christianity combined evangelical conceptions of benevolence and anti-elitism with Jeffersonian rural ideals related to agrarian purity, self-sufficiency, and small-scale commerce to produce "the simple yet powerful idea that economic relationships should be guided by the law of love."[41] As will be explored in more detail in Chapter 3, this strain of religious-based thought heavily influenced Alberta agrarian leader Henry Wise Wood.

Yet, as important as the American social gospel movement was, it is worth noting that the dominance of postmillennial thought within the halls of American Protestantism ended well before the height of the social gospel movement. This was largely due to the arrival of the American Civil War as well as to the rise of scholastic higher criticism (which applied new methods of historical research to the Bible) and eventually to the introduction of the theory of evolution in the second half of the nineteenth century. Indeed, the challenges posed to the biblical literalism central to American evangelicalism, let alone to Christian belief itself by the introduction of higher criticism, on the one hand, and Darwin's theory of evolution, on the other, represented the beginning of a monumental shift with respect to the unity of American Protestantism. The theological reaction these challenges stimulated would eventually blossom into the full-blown fundamentalist–modernist controversy of the early twentieth century. Decades before that controversy erupted, liberal theologians open to the findings of higher criticism and who felt that an outright rejection of Darwin's theory was, in the end, untenable were eager to adopt a notion of evolution within which God's design was firmly encapsulated. Drawing heavily upon the work of English philosopher Herbert Spencer, they arrived at a conception of theistic evolution that accepted the empirical findings of Darwin, but they insisted such progress was the work of the Christian God who set such events in motion.[42] However, the overt supernaturalism of God, the notion that He may again intervene at any point in history to alter its course, began to give way to an evolution-friendly conception of gradual social change driven largely by human action in accordance with the growing presence of a "Christian spirit" on earth. Liberal postmillennialists who adopted this evolutionary framework retained the traditional confidence in the coming of the kingdom of God, as well as a commitment to the basic moral teachings of the Bible, but understood this coming kingdom in a much more secular fashion. The perfection of social institutions in America came to represent the Millennium, or kingdom of God, for many progressive Christians, and the actual physical return of Christ to earth following this period of righteousness seemed to slowly vanish from their theology.[43] The result was a view that remained quite optimistic and continued to motivate social reform, but provided only vague promises of progress that would be realized over long periods of time and was, in the end, quite susceptible to transforming into a secular humanist rather than a traditional Christian outlook.

Yet the decline in popularity of postmillennialism within American Protestant circles was more immediately attributable to the arrival of the Civil War in 1861. In short, conditions suddenly seemed to be getting worse rather than better and the optimism of the liberal postmillennialists seemed misplaced, resulting in a gradual decline of postmillennial thought at the popular level in America.[44] This shift in circumstance, in conjunction with the intellectual and theological gymnastics liberal pastors were performing in the face of the challenges posed by new forms of biblical scholarship and natural science, created a clear opening for the emergence of a new Christian eschatological outlook within evangelical circles. Around the same time, a new premillennial outlook dubbed "dispensationalism" had arrived in America and was slowly gaining followers in certain evangelical circles. It is worth pausing at this point to unpack in more detail this particular stream of Christian interpretation, not only because this was the precise outlook adopted by William Aberhart of Alberta in the early 1900s, but also because the rapid manner by which this outlook largely overtook American evangelicalism says much about the uniqueness of Protestantism in the United States when compared to both Britain and Canada.

Premillennial dispensationalism was not indigenous to the United States but originated in Great Britain in the 1820s. One of its chief founders and the figure perhaps most responsible for its initial spreading to America was John Nelson Darby, an ordained minister in the Church of Ireland who, before founding the British Plymouth Brethren sect in the 1840s, would eventually resign over concerns related to the church's strict insistence on hierarchical organization. It was during this time that Darby would refashion some broad eschatological ideas related to the Second Coming of Christ that existed at the fringes of British Protestantism into dispensationalism, a radical reinterpretation of Christian scripture based on the notion that history has been divided by God into seven separate "dispensations."[45] Within each dispensation, Darby argued, God presented mankind with a different kind of governing relationship and humans in turn were to accept and fulfill a specific responsibility to God within each historical period. Importantly, accurate biblical interpretation would only be possible for those who had come to understand this precise depiction of history because certain verses of scripture, according to this outlook, were applicable only to one particular period of history or dispensa-

48   God's Province

tion. In other words, interpreting the Bible was a far more complex matter than simply assuming every passage was directly applicable to one's everyday life. The great advantage such a reorganization of the applicability of biblical scripture was, or course, that it allowed for so-inclined Christians to continue to adhere to the principle of biblical literalism in the face of contradictions unearthed by biblical scholarship or challenges presented by modern science. In other words, any specific collection of biblical verses that seemed particularly contradictory or unbelievable in the face of newly articulated scientific principles or historical facts was now understood to apply to a different dispensation than the one currently occupied, a feature that undoubtedly enhanced dispensationalism's popularity among evangelical Christians, who were encountering mounting challenges to the notion of biblical inerrancy by the second half of the nineteenth century. Indeed, a central consequence of the surge in dispensationalism's popularity was the resurrection of the literal notion of the coming of the kingdom of God, freeing American Protestants from the claws of evolutionary theory and liberal postmillennialism.

Beyond simply reorganizing the Bible along radically new lines, dispensationalism relied heavily upon a particular interpretation of the prophetic scriptures, especially the Old Testament Books of Ezekiel and Daniel, the New Testament Book of Revelation, and a scattering of Christ's own prophetic murmurings throughout the Gospels, as a way to understand the movement of history. Darby suggested that the present age, which has been dubbed "the Church Age" or "the Age of Grace," represented the second-last dispensation of history and that a proper reading of the prophetic texts unveiled a blueprint of a series of future worldwide events that would unfold as this age came to an end and the final age, "the Millennial Age," the literal kingdom of God on earth, emerged. More specifically, dispensational eschatology foretold of the coming Rapture, Christ's brief reappearance "through the air" to remove His true followers from the earth (a reference to a description found in the biblical book of 1st Thessalonians 4:16–17), a scene that quite literally was expected to be completed in a matter of seconds, leaving those "left behind" utterly stunned and confused. Once the Rapture was complete, the Antichrist, literally the Devil Incarnate, would rise to prominence and torment the world's remaining inhabitants for a period of seven years known as the Tribulation (mentioned first by Christ in the Book of Matthew 24:1, then again in the Book of Revelation 7:14). Christ was then to return with His followers and defeat the Antichrist in the final Battle of Armageddon (Revelation 16:16). This victory would usher in the Millennium, the literal kingdom of God on earth promised in the New Testament (Revelation 20).[46] In other words, the coming kingdom was the literal reign of Christ on earth, but it was to occur in the next and final dispensation, not our own, and any efforts to hasten its arrival in this period through social reform, such as those urged by postmillennialists, were of no use. It was the will of God alone that moved history from one dispensation to the next. In fact, dispensationalists believed that the social conditions of the present dispensation would, according to the biblical prophets, get far worse rather than better, a view that played well in the period following the Civil War wherein social and economic conditions had deteriorated significantly. As the popularity of this outlook grew in the United States, the focus of the country's evangelicalism began to shift from one open to reforming society in a method patterned after Christ's ethical teachings to one far more focused on the health of each individual's soul. Indeed, most dispensationalists were outright opposed to any social activism built upon a postmillennial social gospel foundation because such an outlook operated by way of a faulty understanding of both the movement of history and the degree of agency possessed by humanity when it came to establishing the kingdom of God on earth. To assume that the "good works" of citizens could establish the kingdom of God on earth was the epitome of sinful pride and bound to lead Christians away from their true calling: to build a personal relationship with Christ in this dispensation and await the Rapture.

Despite originating in Britain, dispensationalism has been far more successful within mainstream American Christianity than in Britain or Canada. Darby himself brought this dispensational Christianity to America on at least six occasions between 1859 and 1877, and the prophetic writings of both British and American converts to dispensationalism became popular in the 1870s and 1880s as well. By 1875, American dispensationalists were hosting prophetic Bible conferences in New York and Niagara-on-the-Lake, Ontario, and soon popular American revivalists such as Dwight L. Moody and Leander Munhall were preaching the message of Christ's Second Coming as explained by Darby to thousands upon thousands. Evangelical Bible schools and publications spread the message even farther. Yet no one individual did more to establish premillennial dispensationalism as a bedrock of conservative Protestant belief in America than Cyrus Scofield, a disgraced lawyer who converted to Christianity while in prison before embarking on a career of evangelicalism that culminated with the publication of his infamous Reference Bible in 1909, a work that seamlessly integrated dispensational theology with biblical scripture in a simple fashion. This work would go on to sell as many as 12.5 million copies.[47]

In sum, between 1875 and 1915, premillennial dispensationalism became the central foundation of conservative evangelicalism in America, largely propelling the unique rise of fundamentalist Christianity in the country that continues to this day. Indeed, as the emerging trends in biblical scholarship and scientific discoveries of the late nineteenth century posed significant challenges to biblical literalism, long a bedrock of the populist evangelical Protestantism of America, prominent revivalists and their flock were faced with a conundrum. They could turn to the "modern" interpretations of liberal theologians who sought to rescue a version of Christianity by downplaying the supernaturalism of God and focusing instead on the societal reforms possible should individuals commit to following the moral message of Christ, or they could accept dispensationalism, a mode of Christian interpretation that refused to abandon a literal belief in the virgin birth of Christ, His resurrection, and His foretold Second Coming. For large swaths of American evangelicals eager to protect the tenets of faith they had long held, it was not even really a choice. As one prominent evangelical noted in 1915, dispensationalism represented "the ultimate antidote for all infidelity and the impregnable bulwark against liberalism and false cults."[48] Dispensationalism has been a central characteristic of American fundamental evangelicalism ever since.

Although the precise interpretations of the prophetic scriptures central to dispensationalism have been altered slightly over the past century as various American preachers sought to incorporate ongoing world events into an updated schema, the core prophetic notions of a coming Rapture, Tribulation, Battle of Armageddon, and finally the emergence of the Millennial Age remain central to the outlooks of millions upon millions of American Protestants today. Indeed, Peter Boyer, reporting on the astronomical sales figures in contemporary America of various prophetic Christian books, novels, and magazines that are built upon this eschatological outlook and further noting that approximately 50 per cent of American college graduates await Christ's literal Second Coming, has convincingly demonstrated the manner in which such ideas, born out of premillennial dispensationalism, continue to pervade American thought and culture at the popular level.[49] Noted religious historian George Marsden has gone as far as to argue that Christian fundamentalism, which he defines as a militant opposition to modernism that has been particularly reliant on premillennial dispensationalism, is "overwhelmingly American in the sense that almost nowhere else did this type of Protestant response to modernity have such a conspicuous and pervasive role in the churches and the national culture."[50] Of course, many have noted what an anomaly this really is: a country that is among the most wealthy and educated in the world being so infused not simply with religion but with a fundamentalist brand that is militantly averse to the insights of science and historical scholarship. Why is this so?

This is obviously a complex question, especially with respect to the persistence of such beliefs into the contemporary age, but the initial popularity of these views in America was no doubt related to the populist nature of its evangelicalism, the Common Sense philosophy that sat at its intellectual foundations, and the corresponding anti-intellectualism it subsequently embraced. Marsden digs deeper into this question, acknowledging certain social factors, such as the absence of established churches and "pre-revival" religious traditions that allowed for "the dynamics of unopposed revivalism" to play out in America, before ultimately suggesting that the explanation is related to the fact that America's exposure to philosophical romanticism was largely truncated. This meant that the country, by and large, remained loyal to a Baconian scientific world view shaped by the dominant "common sense realism" of the Scottish Enlightenment rather than to a romantic Humboldtian approach based on natural laws and the process of development that became prevalent in Europe. The result, Marsden suggests, was an understanding of science in the circles of American higher learning as being an inductive activity based on "organizing, classifying, and rationally ordering data" for a time well beyond the point where this approach was largely abandoned in Europe. This was significant because it shaped the manner by which American intellectuals reacted to the findings of Darwin when compared to that of intellectuals in Europe. American thinkers, Marsden argues, were more suspicious of the theories of Darwin because they were derived from a "developmental" type of science largely foreign to them. Marsden paints a more sophisticated and detailed picture than this short synopsis allows, but in essence, this meant that the scientific discoveries that would eventually lead to a more liberal, or modern, approach to interpreting the Bible in much of Western Europe were not treated with the same seriousness by American thinkers, at least in the period immediately following the publication of Darwin's findings. This is turn meant that American Protestants, including highly educated ones, were not so quick to abandon biblical literalism in the face of Darwinism. In fact, faced with a growing onslaught of modern interpretations, large swaths of American evangelicals developed a militantly anti-modern attitude and ferociously defended the literal truth of the Bible in numbers that far, far outweighed any similar opposition one might have found in Britain or elsewhere. The appearance of dispensationalism at precisely this time gave such fundamentalists a lifeline of sort, a theory that explained history in an anti-naturalistic way and allowed for a continued defence of literal interpretations at the precise moment scientific developments were threatening to render such views untenable.[51]

To be sure, premillennial dispensationalism and the broader "militantly anti-modern" Christian fundamentalist approach to biblical interpretation that relies on such a theology have been present in Canadian Protestant circles as well. As William Westfall's observant history of nineteenth-century Ontario Protestantism makes clear, British and especially American premillennialists who preached in Canada in the 1840s, 1850s, and 1860s were able to build an impressive following.[52] Two waves in particular found success. In the 1840s, American premillennialist William Miller and his followers brought their message of the imminent Second Coming of Christ to Toronto and surrounding areas to much fanfare, although the movement would gradually decline in popularity, just as it did in America after Christ failed to return within the predicted window. In the 1850s and 1860s, Darby and his Plymouth Brethren followers renewed premillennial fervour in Ontario with a series of meetings near Guelph, a warm-up act of sorts before the infamous Prophetic Bible Conferences held at Niagara-on-the-Lake beginning in the 1880s that did much to further popularize dispensationalism in the region, especially among Baptists and Presbyterians. Yet most leaders of the mainstream Protestant churches in Ontario, which had been groomed in the more conservative Victorian evangelicalism of Britain, did not fall sway to the arguments of Darby and in fact launched a sustained counterattack against premillennial dispensationalism in the last decades of the century. Central to such efforts was the development of a postmillennial outlook that highlighted the foretold Second Coming of Christ but did so in a way that emphasized the value of human action in this world as a means to hastening this Second Coming. Such efforts were not completely effective at eradicating dispensationalism from Ontario Protestantism, but they certainly went a long way towards limiting its exposure, especially when considering its prominence within American Protestantism at the time. As David Elliott and Iris Miller have noted, despite dispensationalism losing its lustre in the eyes of most church-going Protestants in the region, several prominent Ontario clergymen remained intrigued enough to invite a number of American dispensationalists, many associated with Chicago's Moody Bible Institute, a hotbed of dispensational theology, to speak throughout southern Ontario throughout the first few years of the twentieth century. In fact, this is where William Aberhart, future premier of Alberta, would first encounter dispensationalism, although more will be said about this in Chapter 4.[53]

Those Ontario preachers and laymen who remained loyal to premillennial dispensationalism despite the efforts of the mainstream Protestant churches represented a key component of the fundamentalist branch of Canadian Protestantism from that time onward. Although Marsden has suggested that fundamentalism is an American phenomenon, it is of course true that anti-modern Christian sects emerged in both Canada and Britain in the late nineteenth and early twentieth centuries, some prospering to this day. Indeed, any overview of Canadian Protestantism would be remiss to overlook two prominent Canadian fundamentalists who built impressive followings in the 1920s: T.T. Shields, one-time pastor of Toronto's Jarvis Street Baptist Church, and Oswald Smith, founder of the Peoples Church in Toronto in 1928. Fundamentalist outlooks have also been popular in pockets of the Canadian Prairies. John Stackhouse Jr, for example, has noted rural Alberta's Prairie Bible Institute as an important conservative evangelical centre, established in 1922, that continues to provide post-secondary education today.[54] Yet scholars agree on a broader point: despite the popularity of these individuals and institutions, the prevalence of Christian fundamentalism in both Britain and Canada is but a drop in the bucket compared to that in the United States.[55] In fact, studies of the character of contemporary Canadian Protestant evangelicalism consistently point to its having less conservative leanings, on average, than its American counterpart, a distinction directly related to the fact that fundamentalism, and therefore dispensationalism, has simply not been as strong in Canada as in the United States.[56]

Why has this difference persisted? This is another complex question whose full answer falls well beyond the scope of this section. However, it is worth turning briefly to the work of Canadian religious historian Michael Gauvreau, who, building on the work of Marsden, suggests that the initial roots of Canadian Protestantism relied on distinct intellectual foundations, making it less vulnerable to the temptations of fundamentalism.[57] More specifically, Gauvreau points to a unique strand of Baconianism that was derived from the evangelical movement in Scotland, brought into Canada by Presbyterians, and was more open to romanticism than that stream identified by Marsden as the key to understanding American intellectuals' early rejection of Darwin. This strand of served "as a rhetorical structure promoting caution and reverence" when compared to the American brand. In a wider cultural sense, Gauvreau continues:

> Canada lacked a heritage of revolutionary myths derived from the Enlightenment; Canadian culture was characterized by, in the words of one perceptive observer, an "unusually strong attachment to law and history."
>
> Given these biases, and the fact that neither natural theology nor Common Sense philosophy had ever established a solid infrastructure in Canadian Protestant circles, it was no accident that evolutionary thought in the form of higher criticism found comparatively easy acceptance in church colleges.[58]

This is clearly a quick summary of a complex argument derived from significant research into the development of intellectual currents within nineteenth-century Canada, but the point remains that Christian fundamentalism is essentially an American phenomenon. In other words, despite the undeniable presence of evangelical movements, both the British and the Canadian Protestant traditions retained a stronger conservative and intellectual dimension that prevented the outright victory of an emotional and anti-intellectual revivalism and were therefore also less prone to feeling the need to defend a strict literal interpretation of the Bible. The result has been streams of Protestantism that are both less individualistic and populist than their American counterparts and far friendlier to modern or liberal theology that seeks to build an understanding of God that accords with the realities of science or historical scholarship than what is found in America.

In conclusion, eschatological Christian theology, with a particular focus on the coming Millennium, has been at the heart of American Protestantism since the time of the Puritans. The initial popularity of such views was wrapped up in early expressions of American exceptionalism. For many, the United States was clearly a "New Israel," a true "City on a Hill" whose role was not simply to be a beacon to the rest of the world but also to play a central role in the Second Coming of Christ. Although premillennial sects existed, pre–Civil War American evangelicalism was dominated by an optimistic postmillennial fervour. As will be demonstrated in Chapter 3, the postmillennial eschatology that most influenced the political thought of Henry Wise Wood, president of the United Farmers of Alberta, was a direct import from a liberal American Protestant sect and its American roots gave it a particular populist and republican slant that would have been foreign to both late nineteenth-century Ontario Protestant postmillennialism and the social gospel–based postmillennialism that emerged in Saskatchewan and Manitoba in the early twentieth century. As conditions shifted in America leading up to the Civil War, so too did popular conceptions of how such a Second Coming was to occur. Gradually, a premillennial view overtook a postmillennial outlook and the notion of America as a "City on a Hill" was replaced with a vision of America as being just another nation of individuals who had largely turned their back on God. Although much effort would be expended by Protestant revivalists with the hope of leading as many of those lost souls as possible back to Christ, American evangelicalism has been, since the emergence of dispensationalism, shrouded in a pessimistic view, at least in the short term. The prophetic texts of the Bible foretell worsening social conditions as the world moves closer to the end of days. Those non-Christians who are not plucked from earth by Christ during the Rapture are to suffer terribly at the hands of the Antichrist for a seven-year period. Yet in the long term, those who have authentically accepted Christ as their saviour will enjoy an unprecedented level of peace after the final Battle of Armageddon and the establishment of the millennial reign of Christ on earth. As Boyer and Marsden have both suggested, this is essentially an American interpretation that sits at the foundation of much of America's fundamentalist Christian heritage. Indeed, almost all strands of fundamentalist Christianity that have taken hold in pockets of Canadian society are outgrowths of American movements. In fact, even though William Aberhart, founder of the Alberta Social Credit League, was introduced to premillennial dispensationalism by an Ontario pastor, his fundamentalist theology was clearly derived from the broader American premillennial tradition, a point that will be expanded upon in Chapter 4.

AMERICAN EVANGELICALISM AND THE RELIGIOUS CONTEXT OF EARLY TWENTIETH-CENTURY ALBERTA

Obviously, the above synopsis fails to do justice to the rich and diverse development of either American or Canadian Protestantism, but it does provide an appropriate religious and intellectual context by which one can properly grasp the conceptual and religious framework from which Henry Wise Wood, William Aberhart, and Ernest Manning drew. As will be discussed more fully in Chapters 3 and 4, Wood's religious background was quite different from that of Aberhart and Manning, but all three men adhered to the radically democratic ethos inherent in the broad American evangelical tradition and their thought was also strongly influenced by Christian millennial thinking. It is this influence that helps to place Alberta outside Lipset's general dichotomy and thus differentiates Alberta in an important way from the rest of the Canadian provinces. Of course, the suggestion that Alberta has been influenced by American modes of social, political, or even religious thought is certainly not a revolutionary notion. It has long been assumed by scholars that any exploration of early Alberta political culture must dedicate space to the role of American influence because of the direct impact of significant American immigration. Indeed, nearly 22 per cent of Alberta's population in 1911 had emigrated from the United States.

Of course, significant numbers of Americans would settle throughout the Prairies in the first quarter of the twentieth century, especially in neighbouring Saskatchewan. However, as a portion of the total population, Alberta's collection of American-born residents was by far the largest, a fact Nelson Wiseman has repeatedly pointed to in his effort to explain the differing political cultures of the Prairie provinces. For Wiseman, it was the "radical populist liberalism" brought to Alberta by the significant number of Midwest American farmers who immigrated in the first quarter of the twentieth century that helps to explain Alberta's uniqueness among its Prairie neighbours.[59]

Yet Wiseman and others have had very little to say about the role played by religious ideas crossing the border despite the broad similarities between much of the post-revolution American frontier and early twentieth-century Alberta. Indeed, as W.L. Morton has noted, "Alberta was the frontier of frontiers ... [and] the characteristic frontier malaise of debt, dislocation, and restlessness was active in the province."[60] Just as the participatory and egalitarian evangelical Protestantism emanating out of the American Revolution fit the conditions of the American frontier well, Alberta agrarians, who operated in a space devoid of much traditional denominational influence, seemed predisposed to a similar religious outlook. Add to this rather conducive environment the steady stream of agrarian newsletters and periodicals that made their way from America to Alberta and one begins to see the possibilities of transmission beyond direct immigration.[61] Certainly, as Noll has argued, evangelicalism is not only an agent of democratization because of its internal democratic ethos, it also tends

Table 2.1
Total population and American-born by province, 1911

	Total population	American-born
Manitoba	461,394	16,328
Saskatchewan	492,432	69,628
Alberta	374,295	81,357

Source: Coats and Maclean, The American-Born in Canada: A Statistical Interpretation, 74.

Table 2.2
Total population and American-born by province, 1931

	Total population	American-born
Manitoba	700,139	17,903
Saskatchewan	921,785	73,008
Alberta	731,605	78,959

Source: Coats and Maclean, The American-Born in Canada: A Statistical Interpretation, 74.

to prosper in frontier societies or in Protestant societies that have recently undergone democratic revolutions.[62]

Although scholarly work that focuses on the development of religion throughout the early years of prairie settlement is surprisingly sparse, it is not hard to find census statistics that provide a rough estimate of the numbers of prairie settlers who belonged to each of the five major Christian churches in the early twentieth century. As both Table 2.3 and Table 2.4 suggest, there is nothing significantly exceptional about the religious composition of Alberta in the first decades of the twentieth century when compared to other Prairie provinces, at least at first glance. Yet the usefulness of such statistics is not as apparent as it may seem. As each of these traditional churches moved westward in an effort to win converts, first from the existing Native population and later from the settler communities themselves, the challenges associated with frontier expansion forced competing denominations to co-operate or, at the very least, cede territory. For instance, it was not uncommon for settler community "A" to be served by a single Methodist church, community "B" to contain only an Anglican one, and community "C" to be without any regular church service. It was even common for the minister of one denomination to serve in the church of another when required or vice versa.[63] In other words, the considerable theological differences that make such denominational statistics significant for scholars hoping to assess the potential social or political impact of these established churches on the populations of eastern or central Canada did not necessarily survive the move west intact. In fact, religious historian John Grant has argued that the ecumenical spirit generated by such denominational co-operation in the region ensured that Prairie Protestant churches developed a religious ethos associated with unsophisticated theology, practicality, participation, and community spirit that was quite distinct from the eastern Canadian emphasis on refined sermons, rituals, and the traditional forms of piety that not only reinforced denominational differences but further engrained hierarchical relationships between the church elite and the congregation.[64]

This religious ethos identified by Grant clearly contradicts Lipset's rather simplistic depiction of religious and political values in Canada and is reinforced by the findings of S.D. Clark and W.E. Mann, two sociologists who studied the nature of religious practice in Alberta and its relation to the province's politics in the early twentieth century. Clark attempted to demonstrate a link between the political protest movements of the Prairies (which Lipset's account seems to ignore) and the popularity of non-traditional religious sects in the region, many of which originated in the United States.[65] With specific focus on the religious sects of Alberta around 1930, Clark suggests that such evangelical Protestant organizations took aim at both the traditional theological systems of mainstream churches and their broader social influence within prairie Canada.[66] Implicit within this protest was the same radically democratic spirit one finds in the American evangelical tradition wherein ordinary citizens challenged the position of the traditional church clergy and demanded avenues for increased participation, first in religious services and eventually in social and political affairs. Although Clark suggests that this emerging streak of anti-establishmentarianism among sect members in Alberta was linked to the broader political radicalism within the province, he is also careful to note that religious sectarianism may foster a general attitude of political indifference, especially with regard to specific policy questions. In fact, Clark concludes that such sectarianism impeded the growth of sophisticated political thought and increased general disengagement from policy discussion in areas dominated by sects, an argument that seems to anticipate the later findings of scholars of Prairie populism, who note the ironic existence of an apolitical yet radically populist/anti-establishment political culture in Alberta.[67]

Table 2.3
Religious affiliation by percentage of population across Canada, 1911

Province	Total population	Methodist	Presbyterian	Anglican	Baptist	Roman Catholic
Canada	7,206,643	15.0	15.5	14.8	5.3	39.3
Alberta	374,295	16.5	17.7	14.9	5.2	21.2
Saskatchewan	492,432	15.9	19.6	15.3	3.7	18.3
Manitoba	455,614	15.0	22.8	19.5	3.1	16.3
Ontario	2,523,274	26.7	20.7	19.9	5.3	19.2

Source: Airhart, "Ordering a New Nation and Reordering Protestantism, 1867–1914," 102–4.

Table 2.4
Religious affiliation by percentage of population in Alberta and Saskatchewan, 1921

Province	Total population	Methodist	Presbyterian	Anglican	Baptist	Lutheran	Roman Catholic
Alberta	588,454	15	21	16	5	10	16
Saskatchewan	757,510	14	21	15	3	12	19

Source: These figures are drawn from: Palmer and Palmer, *Alberta: A New History*, 103; and Leona Anderson, Bryan Hills, and Margaret Sanche, "Religion," in *The Encyclopedia of Saskatchewan*, http://esask.uregina.ca/entry/religion.html (accessed 17 November 2014).

To this day, the most comprehensive study on the religious makeup of Alberta remains Mann's 1955 investigation into the province's "exceptional history of religious non-conformity" in the first half of the twentieth century. Utilizing Clark's church-sect distinction, Mann suggests that in 1946 at least 20 per cent of Alberta's nearly 300,000 practising Protestants (and perhaps as many as 35 per cent!) belonged to non-traditional evangelical sects as opposed to mainstream churches.[68] Importantly, the vast majority of the thirty-five sects he identifies as operational in Alberta at the time could be classified as fundamentalist. That is, they were bitterly opposed to modernism in all its forms and held to a "tight ascetic code of morality and belief in the literal truth of the bible, in the personal second coming of Christ ... and the necessity of a dramatic conversion experience." Unsurprisingly, given the vast numbers of Americans who migrated to Alberta in the decades prior, Mann connects these sects to the broader American fundamentalist movement that emerged in the last quarter of the nineteenth century.[69] Mann further draws important parallels between early Albertan religious culture and the American form of populist Christianity discussed above. Central findings include the various sects' penchant for protest against traditional theological formality and a corresponding emphasis on equality and fraternity among members, including the preference for a "folksy" pastor, a "down-to-earth" sermon, and avenues for congregational participation. The impact of this protest against traditional religious authority and practice was significant in the province not simply because there were a large number of sects but, more so, because these sects were very successful relative to traditional churches in setting up Bible schools and commandeering large audiences via radio broadcasting, two vitally important mediums through which the spirit of religious protest and anti-establishmentarianism could easily be spread.[70]

Of course, the success of fundamentalist populist Christian sects owes much to the social conditions of early Alberta. Essentially agreeing with the findings of Grant, Mann points to "the frontier heritage of informal and neighbourly social relations," the lack of considerable traditional church "coverage" over large swaths of the province, high numbers of mobile, newly arrived, and socially marginalized individuals, and various economic crises, especially in the 1930s, as characteristics that created a strong demand for institutions capable to providing a simple Christian message, opportunities for lay participation, and the chance to belong.[71] In fact, the failure of traditional churches in Alberta to adapt to these conditions allowed fundamentalist sects to gradually acquire significant numbers of adherents from their audiences. Indeed, the "stiffness and formality" of traditional church worship and, more importantly, their gradual adoption of the modernist theology that had largely overtaken Ontario Protestant seminaries in the early years of the twentieth century resulted in "a lot of intellectual sermons that 'went over the heads' of the congregations" in the 1920s and 1930s.[72] Subsequently, substantial numbers of mainstream church attendees slowly migrated to fundamentalist services or, in the extreme cases, chose to receive their weekly dose of Christianity by way of the popular fundamentalist radio programs rather than the church. And no Christian radio program was more popular than William Aberhart's fundamentalist *Back to the Bible Hour*, which began transmitting in 1925.

Yet, although it is often assumed that the eventual electoral success of Aberhart owes much to the relatively high number of fundamentalists sects operating in Alberta in the 1920s and 1930s, Harry Hiller has convincingly argued that the general lack of a well-developed class structure and socio-religious unity in Alberta at the time made Aberhart's simplistic "Back to the Bible" message popular beyond such sects and across denominational lines.[73] In fact, a collection of Alberta's most strident fundamentalists, especially those connected with the notorious Prairie Bible Institute, were strongly opposed to Aberhart's entrance into politics. This will be expanded upon in due course, but the broader point I would like to tease out here is simply that early Alberta Protestantism as a whole, given the social conditions of Alberta at the time, was highly susceptible to the populist nature of the message inherent in fundamentalist Christianity despite the fact that census statistics alone suggest that Alberta's religious makeup was not very different from that of other Prairie provinces – or even Ontario for that matter. That Alberta Protestantism was in fact distinct in important ways coincides with David Goa's more recent finding that Aberhart's version of Christianity, which was regularly followed by between 300,000 and 350,000 citizens, gradually colonized many non-fundamentalist Christian traditions in Alberta, resulting in the emergence of a widely shared "great plains evangelicalism."[74]

Taken together, the contributions above hint at a link between sectarian religious protest in Alberta, often infused with elements of the American evangelical tradition, and the broader political and economic populist protest that led to the popularity of a number of non-traditional, populist political parties. The fact that Clark and Mann highlight the distinctly sectarian nature of Alberta's religious history seems, on its own, to strongly contradict Lipset's portrayal of Canada as a land of deference to traditional European Christian theology and, subsequently, to political and economic elites. Add to this sectarian religious history the specific American influence on Alberta that is mentioned in the scholarship of Wiseman and others and it is easy to see why one would expect to find in Alberta a relationship between popular theology and populist political sentiment similar what one often finds in America. This, however, is a broad sociological point that, without further scholarly attention, remains somewhat speculative. Neither Clark, Mann, nor Hiller focus on the specific relationship between the religious interpretation and the political thought of ordinary citizens or particular Alberta leaders. No doubt a more thorough investigation into the thinking of ordinary Albertans would unearth fascinating findings, but this book takes a more focused approach and, over the remaining chapters, argues that American – rather than Canadian or British – evangelical Christian perspectives significantly shaped the political thought of key political leaders in Alberta in the early and mid-twentieth century, thereby helping to set the province upon a political trajectory that was somewhat distinct from that of the rest of Canada.

Of course, it is clear that the social and religious context described above is intimately related to the type of leader that could emerge and gain popular support in the province at the time. Indeed, as mentioned in the previous chapter, the actual "supply" of leaders "is driven by a pre-existing societal 'demand' which the political entrepreneurship of a would-be leader seeks to satisfy." Yet there is often "more than one way to satisfy that demand, or to create an impression that the problem can be resolved."[75] In other words, context such as that described above matters but is not wholly determinate. Leaders possess an element of agency within the political process and thus can be understood as being one of the significant factors shaping the political development of a society. Having provided this brief account of the religious and social context of Alberta in the first half of the twentieth century, which was admittedly fertile soil that leaders such as Henry Wise Wood and William Aberhart could emerge from and operate within, the remainder of this book will focus more specifically on how certain religious outlooks shaped the political thought and action of key leaders, and how this in turn helped to shape Alberta's political development.

3

Religion and the Political Thought of Henry Wise Wood

Liberal Postmillennialism and the Initial Rejection of Prairie Socialism in Alberta

Scholars have typically interpreted the United Farmers of Alberta (UFA), which ruled the province from 1921 until 1935, as an economic and educational agrarian organization that eventually evolved into a dominant provincial political party. Formed in 1909, the UFA sought to improve the economic condition of the prairie farmer, who, in its eyes, were beholden to the exploitation of monopolistic central Canadian industrialists and grain buyers whose financial interests were protected by a distant federal government that showed little sympathy for the concerns of hinterland agrarians. Building upon the gains of the larger North American agrarian movement, the UFA developed into an extensive network of highly participatory "locals," community-level groupings of farmers that sought to protect their economic interests by lobbying government and by pooling both their purchasing power and their agricultural produce in an effort to leverage their way to better financial outcomes. These specific efforts were driven by a broad educational campaign waged by the organization's headquarters, including plain language analyses of the farmers' economic condition and concrete plans to improve it. In 1919, under intense pressure from the popular Alberta chapter of the Non-Partisan League, it was decided that these locals should take direct political action, and in 1921, the UFA – as an "economic group" rather than a "traditional political party" – swept into power. The UFA was initially led by Herbert Greenfield, but he was soon replaced by John Brownlee, who would serve as Alberta premier for nine years. However, the UFA's flirtation with the national Co-operative Commonwealth Federation (CCF) and its inability to spur Alberta's economy out of the eventual worldwide economic depression cost the organization much electoral support, and on the heels of a sex scandal that engulfed Brownlee in 1934, the UFA was swept from office by William Aberhart and the Alberta Social Credit League in the summer of 1935.

That the UFA was perhaps the first and only authentic grassroots participatory movement in Canada to attain political power on the back of an impressive and pre-existing network of community-level groupings of farmers has led to a significant level of attention from academics. In fact, luminary Canadian scholars such as W.L. Morton, Frank Underhill, C.B. Macpherson, Gerald Friesen, Nelson Wiseman, Thomas Flanagan and David Laycock have all studied aspects of the UFA.[1] However, when one takes a step back from the immediate economic and political themes recounted by such scholars and examines the more abstract elements of the overarching vision held by the group's most influential leader, a slightly different picture emerges that has yet to be fully articulated. The UFA was certainly eager to improve the economic position of the Alberta farmer, and it stressed vigorous grassroots participation and education at the local level as a way to meet this goal, but much of its leadership also understood the UFA to be a significant player in a much larger, religiously inspired reform movement that would improve conditions for all people. Indeed, in 1920, the UFA's official periodical declared that the UFA was "the most powerful agency in Canada today for the establishment of the Kingdom of God on earth."[2] Of course, an idealistic mindset that mixed religious notions with broad social reform efforts was not exactly unusual in the early twentieth century, especially on the Canadian Prairies where a number of utopian visions were hatched from the optimism that accompanied a "new start" on the frontier.[3] A good deal of this utopianism was a product of the Christian social gospel message, the broad agreement among progressive Protestants that Christianity was a social religion meant to address the ills of an industrializing society, such as poverty and inequality. The Canadian Prairie version of the social gospel initially emanated out of Winnipeg's Wesley College and the lectures of Salem Bland and onto the pages of the popular agrarian periodical the *Grain Growers' Guide*. Yet the UFA was somewhat unique in that its most influential leader and thinker, Henry Wise Wood, had migrated north from the United States and brought with him a religious perspective that, although similar in many respects, was not identical to what he found in Canada. No doubt William Irvine, a former student of Bland's, played a significant role within the UFA, and for this reason a strand of Bland's more radical "socialistic" social gospel Christianity was present

Religion and Political Thought of Henry Wise Wood

within the UFA from its early years. However, it was the more "American" progressive evangelical Protestantism of long-time UFA president Wood that most influenced the culture and direction of the UFA and therefore of early Alberta as well.

Alberta was very much a Christian society in the early twentieth century, and it is not hard to find some basic Christian teachings at the heart of the Alberta agrarian movement, stretching back well before Wood became UFA president. As early as 1902, there were calls for governments to operate on the principles of Christ as well as assurances to the farmers that God intended profits to flow to those who tilled the soil rather than to the dreaded middlemen.[4] In addition, the influential *Grain Growers' Guide* served as a forum for early advocates of the social gospel to spread their message of a "new social religion," one that demanded that commerce and politics be conducted by way of Christ's golden rule.[5] In 1910, UFA president James Bower insisted that the organization was founded upon the "principle which true Christianity and humanity stand for: namely, the brotherhood of man."[6] W.J. Tregillus, UFA president from 1912 to 1914, regularly echoed this message, quoting from the social gospel message of Salem Bland, calling for a religiously inspired co-operative spirit, and noting that "God has endowed us with intelligence ... to lift humanity to a higher plane and work for the common good."[7] Within a few years of their establishment, UFA locals had become centres of intense social and educational activity, which included their provision of unofficial Christian church services in the many frontier rural areas that had been spiritually underserved. By 1914, this religious presence culminated with the introduction of "UFA Sundays," an annual afternoon picnic featuring both religious and agrarian speakers who emphasized a "practical Christianity" that could be concretely applied to the farmers movement.[8] Thus, as Bradford James Rennie demonstrates, elements of Wood's religiously derived political thought were surely foreshadowed in the pre-existing currents within the UFA.[9] However, it was not until the emergence of Wood as president of the movement in 1916 that the UFA shifted from an organization built upon some broad Christian precepts to one that was, for all intents and purposes, a central player in the quest to establish nothing less than the kingdom of God on earth.

The UFA was a diverse and democratic organization made up of a number of thoughtful and outspoken men and women from different cultural backgrounds, a characteristic that led to there being a noticeable divide between "radical" and "liberal" members.[10] Yet it is not an exaggeration to suggest that Wood, president from 1916 until 1931 and clearly a member of the more mainstream liberal wing, was by far the movement's most respected and influential figure. Indeed, despite refusing the premiership that was offered to him when the organization's political arm won power, Wood would become known throughout the province as "the boss," "the chief," or even "the uncrowned King of Alberta."[11] "The secret of H.W. Wood's extraordinary influence over the rural people of Alberta," observed a curious *Toronto Star* reporter struck by his popularity, "is that he has led them and to a certain extent taught them."[12] The UFA's own periodical expanded on this observation, praising Wood's selflessness, his commitment to humanity, and his insistence on co-operation and local democracy, and claiming that "no other one person in Alberta has done more to arouse the people to accept the responsibility of their own institutions than he."[13] Given this influence, Wood's thought has garnered much interest from scholars eager to make sense of the UFA's highly participatory and democratic nature, its support for economic co-operatives, and its peculiar advancement of "group government." However, although most historians and political scientists have mentioned Wood's religious background, the precise influence of his particular Christian perspective on his political thought has been largely glossed over.[14] Richard Allen, who has taken religious influence far more seriously than most Prairie scholars, did acknowledge that "Wood's whole programme was ultimately theological," yet in the end, he did little to distinguish Wood's thought from key western Canadian social gospel leaders such as Bland, Irvine, or J.S. Woodsworth.[15]

As will be demonstrated, despite broad agreement on the need to import the social teachings of Christ into the political and economic realm, Wood's American evangelical Protestant background would ensure important differences between his thought and that of the mainstream Prairie social gospel crowd, differences that would ultimately help to steer the early political trajectory of Alberta in a distinct direction. Indeed, Wood's opposition to the more radical demands of left-leaning "social gospellers" within the organization was enough to convince most Alberta farmers to reject such policies on numerous occasions throughout his presidency. In fact, it was not until Wood retired and was replaced by the radical former clergymen Robert Gardiner that the UFA veered sharply left, which eventually culminated in the organization denouncing the fiscal conservatism of its own government while simultaneously helping to found the national CCF, a move that might have, quite ironically, sealed the UFA government's electoral demise.

Here, I argue that Wood's personal interpretation of Christianity was a much stronger influence on his political thought – and subsequently on the corresponding practical organization and direction of the UFA and the broader political trajectory of Alberta – than has been previously recognized. Wood's thought did not possess the precision of the thought of a systematic and formally trained philosopher or religious scholar such as Bland, nor was it encapsulated within the confines of a single authoritative text.[16] However, a careful reading of his numerous speeches, letters, and columns reveals a clear pattern of thought that was founded upon his unique Christian interpretation. Of course, religion was by no means the only influence on the UFA, and Wood was not motivated solely by religious concerns. In fact, as he was a relatively well-read individual, his thinking also drew from many of the scientific, economic, and philosophical currents of his day. Yet existing expositions of Wood's thought remain incomplete, for they fail to develop a full accounting of the ways in which his Christian interpretation shaped his social and political thought, from his views on social evolution and democracy, to his advancement of a political system organized around occupational groups, to his aversion to government-sanctioned collectivist schemes. That said, Wood was not religious in the traditional mystical sense of the word. He admitted that his thinking about religion had evolved away from the traditional themes related to personal spiritual salvation or the afterlife that had concerned him in his youth. As he aged, he became ever more aware that the teachings of Christ contained "a wonderful storehouse of practical information," and he therefore defined his religious creed as "a desire to understand [Christ's] natural social law and to live and construct in accordance with that law."[17] In fact, he routinely criticized traditional churches for stressing only individual purity. "Only dull Christians," he argued, "are failing to see that ultimate Christianity is social rather than individual," a belief he shared with the broader Prairie social gospel crowd who also largely operated outside the traditional church.[18] This shared emphasis on the social aspects of Christ drew from the American liberal and postmillennial evangelical Protestant tradition that emerged in the second half of the nineteenth century. As discussed in Chapter 2, this particular strand responded to the challenges posed by both Darwin and *higher criticism* by gradually abandoning the overt supernaturalism of God and instead adopting an evolution-friendly conception of social change driven largely by human action in accordance with the moral teachings of Christ. Central to this interpretation was a view of the ordinary individual possessing the agency required to slowly reform social institutions according to the dictates of Christ's moral message, culminating with the establishment of Christ's promised kingdom on earth. Importantly, however, Wood harnessed this particular postmillennial interpretation to a more traditional and conservative American evangelical stream of thought that emphasized both democratic participation and individual responsibility, the latter characteristic helping to set Wood apart in important ways from the Prairie social gospellers.

The following paragraphs provide a brief re-examination of Wood's religious and political background in order to contextualize the detailed reconstruction of his social and political thought that comprises the greater part of this chapter. Not only does this reinterpretation present a more complete picture of the religiously based strand of political thought that stood behind the UFA's emphasis on local organization, participation, education, and voluntary co-operation, but it further demonstrates an important link between the American evangelical Protestant tradition and the early political development of Alberta. The broader political implications of Wood's religious-based thought and its impact on the political direction of the UFA and Alberta's early political trajectory are discussed in the concluding section.

WOOD'S POLITICAL AND RELIGIOUS BACKGROUND

Wood was, like many of his UFA contemporaries, a recent immigrant from the United States, and his particular upbringing in Missouri, where he lived until the age of forty-five, had exposed him to three unique, although related, strands of religious-based thought from which his own particular interpretation would draw.[19] The first of these strands was encapsulated within the agrarian populist movement of the American South and Midwest that he had supported as a young man. Although not a significant player in the movement, Wood was a participant in his local of the Farmers' and Laborers' Union in Ralls County, Missouri, and a careful observer of the broader populist crusade that clearly influenced his eventual analysis of the economic and political conditions faced by the Alberta farmers.[20] Although Wood's brush with the populist movement has been mentioned by nearly all who have written about him, most commentators, having relied upon the standard historical accounts of the American movement penned by the likes of John D. Hicks, Norman Pollack, and Lawrence Goodwyn, have failed to emphasize the strong religious current that ran through it.[21]

However, recent scholarship has done much to highlight the significant religious dimension of the American agrarian movement from which Wood emerged.

As Rhys Williams and Susan M. Alexander have argued, the moral and philosophical foundations of the American agrarian populism movement were significantly influenced by evangelical Christianity in the American South and Midwest.[22] Joe Creech, who has thoroughly documented the evangelical Protestant "patterns of thoughts" that sat at the foundation of the populist movement, has furthered this point by noting the manner by which the agrarians were strongly moved by the evangelical belief in the capacity of the "common man" not only to interpret sacred scripture but, more importantly, to apply it to day-to-day circumstances. Thus, the populist agrarians were provided with both the confidence and the divine inspiration required to challenge traditional forms of political and economic authority in the name of Christian justice.[23] In addition, beyond this evangelical Protestant foundation that emphasized their individual capacities to challenge a system responsible for their hardships, the evangelicalism of the rural South and Midwest also offered particular solutions. Indeed, Richard Goode and Paul Harvey have both demonstrated the manner by which American populist agrarians drew on a "rural social gospel" that was distinct from and less sophisticated than the northern and urban and largely academic social gospel espoused by the likes of Washington Gladden and Walter Rauschenbusch. This rural social gospel drew heavily from the evangelical values of individual autonomy and piety but shared with the northern social gospel a social condemnation (based on the golden rule of Christ) of the political and economic conditions imposed upon the plain people by an ever-industrializing economy.[24] Creech also distinguishes the evangelical social Christianity that motivated the American agrarians from the more sophisticated combination of theological liberalism and progressive economic theories that emerged from the oft-cited northern social gospel movement. This common folk social Christianity combined evangelical conceptions of benevolence and anti-elitism with Jeffersonian rural ideals related to agrarian purity, self-sufficiency, and small-scale commerce to produce "the simple yet powerful idea that economic relationships should be guided by the law of love."[25]

The strong evangelical basis of this sentiment ensured that agrarian populists remained fixated on individual piety even when sternly challenging a political and economic system they viewed as corrupt and oppressive. In fact, the anger of agrarians was largely directed at economic and political elites who had failed to embody the moral axioms of God and had thus allowed their corporations and political parties to operate in manners contrary to God's principles. The agrarians did not, therefore, view state-led regulations on industry or private property as the answer. Instead, "a permanent change in the economic system required a change in the hearts of individuals and then through those individuals a change to political and economic organizations." Thus, Creech continues, "through a process of moral suasion, discipline, and education, the [agrarians] hoped to create an army of enlightened individuals and then to provide pathways for those individuals, acting co-operatively, to effect change in the political economy.[26] As will become clearer as this chapter progresses, it is difficult to overstate the degree to which this particular evangelically based remedy for social change, articulated by American agrarian populists in the 1890s, foreshadowed the essence of Wood's unique social and political thought made manifest in Alberta three decades later.

In addition to this evangelical Protestant dimension of the American populist movement, Wood was also exposed to a second strand of religious-based thought by way of his membership and active participation in the Missouri branch of the Disciples of Christ.[27] The Disciples, a sect stretching back to Alexander Campbell and the American Restoration Movement of the early nineteenth century, had as their mission the reconciliation and unification of the various denominations of the Protestant Church by stressing a return to "primitive Christianity" based solely upon the teachings of Christ in the New Testament.[28] Primarily rural in nature, the Disciples in the American South and Midwest in the late nineteenth century were, in the words of historian David Harrell, "a case study of the Protestant ethic," embracing small-scale laissez-faire capitalism, individual responsibility, honesty, and frugality, as well as a distinctly "lower class prejudice" that singled out the unethical practices of "plutocrats."[29] Combined with this traditionally conservative evangelical outlook, however, was the Disciples' prototypical post-revolution religious preference for an organization that rejected the cold, formal, and hierarchical nature of traditional Christianity and its tendency to elevate the learned clergy. In its place grew an ecumenical and co-operative sentiment within the church as well as a broader democratic tendency towards anti-establishmentarianism and a decentralized congregational organization that demanded layman participation. This was founded upon a strict adherence to a "populist hermeneutic" that understood the common individual as one who possessed the intellectual capacity required to interpret the teachings of Christ for him or herself.[30] The social and economic thought of the Disciples that grew from this populist hermeneutic, which Keith King describes as a "Christianized, Jeffersonian agrarianism marked by antimonopoly sentiments and frontier egalitarianism," ensured that members of the Disciples' congregation were avid participants in the broader agrarian populist movement.[31] As will become apparent, it is not difficult to discern a distinct version of this Christianized Jeffersonian agrarianism in the eventual political thought of Wood, although he would also draw from a more radical interpretation of Christianity.

In the final decade of the nineteenth century, young liberal Disciple ministers began to explore the "kingdom theology" emanating out of the early northern social gospel movement and preached the "brotherhood of man" message to their congregations. The Disciples' traditional emphasis on the social teachings of Christ and their broader evangelical-based insistence on the dangers of centralization ensured that Wood and his fellow Disciples were particularly well-suited to embrace elements of the broader social gospel message, and before long, the works of early social gospel stalwarts Washington Gladden, Josiah Strong, and Richard T. Ely were printed and discussed in the Disciples' press.[32] Related to the introduction of social gospel themes was the Disciples' new commitment to the principles of the Enlightenment, most especially the notion of a "scientific method," which gained significant traction in nineteenth-century America from a Christian perspective. Just as the establishment of a proper method of scientific inquiry would lead all rational humans to agree on the laws at work in nature, a focus on the New Testament alone, without the interference of traditional clergy, would lead the common people to the true Christian message and the laws it contained.[33] In fact, this emphasis on the "natural laws" contained within scripture, in conjunction with the broader rural-based lower-class prejudice that ran though the sect, led the Disciples to embrace the notion that the Antichrist was working through the elites in society in order to prevent the coming kingdom of God, a central theme eventually found in the thought of Wood.[34]

Wood's exposure to Christian-based natural law theory was furthered by his exposure to a third strand of religiously infused thought by way of his studies at Christian University in Missouri, where, according to his brother, he was deeply moved by professors who taught that co-operation rather than competition was the true social law and that the inspiration for this philosophy "was not the communist saint, Karl Marx, but the Christian saint, the Apostle John."[35] Wood completed only two

72   God's Province

years of university before returning to full-time farm life, but he remained a voracious reader throughout his lifetime. In addition to close
personal study of the Bible, especially the gospels of Christ, which, he
declared, "have been the greatest influence of my life," Wood studied
the works of Adam Smith, J.S. Mill, Karl Marx, and Herbert Spencer
alongside American progressives Frank Norris, M.P. Follett, Henry
George, and Washington Gladden, among others.[36] The lessons Wood
drew from this personal study were added to many of the central religious themes he was exposed to in both the agrarian populist movement and the Disciples of Christ sect. The result was a pattern of social
and political thought that retained a striking similarity to the central
tenets of the liberal postmillennial stand of American evangelical theology but was also tinged with aspects of the more sophisticated northern social gospel movement. This puts his religious views in a category
separate from the more orthodox and less populist evangelical Protestantism of Ontario and much of the western Canadian social gospel
movement, both of which had a more European and less individualistic and democratic flavour. In the sections that follow I spell out in far
more detail the particular religious views of Wood and how they influenced his own social and political thought that began to take concrete shape upon his move to Alberta in 1905 and his eventual
participation in, and leadership of, the UFA. It is only by way of such detailed investigation that one can come to see the manner by which
Wood's unique interpretation helped to set Alberta on a unique path
when compared to that of Alberta's neighbouring Prairie provinces and
more distant eastern ones.

RELIGION AND THE SOCIAL THEORY OF WOOD

The social thought of Wood was grounded on two fundamental assumptions drawn from his exposure to natural law theories within the
Disciples of Christ sect as well as his former Christian University. First,
Wood believed that human beings are naturally social beings who are
destined to construct a proper social system within which they can
flourish. This was necessary given that the war and financial oppression that had become so prominent at the time "originate[d] in a wrong
principle that [lay] somewhere at the foundation of the social structure."[37] Luckily, nature has provided humans with certain intellectual
faculties as well as a blueprint in the form of natural laws in order to facilitate the construction of a proper social system, "but it is up to [them]
to do the construction work. [They] can do this only by using [their]

Religion and Political Thought of Henry Wise Wood

faculties under the guidance of those natural laws."[38] Second, the history within which humans find themselves, argued Wood, progresses in a linear fashion and has been characterized from the beginning by a cosmic struggle between two opposing forces, the true and false laws, those of co-operation and competition, that will eventually collide one final time, producing a definite victory of good over evil. Wood writes:

Competition is the false social law, and no social system based primarily on this law can ever reach perfection. Co-operation is the true social law, and a true social system must be founded primarily on that law. All past social progress has been founded primarily on the law of competition, but the law of co-operation has been operating secondarily. These laws are ever acting and reacting upon each other, the destructiveness of competition forcing co-operation to higher development, and this in turn increasing the destructiveness of competition. Competition is the law of destruction, and all the destruction that has ever been wrought by man against his fellow man has been wrought by competition. All construction of social strength has been done by co-operation.[39]

He continues:

Democracy can be established only on the basis of co-operation. The great masses of people have failed in their competitive struggle ... [but they are now] marshaling their forces in stable groups.
    When these forces are finally thus marshaled the irrepressible conflict will be on. The conflict between democracy and plutocracy; between civilization and barbarism; between man and money; between co-operation and competition; between God and Mammon. To say that democracy will fail will be to say that the design of nature in creating a social being and bringing him into obedience to social laws has failed. It will be to say that nature has failed in her supreme effort; to say that wrong is stronger than right; error stronger than truth; Mammon stronger than God.
    It will not fail. It cannot fail, because the Supreme Power ... will not let it fail.[40]

This particular teleological interpretation of both humanity and history was heavily influenced by the work of Herbert Spencer, the English evolutionary philosopher and favourite of Wood's. Following

Spencer's general argument, Wood understood history to be unfolding by way of an evolutionary process that had as its end the creation of the morally perfect individual within a perfectly moral society. This perfected society, governed by the social law of co-operation, would "be a living thing, not one that lives, reproduces and dies. Its life will be eternal and in it human well-being will be established."[41] The positive progression of humanity and society was thus a natural process that occurred according to natural laws in the same way physical evolution takes place. However, Wood did allow a vital role within this understanding for human agency. The rate at which this positive progression would take place was related to the degree to which humanity could properly identify and follow the natural social laws. Much work had already been done to unearth the operation of the natural physical laws, but according to Wood, an exploration of the natural social laws, what he deemed "the realm of spiritual science," was still required for it is here that "man will eventually gain an understanding of the truth that will make him free."[42] Even a quick glance at human history confirmed for Wood that humans had failed to comprehend, let alone follow, the natural social laws:

We look into the universe and see everywhere the works of nature and we see them all in obedience to natural law. Till we come to man, the creature that was created as a social being. There we see the great exception. Man to the present time has stubbornly refused to come into obedience to natural social law. Now there is one of two things that is going to happen ... man is going to come into obedience of nature's laws or else he is going to become self-destructive. No work of nature can exist and can continue to violate natural law.[43]

Thus, the articulation and exposition of these natural social laws became the central focus of Wood's social thought, a task made all the more necessary given the unprecedented magnitude of death and destruction occurring in the Great War of Europe. For Wood, the technological machinery required to produce death on such a scale only confirmed his thesis that mankind had progressed by great strides in the field of natural sciences but remained stuck in a state of social competition and barbarism. It was in this personal quest to identify and make known the natural social laws that could end such competitive misery that his thought took a distinctively Christian turn. Indeed, upon assuming the presidency of the UFA in 1916, he was adamant about the centrality of Christ's message in this quest:

> We believe that our organization represents a reform movement and that reform movements are efforts to make adjustments in accordance with the principles of right and justice; and no matter what a man's orthodox opinion may be, if he is investigating the laws of right, he cannot afford to ignore the teachings of Christianity ... [T]hese are the great lights by which reform must be guided. More men now than ever before are coming to believe that His teaching is the one and only key to the true and final adjustment of the elements of human affairs, social, economic, and political.[44]

The following year, while instructing the Christian ministers who would preside over UFA Sundays across the province, Wood urged them not to simply preach about personal righteousness but rather to make clear that "through His [Jesus'] leadership alone, we have hope of reorganizing institutions and building a perfect civilization." Indeed, he continued, "the only thing Jesus ever taught us to pray for was this regenerated perfected civilization."[45] Yet, rather than investigate this religious influence, the vast array of scholars who have considered the thought of Wood within the context of the UFA have tended to begin their own analysis of his political prescriptions at this point, thereby largely overlooking this central foundation.

For Wood, history began with primitive man, who, although provided with an intellectual or reasoning capacity, was initially guided by the spirit he inherited, the animal spirit, the law of the beasts, of competition, of every man for himself. However, implanted within man was also a "germ" of something purer, a capacity to eventually hear "the call of nature for co-operation."[46] This call would come from Christ, whose appearance and teachings on earth represented the first stage of the positive moral progression of humanity. According to Wood, this call is issued most authoritatively in the Sermon on the Mount, the most substantial collection of Christ's ethical teachings recited in the Book of Matthew. Christ's intention in this sermon, Wood argues, is the eventual establishment of the kingdom of heaven, which, importantly, is not to be found in a mystical heaven in the afterlife: "He instructed them to pray for the coming of the Kingdom, and the doing of the Will of God on earth. This locates the Kingdom on earth, and makes it a practical institution. This can mean nothing less than a social structure built in conformity with natural, social laws."[47]

However, this kingdom on earth will not come along by way of prayer alone. The natural development of the kingdom was, for Wood, a two-stage process. First, humanity must come to abide by natural social laws, the moral laws of Christ delivered in the New Testament. At the heart of these teachings is the call for repentance, the beginning of individual regeneration wherein the individual turns away from the primitive animal spirit that is the law of Satan and embraces the demand of Christ to "be ye perfect as your father in Heaven is perfect" by bearing one another's burdens and following the golden rule by "doing unto others what you would have them do to you."[48] This revelation by Christ represented "the climax of the true principles governing individual relationships."[49] Such social commands were "natural" because humans are social beings and it is their natural end to evolve into morally perfect social beings by treating their fellow human beings in the proper manner, the manner taught by Christ. Once they complete this individual regeneration, they are ready to contribute to the second phase of the development of the coming kingdom:

> When man comes to act naturally and normally under the guidance of the true spirit he will be ready to begin construction of the Kingdom. The call to repentance was a call to man to turn away from the dominion of the animal spirit that has led him into the bondage and darkness or barbarism – the world, and to turn to the true social spirit that would eventually lead him into the light and liberty of true civilization – the Kingdom.[50]

The second phase required of the coming kingdom – social regeneration – would thus be initiated by those who have already accepted the teachings of Christ and are therefore "born again" as moral humans acting in accordance with the natural social law. The social system they build will be founded upon the call for social co-operation issued by Christ. However, Wood was adamant that such construction would take place not by way of a quick and violent victory but rather by a gradual, evolutionary process wherein the spirit of co-operation overtakes that of competition. This rejection of violent revolution is again based on the teachings of Christ, most especially his "parable of the tares" recited in Matthew 13:24–43 in which a farmer, eager to separate the tares, or weeds, from his wheat field, is instructed by Jesus to avoid immediately pulling at the weeds, for such an action will disturb the wheat as well. Instead, the farmer is to allow both plants to mature, at which point it will be possible to extract the weeds without damaging the wheat. Wood, understanding the weeds to represent the spirit of Satan, the false social law that currently dominates the world, and the wheat to be that which is good and associated with the kingdom of God, writes:

> When both [seeds] were sufficiently mature, the false would be carefully separated and destroyed, the true only remaining. In the destruction of the false the "world" would disappear and the Kingdom only remain. This is a gradual evolutionary process. The uninformed servants, on discovering the evil tares in the field, wanted to go out and eradicate them by violent force or by revolutionary methods. The householder informed them that revolutionary violence would not only destroy the evil, but would destroy the good with it.[51]

Relating this interpretation to the point in history he finds himself in, Wood writes: "At the present time the good and evil in our social system are so interrelated and interwoven with each other that to undertake to destroy the evil by violence would be impossible without destroying the good also. But, by the evolutionary process of gradually building up the good, the evil can as gradually be eliminated."[52]

To add further credibility, as well as an air of inevitability, to his particular interpretation of Christ's teachings Wood offered a unique reading of the Book of Revelation that radically departed from traditional literal interpretations popular in fundamentalist evangelical circles. For Wood, the Book of Revelation depicted the coming battle between the "true" and "false" social laws, culminating in "the most wonderful picture of the development of a social system, from the false social system on up to a perfect civilization."[53] In Wood's interpretation, Babylon, the evil city that is toppled by the true forces, encapsulated the competitive nature of commercialism found in present-day society and its prophesized fall in Chapter 18 of the Book of Revelation signals that "the superstructure has been changed from a false foundation to a true one."[54] Despite a last-gasp effort on the part of Satan and his minions to retake control, the forces of God withstand their advances and the evil one is "cast out forever, into a bottomless pit, and a social system was founded absolutely."[55] This is represented by the establishment of the New Jerusalem described in Chapter 21 wherein "the laws of Christ were put into complete operation ... [I]t

78   God's Province

was the ultimate accomplishment of perfect spiritual life. There was no
darkness; man understood the spiritual laws of life; they didn't walk in
darkness anymore, but walked in the light of truth."[56] This was the perfect social system, for its construction is guided by the "ultimate
knowledge of the truth as taught by Christ," and its development takes
place "in perfect harmony with nature's laws, which are the laws of
God."[57] Thus, Wood adhered to a clear evangelical postmillennial
Christian interpretation wherein humanity was to bring about a perfect social system, which he equated to God's kingdom on earth, by
way of personal, and eventually social, devotion to the co-operative
message of Christ. The practical details of how this process was to be
undertaken by the agrarians of rural Alberta are made apparent in
Wood's more precise political thinking, to which we now turn.

RELIGION AND THE POLITICAL THOUGHT OF WOOD

As noted above, Wood's interpretation of the direction of history, guided by his personal reading of the New Testament, points towards the
gradual coming of a new age highlighted by the creation of a perfect social system. Although he is clear that humans have a substantial role to
play in this development, very little is said in the way of a detailed plan.
Surely the process begins with "individual regeneration," the spiritual
rebirth of the individual who brushes aside selfish impulses and follows the social edicts delivered by Christ in the Sermon on the Mount.
This individual rebirth paves the way for "social regeneration," whereby a collection of such people begin to work together so that the co-operative social spirit they have learned from Christ is extended to more
and more groups of people, thus building a certain momentum that
ensures this spirit begins to overtake public life, eventually resulting in
its complete domination over the spirit of competition. But this seems
to be where the divine instruction stops. Wood writes: "Christ did not
go into details in regard to social reconstruction, but many of His say-
ings prove conclusively that He had a clear understanding of the underlying principles of that process. After all, these principles are eternal
and of primary importance, and while details will change as conditions
change, it is up to us to work them out."[58] Wood was therefore left to
his own devices to work out these details in accordance with the conditions in which he found himself, those of the agrarians in rural Alberta. It is thus not surprising that he turned to the already existing UFA
as an outlet for his broader goal of establishing a kingdom of heaven on
earth. Consequently, many of his practical political and economic de-

mands were made with the Alberta farmers in mind. However, before the concrete link between Wood's interpretation of Christianity and the practical work of the UFA under his guidance is established, the theoretical implications of his religious beliefs upon politics must first be made apparent.

Although Christ provided no specific blueprint for the creation of perfect political institutions, Wood was convinced that the moral teachings of Christ demanded, at minimum, a democratic system. "I believe with all my heart," professed Wood,

> that there has never been any living man that had an absolute clear understanding of the fundamental principles of democracy except Christ himself; and I believe that our only hope is in Christ and his teachings, his philosophy. Without that hope I believe we have a future without hope. I would ask you to read for yourself Christ's teachings, study them, try to understand them, try to see how absolutely they fit with every principle and ideal that you can imagine of real democracy, and how every principle that He taught has got to be developed before we can hope to have a real and ideal democracy.[59]

He would later expand on this contention with more detail:

> Real democracy and co-operation are not one, but they are inseparable. Democracy cannot be established or maintained except through co-operation.
>
> This conflict [between the spirits of co-operation and competition] can be repressed only by establishing the true social law. Christ understood this and taught the true law and upheld the ideals of democracy. What could be more expressive of the true ideal of democracy, and the true function of democratic leadership than [Christ's demand that]: "whosoever will be great among you, let him be your minister; and whosoever will be chief among you, let him be your servant?"[60]

Although Christ failed to provide a more specific description of democratic governance, Wood's overall interpretation requires that, whatever its practical manifestation, it must be based upon the social law of co-operation rather than upon competition. A system dominated by competition, the law of Satan, is autocratic. It is ruled by those who excel at competition, those who can dominate the weak. Any further practical details regarding the workings of a proper democratic system require a study of present conditions.

For Wood, this study from the perspective of a prairie farmer quickly revealed that Canada was not an authentic democracy but rather an autocracy ruled by the wealthy *plutocrats*. This "money power," made up of large groups of industrialists and grain-buyers from central Canada, held strong monopolies in their respective fields that enabled them to exploit western Canadian farmers. Furthermore, their wealth allowed them to control politicians within the democratic system by way of the lobbyist, and thus it was the money power that, in effect, ensured the survival of the much-hated national tariff, which protected their monopolistic position.[61] This outcome was rendered possible by the current structure of the Canadian political system. Although a democracy in the sense that the people's representatives were chosen in free elections, Canada's particular evolution of the electoral system along competitive lines actually inhibited authentic democracy, according to Wood. Despite their comprising a group of individuals seemingly working towards a common end, political parties failed to deliver accurate or honest representation of the people because, ultimately, they lacked unifying principles and were, in the end, simply large vote-seeking organizations offering anything to anybody in their search for power. Here Wood touches on a concern that has hounded contemporary democratic theorists with respect to parties:

> False appeals are frequently made in the name of the most sacred things. Prejudices and passions are appealed to. Patriotism is prostituted to the services of the most selfish interests and designs. Few questions are seriously discussed on their merits. Truth is frequently not sought after, but systematically concealed in a mass of confusion.
>
> [Citizens] have been like the sands of the desert, blown back and forth by the changing winds of false propaganda.[62]

It is within this confusion that the wealthy industrialist gains control of individual politicians eager to accept the donated funds of industry in order to finance their electoral campaigns or simply line their pockets. The result is autocracy, or more specifically, plutocracy. The interests of the masses become subservient to the greed of the wealthy and the politically powerful. Because the individual citizen is too weak to challenge the plutocracy and traditional political parties are susceptible to such corruption, Wood was convinced that the masses must form their own groups capable of providing proper representation within the political realm in order to overthrow the money power. The basis on which these groups were to organize and operate within the political system has since been recognized as Wood's most original contribution to Canadian political thought, that of "group government."

Of course, articulating the need for occupational groups to replace traditional political parties within the legislature did not organically sprout from Wood's social theory; rather it was a pragmatic response to the growing pressures in Alberta for the UFA to enter the political realm, pressures generated most significantly by William Irvine and the radical left-leaning Non-Partisan League (NPL). Wood had resisted early calls for the UFA to enter politics directly, convinced from his first-hand study of agrarian-driven politics in the United States that such action could destroy all the good the UFA had achieved as a community-level educational and lobbying group.[63] Sensing the political will of the membership, however, Wood acquiesced, and the UFA endorsed direct political action at their 1919 convention. Despite failing to persuade members to avoid such a move, Wood did emerge from a series of debates with Irvine with a significant victory of his own. It was at this point that Wood began to generate his theory of group government – a theory that he subsequently successfully used to convince farmers that it was in their best interest to remain a strictly agrarian organization – ignoring the pleas of Irvine and the broader NPL to create a new progressive party open to non-farmers. In an ironic twist, Irvine would largely accept this argument, at least for a time, and would play an instrumental role in popularizing the idea of group government with his book *The Farmers in Politics*, published in 1920.

Wood's specific proposition that the UFA remain an agrarian organization within politics rather than be a political party was founded upon his contention that groups designed to articulate a political viewpoint can only remain stable, and thus effective, if they are organized around that which is of supreme interest to all and "at the present time humanity's greatest general interest is economic."[64] But Wood, understanding that it was not realistic to assume that all people could agree on a single economic viewpoint, argued that group organization should be subdivided by economic class. This idea did not refer to an upper, middle, and lower class or a bourgeoisie and proletariat class but rather to something akin to general occupational classes. The Western world had developed as a "trading world," and its evolution had produced distinct groups of people who produced certain goods or services, such as farmers or bakers or labourers engaged in manufacturing. Each of these groups had particular economic interests, and it was these common interests, shared by members of each respective group, that would encourage them to co-operate with their fellow farmer or baker or labourer within their own organization. Of course, Wood never did spend much time focusing on the makeup of particular groups outside his own "agricultural class," a weakness that C.B. Macpherson picks up on in his insightful critique of Wood's overall group government scheme.[65]

Although a number of scholars have noted Wood's critique of the traditional party-dominated Westminster system, they have largely overlooked the way in which the theory of group government was very much connected to his broader Christian-inspired social outlook. Indeed, the formation of this agrarian occupational group represented for Wood the initial stage of the social regeneration process described above whereby Christ's true social law of co-operation would be introduced into the political realm. Once "people learn to speak through a properly developed group," he argued, "the group becomes the voice of the people, and the voice of the people becomes the voice of God."[66] But such co-operation does not only guide humans closer to the long-term goal of a perfected society built upon the true social law; in the immediate term, it would also ensure a stability within each occupational group that would subsequently allow them to maintain and articulate a consistent message in the political realm, something traditional political parties were unable to do. These groups would thus be resistant to the seductions of the industrial lobby and would contribute to an authentic democratic dialogue by making heard the voices of the masses, at least with respect to their economic demands. The distinct economic groups, already consisting of individuals co-operating at a local level, were to co-operate with each other in the political realm or legislature in order to secure the most just outcome with respect to particular policy decisions. This was the logic behind Wood's radical recommendation that occupational groups replace traditional parties within the legislature. It was also the reason behind Wood's insistence that the UFA remain an economic group that would participate in politics rather than a traditional political party that would seek broad-based electoral support.[67]

Importantly, for Wood, the health and viability of such economic groups within the legislature depended upon the lengths such organizations went to ensure sufficient influence from the deliberative, community-level groupings of occupational members, or locals. It was only through intense grassroots participation and significant avenues

Religion and Political Thought of Henry Wise Wood   83

for membership control that such a political organization could avoid the fate of traditional political parties and resist manipulation by outside interests. As Laycock has noted, although the implementation of true group government within the Alberta legislature fell short, the UFA itself operated as a highly participatory and deliberative institution that maximized the democratic potential of community-level involvement by ensuring that the locals maintained significant influence over the UFA's central leadership.[68] In fact, Frank Underhill went as far as to claim that the UFA "had worked out a method of combining constituency autonomy with group solidarity, and local initiative with central direction, which no doubt is not perfect, but does achieve the most complete and real democracy that we have yet seen in Canadian politics."[69]

Of course, the notion that citizens were to co-operate with their neighbours and participate in community-level endeavours was certainly not foreign to the farm families who were attempting to carve out a living on Alberta's unforgiving frontier. In fact, UFA locals had a long and impressive history of grassroots co-operative experience in the selling of produce, the buying of supplies, the provision of crop insurance and even the extending of credit.[70] However, the UFA's emphasis on such local activity as a prerequisite not just for economic survival but for good democratic government and improved social conditions was championed most strongly by Wood. Indeed, in providing his blessing for political action, Wood was adamant that people were not to lose focus on their individual responsibilities at the local level. "All democratic organization," Wood argued, "begins at the bottom and works upward … Now, beginning at the real bottom, democratically speaking, means beginning with the individuals and organizing them in local units."[71] Responsibility, he continued elsewhere,

begins with yourself. You must realize that as a social being you owe a duty to the development of a social system in which the future generations of your posterity will be protected in the rights of life and the pursuit of happiness.

But where does your social work begin? It begins right where you are located. If you are in a local rural community, your responsibility and work lie there. All democratic social development is from the bottom up. The individuals spring into a local, these locals grow into larger units, and these larger units into still larger ones, until the whole is embraced in one complete system.

84   God's Province

> Fill Alberta with the UFA locals in which every man and woman
> is taking his and her full responsibility in organization and co-op-
> eration and nothing can hold our organization back. It will flour-
> ish like a green bay tree.
> This is where social responsibility begins. It ends in a perfect so-
> cial system.[72]

Going forward, Wood would remain unyielding in his view that the
locals were the "Heart of the UFA,"[73] eventually arguing that "[i]f one
UFA Local could establish a purely co-operative community where all
community affairs, both social and business, were dealt with in a practical co-operative way, that pioneer Local would be contributing more
to right social construction and human welfare, than any individual
that has ever lived."[74] Therefore, for Wood, the introduction of group
government, built upon a network of participatory and co-operative
locals, would ensure not only enhanced economic well-being for farmers but also a co-operative spirit in politics and an authentic vehicle of
political representation. Thus, Christ's natural social law of co-operation, the economic well-being of agrarians, and the establishment of
true democracy perfectly coalesced in Wood's political theory. In fact,
Wood argued, "The Kingdom of Heaven and perfect democracy are syn-
onymous terms."[75]

Yet, despite the very real success of a number of co-operative efforts
at the local level, Wood's ideal group government scenario, wherein
the political arm of the UFA would be controlled by local members,
was largely abandoned in practice shortly after the organization
gained political power in Alberta in 1921. In essence, the rigidity of
the traditional Westminster system as well as the economic realities
facing the province at the time led to a surprisingly conservative administration characterized by cabinet supremacy rather than considerable local control. By 1923, much member enthusiasm for the UFA
government had faded and the vast majority of grassroots farmers,
alongside many of the most talented UFA organizers, turned their attention instead to the Alberta Wheat Pool, a farmer-owned wheat
marketing co-operative modelled after successful American voluntary
marketing pools and actively supported by Wood.[76] Wheat marketing was a central concern of all prairie farmers, and various experi-
ments with mandatory federal government-regulated wheat boards
in the second and third decades of the twentieth century had split the
allegiances of farmers. For instance, whereas Saskatchewan agrarians
became enamoured with mandatory pools that offered a fixed price

Religion and Political Thought of Henry Wise Wood   85

guaranteed by governments, Wood, although supportive of such pools as a temporary measure, was resolute in his contention that the only long-term solution for agrarians was a voluntary pool built upon the broader co-operative principle that underlay his support for group government.[77] Ultimately, mandatory government-regulated wheat pools violated Wood's strong belief in individual liberty and, most importantly, the first stage of the two-stage process of social regeneration. The kingdom of God was not to be built via government regulation but rather, first, by large-scale voluntary individual regeneration, or rebirth, and second, by the co-operation of those regenerated individuals within voluntary organizations. His emphatic support for a voluntary wheat pool, which led to its adoption by Alberta farmers in 1923, was simply an extension of this logic. Indeed, in his 1927 UFA presidential address, he noted:

The UFA political movement and the Alberta Wheat Pool are the two greatest achievements of the United Farmers of Alberta ... [and] they are both founded on the same general basic principles ...
    Each of these institutions represents an organized, co-operative citizenship effort. The object of the political movement is to use our united citizenship strength in our own way, for the purpose of bettering our own condition and that of society in general, in the political field. The object of the Wheat Pool is to use our united strength for the purpose of bettering our own industrial conditions, and those of industry in general.
    We have decided to act collectively in both fields of action, and the reasons for doing so are exactly the same in both instances ... In our political activities we are opposed by those who hope to profit personally by the use of our franchise. In the co-operative marketing of our produce we are opposed by those who hope to profit by the buying and selling of our products.
    The opposition of these two forces we cannot hope to escape. All along the way we will have to consider this and be ready to meet and overcome it. This we can hope to do only by keeping on the basis of right principles, in obedience to natural social law.[78]

Thus, given Wood's Christian understanding of natural social law, it should come as no surprise that he conceived the Alberta Wheat Pool, over which he presided from its inception until 1931, to be "just as much a religious organization as the Church."[79]

Wood's identification of group government by economic class as a practical solution to the undemocratic nature of the political system, as well as his support for the voluntary Alberta Wheat Pool, introduces an additional aspect of his political and economic thought. Much to the chagrin of the more radical advocates of the social gospel, who called for the introduction of a variant of socialism on the Prairies, Wood never questioned the economic foundation of the Western world. As Macpherson notes, Wood's theory remained faithful to a basic economic liberalism and was essentially built upon the assumption that a human being is a "trading animal."[80] Indeed, Wood interpreted the beginning of human progress to be the point at which "a primitive savage conceived the idea of trading some article he possessed beyond his immediate needs, for something he wanted that another savage had." This initial trade represented the "discovery of the great central institution of present civilization, namely, trade and commerce."[81] From then on, social institutions have been built up with the specific purpose of governing this method of exchange, the free trade of goods and services. Because the origins of this trading system appeared to Wood to be natural, he never once considered the merits of an economic system built upon anything other than the market. Thus, any social or economic problems that developed in society could not be attributable to the natural practice of trading, but rather to the unnatural development of the social institutions that determine how trading takes place.

This element of Wood's thought contrasted sharply with the views of the main spokespeople of the Prairie social gospel movement, notably Salem Bland, J.S. Woodsworth, and Alberta's own William Irvine. Bland, who had studied at both Queen's and McGill Universities and had served as a Methodist preacher in Ontario and Montreal before taking a post as a theology professor at Winnipeg's Wesley College in 1903, was easily the Prairie social gospel's most intellectually sophisticated spokesman. As biographer Richard Allen notes, "the complex moving body of Salem's thinking" drew from multiple intellectual sources over a long period of time, producing "a new type of liberal Protestant" who embraced modern biblical interpretations informed by reason and science and was eager to apply the message of the New Testament to the economic and social structures of the day.[82] Indeed, the progressive Christianity that emerged in Bland led to his eventual declaration that capitalism was a corrupt system "contrary to the spirit of Christ."[83] He added elsewhere, "[T]he ethics of Jesus demand nothing less than the transference of the whole economic life from a basis of competition and profits to one of co-operation and service," a con-

Religion and Political Thought of Henry Wise Wood   87

tention he explored colloquially within his regular column, entitled "The Deeper Life," in the *Grain Growers' Guide* between 1917 and 1919 and also academically in his strongly pro-labour work – *The New Christianity* – published in 1920.[84]

This line of thinking similarly generated a very real commitment to Christian-inspired anti-capitalist social and political activism, leading to his decision to address the conventions of the Manitoba and Saskatchewan Grain Growers' associations in 1912 and 1913, to his brief role as organizer – alongside his former students Woodsworth and Irvine – for the left-wing NPL in Alberta, to a summer of "Chautauqua" speeches on applied Christianity across the Prairies alongside Wood in the summer of 1918, to an influential role in the Winnipeg General Strike in 1919, and eventually to his role as advocate for the CCF in Ontario in the 1930s.

Irvine, an influential newspaper editor and NPL proponent who played a key role in pushing the UFA towards direct political action in 1918–19 before embracing the unofficial title of leader of the radical contingent within the UFA, was a personal friend of Woodsworth's and a former student of Bland's at Wesley College and much of his social commentary within Alberta periodicals matched that of his former teacher.[85] Irvine routinely chastised traditional churches and their "gaunt and emaciated theological conceptions of the past" that prevented them from emphasizing the "living principles of Christ" articulated most thoroughly by his mentor Bland, who "demands we struggle against selfish individualism and for righteousness against the industrial and political crimes of our age."[86] Although Irvine often lauded Wood's emphasis on the social nature of Christianity and broadly supported the commitment to the principle of co-operation inherent in Wood's conception of group government, the two men did not share the same feelings towards the market system. Indeed, Irvine was more closely aligned with the radical anti-capitalist tendencies of Bland and Woodsworth, and this strain of thought would emerge in aspects of his *Farmers in Politics*, wherein he explored Wood's conception of group government but also attempted to radicalize it by expanding the economic analysis to include farmers and workers and further noting that capitalism was "the common enemy of all industrial groups" and its eventual downfall was certain, a proclamation Wood would never himself make.[87] In fact, he would eventually publish a short book entitled *Can a Christian Vote for Capitalism?* within which he was far more blunt, arguing that the capitalist economic system was "ethically indefensible" in the face of the teachings of Christ.[88] Irvine would go on to lead a

88   God's Province

dedicated group of radical left-leaning followers within the UFA who
shared his interest in a religious-based strain of what Laycock has labelled an "agrarian socialism." Followers of this line of thought were
careful to avoid questioning the right to private ownership of land by
farm families, but would simultaneously demand the public ownership
of banks, transportation and utility companies, grain elevators, and certain natural resource industries.[89] Although the bulk of Alberta farmers remained loyal to Wood and his attachment to the market system
and thus largely rejected such motions, Irvine would continue to push
for an anti-capitalist alliance between farmers and urban labour, an effort that would eventually culminate in the newly formed national CCF,
within which he took a leading role in the early 1930s.

    From the perspective of Macpherson, the fact that Wood was a long-
time farmer whereas Bland, Woodsworth, and Irvine, although familiar with and supportive of small-scale agriculture, were urban-based
writers and clergymen, most likely goes a long way towards explaining
their divergent attitudes towards capitalism. For Macpherson, Wood
and the bulk of the UFA membership were simply unable to break away
from the standard economic conservatism inherent in what he labelled
"petit-bourgeois agrarian radicalism."[90] Because the particular style of
small-scale agriculture practised by prairie farmers in Canada and the
United States had traditionally depended upon a system of private
property and a market capable of selling their produce, the notion of increased co-operation, as opposed to outright socialism, represented the
only reform they considered viable. Bland and his followers, personally unencumbered by a perceived dependence of small-scale private
property and more acutely aware of the injustices committed upon
urban labour by owners of industry, were able to avoid this "inherent
conservatism" and seek a true alternative, the replacing of the capitalist
system with a particular variant of socialism.

    There is little doubt that Macpherson had uncovered an important
explanatory variable in his analysis when he pointed to the nature of
Wood's occupation and its position within the market system, but the
divergent views towards capitalism between Wood and the more mainstream social gospel proponents also owe something to the distinct
religious interpretations of Wood and Bland. As Allen has noted, Bland
derived much of his social interpretation of Christianity from European
rather than American intellectual sources, which resulted in his having
a less individualistic viewpoint when approaching societal ills.[91] In fact,
Bland's reading of the Bible in conjunction with social conditions led
him to conclude that capitalism itself was to blame for the economic

Religion and Political Thought of Henry Wise Wood 89

oppression of the plain people, not simply the "original sin" of man, and thus the essential task of "true" Christianity was not only individual regeneration but also the abolition of capitalism and the introduction of public ownership.[92] In other words, Bland's vision of the social gospel, with its particular theological and social roots and its tendency towards socialism, was not the same strand of Christianity that Wood adhered to. Although Bland, Woodsworth, and Irvine, on one hand, and Wood, on the other, shared a basic rejection of the otherworldliness of Christianity, an appreciation for certain elements of the American, urban-based social gospel movement, and an overall desire to see better conditions for the plain people of the Prairies through increased co-operation by way of Christ's moral teachings, Wood's interpretation was derived primarily from the evangelical social Christianity he had experienced in the American South. This was a more conservative interpretation that combined a basic co-operative "brotherhood of man" ethos with a more traditional evangelical embrace of individual piety and a Jeffersonian appreciation of small-scale commercial self-sufficiency rather than a wholesale restructuring of the economic system. In fact, Wood framed his solution to the problems of the market around his broader postmillennial understanding of social life and the need for individuals and groups, motivated by the message of Christ, to embrace co-operation.

"Commerce," Wood argues "systematically used in accordance with the true social laws of life, would be the greatest binding tie in the social system."[93] However, the economic system had become dominated by the false social law, the spirit of competition, and the terms of trading had thus been engineered to favour those who, driven by incessant greed, excel at competition and are therefore able to build up monopolies that exploit the masses. The solution, therefore, did not lie in a radical retreat from traditional conceptions of private property and free trade, as demanded by the likes of Bland, Woodsworth, and Irvine, but rather in a straightforward shift in spirit on behalf of individuals and the groups they participate in. Indeed, individual responsibility was paramount in his vision. Ultimately, humanity's salvation lies in "self-help" undertaken by "regenerated" individuals, not government assistance. Thus, Wood's thought comes full circle as he returns to his foundational belief in the teachings of Christ to offer a solution to the economic troubles the masses were facing:

Until the problems of trade are solved according to the laws of Christ, His will cannot maintain on earth, and His great prayer cannot be answered.

90   God's Province

The solutions of the economic problems must be spiritual,
rather than intellectual. Henry George cannot solve them, neither
can Carl Marx [*sic*]. Both may, and will give valuable assistance, but
the solution is beyond them. Christ can and must solve them.[94]

Therefore, the co-operation of economic groups within the political
system made possible by the initial spiritual rebirth of individuals demanded by Christ would move humanity closer to the coming kingdom:

If the relationships between economic classes can be adjusted in accordance with the true social laws of life, other social problems will
almost automatically adjust themselves. When we learn to trade
right we will have largely learned to live right. When man trades
with man, class with class, and nation with nation in accordance
with the true principles of trade, the world will be living in accordance with true social principles, and civilization will be perfected.
As long as trade is carried on barbarously our so-called civilization
will never rise above the level of barbarism.[95]

This perfected civilization would be the culmination of the process of
individual and social regeneration highlighted in the previous section.
The practical construction of this civilization was to be completed by
citizens who, over time, evolved into their natural "co-operative" state by
following the teachings of Christ and, in the context of commercial
North America, organizing themselves in appropriate occupational
groups that would overtake competitive political parties within the
democratic system of governance. In this way, the UFA, as a particular
occupational group participating in the political and economic realms,
was, in the view of Wood, striving toward something well beyond the
immediate economic interests of Alberta agrarians. It was an organization dedicated to ushering in the perfect democracy, the kingdom
promised to humanity by Christ.

CONCLUSION:
THE POLITICAL THOUGHT OF WOOD
AND THE INITIAL TRAJECTORY OF ALBERTA POLITICS

For Wood, the notion that religion must be held out of politics or economics was unthinkable. Christianity, he noted very early in his presidency, is a "capable physician, able to heal all the ills of our social an
economic body."[96] Indeed, Wood's entire system of thought, from the

initial regeneration of the individual to the transformation of the social realm by way of group government and co-operative "pools," was built upon a particular interpretation of Christianity. Yet, for the long list of scholars who have studied the thought of Wood and the practical achievements of the UFA, the role played by religion has been largely shuffled to the side. It is true that nearly all those who have written about Wood or the UFA have mentioned religion, but for the most part, these brief references have tended to imply that the UFA was part of the broader social gospel movement that swept through the Prairie provinces in the first quarter of the twentieth century. There is little doubt that the social gospel movement touched the UFA in important ways, but as was discussed above, Wood's Christianity and his subsequent conclusions regarding social reform drew from the American evangelical tradition and were therefore distinct from the interpretations of Bland, Woodsworth, and Irvine, the central purveyors of the mainstream social gospel message on the Prairies.

Wood's interpretation of Christianity drew from the distinct American evangelical Protestant tradition in a number of ways. Most fundamentally, he agreed with the general evangelical Protestant contention that humans are born as imperfect beings, guided initially by "the animal spirit." It was the dominance of this spirit in public and economic life, not the capitalist economic system, that required attention and reform. Given humanity's "fallen" condition, the individual required a personal conversion or rebirth through Christ to ensure they were "regenerated" as individuals. Of course, Wood's notion of conversion was not the deeply emotional, mystical, or immediate experience it was for many of the American evangelical revivalists, nor did it promise salvation in the afterlife. It was instead a gradual acceptance of the "co-operative spirit" that was at the heart of Christ's teachings required for earthly salvation. Nevertheless, embracing the populist and egalitarian sentiment inherent in the post-revolution American evangelicalism from which he emerged, Wood understood this conversion to occur by way of the individual's free will. Once common individuals dedicated themselves to the teachings of Christ, they could be reborn in a way that did not require elitist education or the blessing of the traditional clergy. Regeneration was provided to those who carefully read and took to heart the New Testament and most especially the parables of Christ. By structuring the parables around everyday situations, surely Christ intended them to be understood by ordinary people.

By suggesting that social regeneration – the victory of Christ's spirit of co-operation over Satan's competitive spirit within society – rather than individual conversion was the true end for humanity, Wood also embraced a radical and progressive Christianity akin to that espoused by mainstream social gospel advocates. However, even this dimension of his Christian interpretation had strong roots in American evangelicalism. It was the liberal Christian thinkers in mid-nineteenth-century America who emerged from the revivalism of the Second Great Awakening who first articulated a modern postmillennial interpretation that viewed humans, following the teachings of Christ, as possessing the capacity to establish the kingdom of God on earth. Furthermore, Wood interpreted this process through an evolutionary framework, just as those liberal evangelicals in America had when confronted with the challenge of Darwin. Similarly, the physical return of Christ following the establishment of this kingdom was noticeably absent from Wood's vision. Christ had already intervened in human history to provide the natural social laws required to achieve the kingdom, those of co-operation. The cosmic struggle between God and Satan would be decided gradually as this natural law identified by Christ slowly overtook humanity and they, in turn, directed their social efforts towards co-operation rather than competition and thus defeated the Antichrist in the form of a competitive spirit. Personal salvation in the foretold kingdom would thus be found on earth at the culmination of a long historical process that was bound to produce a perfect democratic society in which Christ's social teachings reigned supreme.

There can be little doubt that the broad parallels between post-revolution American evangelicalism and the thought of Wood are attributable to Wood's general exposure to the evangelical Protestant culture of the American South and Midwest, including the agrarian populist movement of the late nineteenth century, and his particular upbringing in the Disciples of Christ sect. The anti-elitism generated by a belief in the capacity of the common individual, the defence of individual autonomy and small-scale commercial self-sufficiency, the emphasis on personal piety and responsibility, and the related embrace of individual-level regeneration as the appropriate tool for social change were themes central to rural evangelical Protestantism in the American South and Midwest. The intense focus on the gospels at the expense of the remaining scriptures, the emphasis on meaningful participatory democracy and co-operation at the local level, Christianized theories of natural law, and the notion of the Antichrist working through societal elites and oppressing the plain people were all staples of Disciples of Christ theology. To this foundation Wood mixed ideas from the northern American social gospel tradition (particularly notions related to the kingdom of heaven on earth) and broader philosophical currents (particularly Herbert Spencer's progressive evolutionism and Adam Smith's defense of laissez faire capitalism) to produce a thoroughly unique liberal and postmillennial Christian interpretation. When applied to the particular conditions that Wood found himself in as a farmer in Alberta, he eventually developed the theory of group government. It was this arrangement that could lead to the construction of an authentic co-operative and democratic society built upon the laws of Christ, within which ordinary people retained the right to participate in government through local avenues and to trade freely within the marketplace while slowly chipping away the competitive spirit that oppressed the common people.

Although there is little evidence to suggest that Wood's peculiar interpretation of history, complete with the cosmic struggle between antithetical social laws foretold by the Book of Revelation, was shared, or even fully understood, by the majority of farmers who toiled in the various locals of the UFA, the strong religious message it contained was an easy sell in the overwhelmingly Christian province, especially one with such a strong American presence. Of course, the transformation to a "group government" legislature attempted by the UFA following its 1921 electoral victory was not a success. In addition, the UFA provincial government, facing increasingly tough financial conditions, was unable to offer much in the way of radically co-operative policies, with the exception of some assistance to agrarian co-operatives, including the Alberta Wheat Pool.[97] Indeed, by the mid-1920s, UFA membership rolls had decreased significantly and by the early 1930s a noticeable divide had emerged between the UFA's political arm and its executive following Wood's retirement and the emergence of the more radical Robert Gardiner as president in 1931. And, in 1935, the UFA government would famously be swept aside by William Aberhart's Alberta Social Credit League, losing every single riding it contested before officially withdrawing from politics two years later. So what then of the influence of Wood's religious-political theory with respect to the early trajectory of Alberta politics?

First, regardless of the difficulties the UFA government faced in attempting to implement Wood's vision within the constraints of a pre-existing, party-dominated parliamentary system, Wood's theory did underlie the highly successful actions of the broader UFA movement outside the legislature. By 1921, the UFA had over 37,000 male mem-

94   God's Province

Table 3.1
Alberta population, urban and rural, 1911–1941

Year	Total population	Urban	Rural
1911	374,295	137,662	236,633
1921	588,454	222,904	365,550
1931	731,605	278,508	453,097
1941	796,169	306,586	489,583

Source: "Population, Urban and Rural, by Province and Territory (Alberta)," Statistics Canada,
http://www.statcan.gc.ca/tables-tableaux/sum-som/l01/csto1/demo62j-eng.htm (accessed 25 October
2014).

Table 3.2
UFA male membership, 1912–1935

Year	Total male members (approx.)
1912	7,190
1918	18,000
1921	37,000
1935	< 10,000

Source: Palmer and Palmer, Alberta: A New History, 151, 184, 194, 265.

bers, representing roughly 40 per cent of Alberta farmers, all toiling in
approximately 1,200 locals throughout the province. This was in addition to the over 4,000 females who had joined the United Farm Women
of Alberta.[98]

The success with which these locals pursued legitimate co-operative
ventures, including the Alberta Wheat Pool, while simultaneously engaging and educating citizens in the political and economic issues of
the day has been clearly documented by scholars, although not yet
through the lens of Wood's religious-based political thought. Once this
religious foundation is made apparent, it is easy to see how the intense
participation and co-operation at the local level stressed by Wood were
not simply tools to be utilized in the quest for economic stability on the
part of the agrarians; rather, co-operation between citizens was the key
activity required of humanity in their struggle to establish the millennial kingdom of God on earth. In fact, once individuals had made the
choice to be reborn – to accept the call for co-operation issued by Christ
– they would be naturally inclined to co-operate with their neighbours
and this would lead to the establishment of the local that, in turn,

Religion and Political Thought of Henry Wise Wood 95

would nourish the provincial organization and society at large by applying the co-operative message of Christ to the social and political realms. Co-operation demanded intense participation from UFA members, and this in turn fostered a highly participatory and deliberative democratic structure. This was authentic grassroots democracy where concern for the public good was paramount and citizens were expected to devote much energy towards it, the payoff being the establishment of the ultimate common good, the kingdom of God on earth. Although this emphasis on meaningful community-level participation would eventually wane under the Alberta Social Credit League (as will be discussed in Chapter 4), Rennie has noted that the UFA's emphasis on such participation "entrenched a populist bias for grassroots democracy in Alberta political culture that lingers to the present."[99] Surely Wood was not the only member of the UFA to actively encourage this participatory sentiment, but as the UFA's own periodical observed in 1920, "no other one person in Alberta has done more to arouse the people to accept the responsibility of their own institutions than he."[100] And Wood's insistence in this regard was directly related to his interpretation of Christianity.

Second, despite advocating a system of commerce based upon co-operation rather than competition, a notion that clearly seems quite progressive from our contemporary perspective, Wood did much to ensure that the UFA rejected the more radical demands for socialism or increased state ownership, at least at the peak of its political influence. For Wood, not only was commerce a natural institution, the notion of centralizing more economic control in government went against his evangelical populist impulses, which stressed the problem-solving capacity of ordinary people and the ultimate importance of individual responsibility. More practically, as Wood's preference for a voluntary rather than compulsory system of grain-pooling among Alberta agrarians made clear, socialistic arrangements impeded individual liberty and opened the door to manipulation by the political parties of the day, which were controlled by wealthy industrialists.[101] Surely this perspective was partly rooted in Wood's particular American agrarian and Jeffersonian liberal upbringing, but by arguing that the only authentic solution to the problem of the economic oppression of the plain people began with spiritual regeneration at the individual level, Wood drew directly from the American evangelical Protestant tradition. By instructing agrarians to embrace the teachings of Christ and "be ye perfect as your father in Heaven is perfect," Wood rejected both the secular intellectual solutions of Marx and the Christian-based social gospel calls for socialism and placed the onus squarely on the individual to bring about the perfect democratic and economic system. In doing so, Wood helped to steer early Alberta society in a decidedly anti-socialistic and more individualistic direction by harnessing the Prairie-wide utopian and co-operative hopes of Alberta agrarians to a stern emphasis on individual responsibility.

The concrete work of Wood in this regard can be traced all the way back to 1919 and his victory over Irvine and other NPL radicals who had demanded that the UFA's newly formed political arm open itself up to labour leaders and socialist intellectuals. In resisting this push, Wood was successful in minimizing the influence of the socialist faction within the organization from the beginning.[102] Although Irvine would subsequently become one of the UFA's most well-known spokesmen, Wood was also successful in ensuring that strong left-wing proposals that emerged from the radical wing (such as the re-establishment of a mandatory wheat board, state ownership of utilities, the establishment of a provincial bank, debt moratoriums, and even an official recognition of Communist Russia) were defeated at UFA conventions in 1923, 1924, and 1928. As Wood's biographer has noted, the failure by such radicals to change the course of the organization was largely due to Wood's supreme influence over the individual farmers within the organization: "If 'the chief' did not believe in the value of a particular reform, the vast majority of delegates usually rejected it."[103]

As mentioned above, Wood's preference for citizen-driven as opposed to state-driven collective action was also central to his impassioned arguments in favour of a non-compulsory wheat pool. This ultimately culminated in the formation of the voluntary Alberta Wheat Pool in 1923 despite demands for a compulsory pool from certain radical corners of the UFA. Mandatory government-regulated wheat pools violated Wood's strong belief in individual liberty and, most importantly, his contention that the kingdom of God was not to be built via government regulation but rather, first, by large-scale voluntary individual regeneration, or rebirth, and second, by the co-operation of those regenerated individuals within voluntary organizations. The popularity in Alberta of Wood's argument on this matter was significant given the very different line of thinking that emerged out of neighbouring Saskatchewan's primary agrarian organization, the left-leaning United Farmers of Canada (Saskatchewan Section). Saskatchewan farmers had followed Alberta's lead and created their own voluntary pool, the Saskatchewan Wheat Pool, in 1923, but a large contingent of radical farmers became enamoured with the notion of a mandatory pool that offered a fixed price guaranteed by government, an outlook consistent with the broader influence of a more state-friendly social democratic strain of social gospel–infused thought in Saskatchewan. This strain, which favoured a variety of public ownership schemes as well as a broader farmer–labour alliance in addition to farmer-led co-operatives, was similar to the views of radical UFA spokesman William Irvine and his Christian-inspired hope to utilize the state to improve the conditions of the common man.[104] Indeed, in 1932, the United Farmers of Canada (Saskatchewan Section) would merge with Saskatchewan's Independent Labour Party, eventually becoming the provincial CCF party that swept to power under another social gospel devotee, Tommy Douglas, in 1944. This bit of Saskatchewan political history aside, it is worth noting that, as recently as 2007, the government of Saskatchewan has been an avid supporter of the Canadian Wheat Board (CWB), the mandatory "single desk" marketing authority to which all prairie farmers have been required to sell their wheat and barley since its inception, largely at the bequest of the Saskatchewan agrarians, in 1935. Interestingly, the Alberta government (indirectly following the lead of Wood) has long been an opponent of the mandatory nature of the CWB, going so far as to launch a $650,000 campaign in the early 2000s that urged grain farmers to fight the CWB monopoly.[105]

Perhaps the most notable testament to Wood's influence over the agrarians of Alberta in this regard can be witnessed through the lens of the UFA's radical shift in direction upon his retirement from the presidency in 1931 and its subsequent fall from power. Just prior to the election of Wood's successor and in the face of an unexpected rival in the radical Farmers' Unity League, which had originated in Saskatchewan and was now growing in popularity in Alberta, the UFA issued a manifesto that referred for the first time to the need to develop a "cooperative commonwealth." This phrase had been used at the United Farmers of Canada (Saskatchewan Section) the year prior to refer to the need for a complete and radical overhaul of the capitalist system. Importantly, however, the UFA was careful in suggesting that such a phrase was meant to imply continued support for Wood's call for co-operation between farmers as opposed to a demand for socialism.[106] This was essentially the last act of deference to the economic conservatism inherent in Wood's thought that would emanate from the organization. Shortly thereafter, the more radical UFA member of Parliament Robert Gardiner and former Methodist and United Church minister Norman Priestly would take over the executive. Both Gardiner and Priestly, close acquaintances of Woodsworth and Irvine, were followers of the main-

98   God's Province

stream Prairie gospel movement and were quick to denounce the fiscal
conservatism of the Brownlee-led UFA provincial government and demand the implementation of a variety of nationalization and public
ownership schemes. Indeed, a wide gulf quickly emerged between Premier Brownlee, a close friend of Wood's who shared a hesitation around
the emerging calls for large-scale state involvement in the economy, and
the now radical UFA executive. In fact, as the broader organization passed
resolutions from 1931 onward that were favourable to various degrees
of public ownership and state intervention and overtly supportive of
the newly formed national CCF (whose formation owed much to the
participation of Irvine, Gardiner, and Priestly), the UFA government remained completely ambivalent regarding such measures, continuing
down a fiscally conservative path even after the UFA officially affiliated
with the CCF in 1933.[107]

Perhaps more interesting than the gulf between the broader UFA organization and the UFA government, however, was the gulf that
emerged between the organization and most Alberta farmers. By this
point, the vast majority of agrarians who had been so active in the
group's early years had allowed their membership to lapse, most now
directing their energies instead towards the management of a variety
of farmer-run marketing and purchasing pools, encouraged by
Wood.[108] Thus, this radical incarnation of the UFA was not actually representative of the majority of farmers it claimed to represent. Indeed,
as numerous observers have noted, most Alberta farmers, who had
been bathed in the political and economic thought of Wood since
1916, were shocked by the radical socialist elements of the CCF platform endorsed by the UFA in 1932/33.[109] Brownlee's biographer went
as far as to suggest that the UFA's "attempt to foist upon Alberta the
godless, materialist doctrines of European socialism under the guise of
the CCF ... [was] fundamentally distasteful to most of those who once
filled the zealous ranks of the UFA."[110] Wood himself reportedly observed that "the farmers' movement [has been] turned back forty years
by [this] UFA-Labour combination."[111]

Clearly, the UFA's eventual electoral demise in 1935 was strongly tied
to its inability to offer meaningful economic relief from the Depression (in addition to the appearance of the persuasive William Aberhart
and his seductive promises to end the Depression with a panacea labelled "social credit"), but the UFA executive's decision to affiliate with
the CCF in 1932/33 was a factor as well. The socialism of the CCF was
simply not popular with most Alberta farmers, who had initially followed Wood so devoutly and, in 1935, would switch their allegiance

to Aberhart and his anti-socialist (at least in rhetoric) Social Credit League.

Of course, it would be a significant oversight to suggest that this hesitancy with respect to the left-leaning platform of the CCF had little to do with the cultural makeup of the province or the UFA itself. Indeed, I wholly support Wiseman's contention that the large influx of American immigrants into Alberta in the first decades of the twentieth century, bringing with them a distinctly individualistic and laissez-faire sentiment, should be considered an incredibly important factor in the early political trajectory of the province.[112] In fact, in the organization's early years, American-born Albertans were overrepresented in both the general UFA membership and the UFA executive relative to their overall percentage of the population.[113] However, I again follow Masciulli, Molchanov, and Knight in asserting that although contextual factors such as the cultural or demographic makeup of a society often generate a certain demand for a particular kind of leader to emerge, there is often room for a variety of ideologically varied leaders (within a certain range) to meet that demand.[114] In other words, Wood's rise to such an influential perch among the Alberta agrarians is no doubt related to the similarity between his particular views and the general views held by the bulk of American immigrants in the province. That is not to say, however, that it would have been impossible for Irvine's views, which were similar to Wood's in many ways, to attain a more influential status should Wood not have put his name forward for the presidency in 1916 or had his leadership skills not been so finely tuned. Context certainly matters, but there are moments when the actions and arguments made by such leaders can and do influence the social and political trajectory of the community of which they are a part. The challenge is to identify such moments and demonstrate how and why a particular leader helped lead his or her community along path X rather than path Y. As I have argued above, between 1919 and 1931, there were several such moments where the UFA faced a crossroads, having to decide between a more or less radical path. Wood stepped in on each of these occasions to ensure that the more radical views of Irvine and his followers were not, in fact, adopted by the UFA. Upon Wood's retirement, the UFA executive was overtaken by more radical leaders, and Alberta's agrarians, having been nurtured on the less radical arguments of Wood for so long, largely abandoned the organization. This was partly because of their American background, but it was also partly owing to the influence of Wood as a successful leader and to his social and political thought, founded upon an individualistic evangelical Protestantism that would imply a rejection of the type of large-scale state intervention required by the social gospel–infused socialist planks of the CCF. Thus, Macpherson's famed argument pointing to the economic conservatism inherent in what he labelled "petit-bourgeois agrarian radicalism" as the central factor in Alberta's initial rejection of socialism misses the mark in some important ways.[115] Indeed, it overlooks the subtle yet significant differences in outlook one finds between the religiously inspired thought of the more radical social gospellers, like Bland or Irvine, and that of the highly influential Wood and how this difference was played out in a concrete way between 1919 and 1935. As will become clearer in the next chapter, utopian dreams of a perfected co-operative society on earth so central to Wood's message would quickly fade from the Alberta political landscape under a Social Credit government, but a distinct antipathy towards socialism would only grow more powerful as the province continued to chart a political and economic course distinct from its Prairie neighbours.

Third, and closely related to the points made above, the broader aspects of Wood's religiously inspired political thought helped to solidify an adherence in Alberta to a unique variant of conservatism, one at odds with the British-based Tory conservatism that played such an important role in the ideological development of much of the rest of English Canada.[116] Indeed, Wood's thought represents in Alberta an early strain of an American-born "populist conservatism," discussed in Chapter 3. This is a variant of conservatism that shares with the Tory strain a Christian foundation and thus a subsequent respect for the institutions capable of spreading its moral message in the name of social stability, but it does so from an individualistic and egalitarian perspective that rejects the hierarchical tendencies of Tory conservatism. In fact, this populist strain of conservatism stresses the capacity of common individuals and the need to ensure their freedom from the oppressive nature of certain established authorities. Wood's political thought, built upon an American evangelical foundation, insists that only through an individual's rebirth in Christ could society begin to improve, and it thus stressed personal study of the gospels and an individual dedication to the moral code demanded by Christ. The most obvious lesson to be derived from such study was that of co-operation, but Wood and the UFA also focused much energy on educating agrarian youth with respect to the parables of Christ and the broader Protestant ethic, including the hard work and self-discipline required to become proper, contributing citizens.[117] By demanding personal responsibility, guided by basic Christian precepts, the UFA could conserve the institutions of democratic governance and commercialism that were "natural" but in need of reform. However, this reform was to come gradually, for revolutionary violence would surely destroy both the good and bad in the social system and humanity would be left in a state of dangerous anarchy.

On the other hand, the appeal to individuals and their capacity to interpret both the moral lessons of the Bible and the nature of the political and economic problems they faced offered a radical challenge to the more traditional attitude of deference to the established power present within orthodox versions of conservative political thought. This egalitarian and dissenting sentiment, in conjunction with Wood's post-millennial sympathies related to the social aspects of Christianity and the coming kingdom, put a more radical stamp on his thought. The conception of citizenship that Wood's political theory implies shared this tension. In abstract terms, citizenship required emulating Christ and thus co-operating with those in their community. More practically, this meant contributing to one's local and educating oneself with respect to the gospels in addition to keeping up with current political and economic problems. By doing so, one worked towards the success of the UFA, and on a higher plane, this was the same as working towards the coming kingdom of God and the establishment of a just society. The role of the citizen therefore implied a duty one must fulfill in order to advance the interests of the whole society, but it also contained a more radical interpretation of the common individual as a person of significant moral and intellectual capacity, a stance often denied by orthodox conservatism.

Thus, Wood's political thought, derived from his religious perspective, maintained both the conservative religious-based demand for individual moral responsibility and the populist anti-establishment and egalitarian orientation that blossomed in post-revolution evangelical America. Although unsuccessful when it came to permanently instituting Wood's vision of group government within the political realm, the Alberta populace has, to this day, remained faithful to the populist variant of conservatism inherent in Wood's political thought, including the radical emphasis on the virtue and capacity of the common people and the more conservative demand that individual and societal well-being is dependent upon the exercise of individual responsibility as opposed to state intervention and socialistic arrangements. This is evidenced not only by the electoral success in Alberta of "populist conservative" parties such as Preston Manning's federal Reform Party or Ralph Klein's Progressive Conservatives, but also by recent survey research that points to the popularity of such views.[118] As will become apparent in the following chapter, this simultaneous focus on the moral and individual capacity of the individual and on the need to encourage individual responsibility helped to lay the broader political and cultural foundations upon which Alberta Social Credit, another religiously infused movement, would emerge and hold power for a remarkable thirty-six years. In fact, although the UFA and Social Credit were founded upon distinct Christian millennial perspectives, their shared American evangelical Protestant heritage would ensure important threads of continuity that helped to shape the broader political culture of Alberta in significant ways that remain apparent even today.

4

Religion and the Political Thought of William Aberhart and Ernest Manning

Fundamentalist Premillennialism and Anti-Socialist Sentiment in Alberta

In August 1935, on the heels of a sex scandal involving UFA premier John Brownlee and in the midst of the Great Depression, the Alberta electorate swiftly turfed all thirty-nine UFA MLAs from office and handed power to Calgary schoolteacher and Christian fundamentalist radio evangelist William Aberhart and his Alberta Social Credit League, which claimed fifty-six of the legislature's sixty-three seats.

In 1932, Aberhart had become interested in the "social credit" economic theories of British engineer Major C.H. Douglas, who essentially argued that the Depression could be solved by the state issuing individual citizens additional credit to enhance their purchasing power. Aberhart spent three years attempting to convince the governing UFA to adopt this economic strategy, but after being rebuffed on numerous occasions, he took to politics himself and led his newly formed party to victory on his promise to end the Depression. Although constitutional roadblocks ultimately prevented the implementation of social credit financial reforms, Aberhart's protegé and successor Ernest Manning relied on growing oil revenues and a stern anti-socialist message to build a dominant electoral machine that would hold power until 1971, significantly shaping Alberta's political culture along the way.

As with the UFA, there already exists a substantial academic literature on Alberta Social Credit that examines the rise and fall of the party, the unique social credit economic theories adopted by Aberhart, and the subsequent abandonment of social credit theory by Manning following Aberhart's death. Unlike most academic treatments of Henry Wise Wood and the UFA, however, the scholarly treatment of Aberhart affords significant attention to his religious activities. Indeed, a whole host of works tell, and retell, the story of Aberhart as a devout Christian who was introduced to a particular version of Christian premillennial fundamentalism in his home province of Ontario before moving to Alberta, where he embarked on a successful career as school principal and radio preacher before becoming premier in 1935, a position he would hold until his death in 1943. In addition, nearly all commentators mention the unusual mix of radical economic theories and prophetic Christianity that he would eventually blend together on his popular religious radio program. Yet, rather than exploring the precise relationship between Aberhart's Christianity and his political thought, the vast majority of this scholarly work on Aberhart's religious beliefs has focused most intensely either on the role Aberhart's radio ministry played in popularizing his particular religious-economic message in Alberta, on the manner by which his religious message spoke to the hopes of an economically insecure population in a Depression-ridden province, or on the broad philosophical similarities between Aberhart's Christian interpretation and the economic theories of Major Douglas.[1] Of course, the lack of scholarly interest in the relationship between Aberhart's religious interpretation and his political thought is somewhat understandable given that Social Credit campaign literature consistently avoided religious references.[2] Yet the secular language utilized in such literature belies the decidedly religious motivation one finds operating just below the surface. Although the electoral success of both Aberhart and Ernest Manning (the latter would become premier upon Aberhart's death in 1943 and lead Alberta until 1968) owes more to the material benefits they promised citizens than to their particular religious beliefs, this chapter seeks to highlight the specific manner by which their political thought and eventual policy decisions were significantly influenced by a shared religious foundation. In fact, to overlook this religious foundation is to overlook one of the more important, although thoroughly underappreciated, factors that has helped to shape Alberta's decidedly anti-socialist political trajectory.

In short, both Aberhart and Manning subscribed to a fundamentalist, premillennial Christian perspective that significantly influenced their thinking with respect to the nature of politics and the proper ends of the state. In contrast to the postmillennialism of Wood, the religiously inspired political thought of Aberhart and Manning did not aim towards gradually perfecting society through works based upon the teachings of Christ. Rather, Aberhart and Manning's premillennial theology insisted that Christ alone, rather than humanity, would bring about the millennial kingdom of God on earth. Therefore, they utilized their religious radio program to encourage individual Albertans to seek the eternal salvation offered by God prior to the point at which He would establish the Millennium. Yet this goal also demanded that certain political conditions be implemented to facilitate the personal conversion of those individuals who had not yet "found" God. More specifically, Aberhart and Manning were convinced that the fundamental purpose of the state was to protect the individual's God-given right to freedom, a condition the individual needed in order to seek out and build a relationship with God that would lead to rebirth and therefore salvation. It was this desire to protect individual liberty that motivated Aberhart and Manning in the political sphere and ultimately generated a visceral anti-socialistic sentiment that shaped Alberta's broader political culture in important ways. However, this religious perspective did grow out of the same broad tradition of American evangelical Protestantism that produced Wood's religious outlook. Thus, it shared the same emphasis on the moral and intellectual capacity of the ordinary individual as well as the same tensions between this more radical populist understanding and the conservative tendencies inherent in the Christian faith that characterized the history of American evangelicalism. This populist conservatism helped to distinguish America from many other Christian nations, and it similarly helped to position Alberta on a unique trajectory when compared to the rest of Canada.

The remainder of this chapter expands on this assertion by first examining the shared theology of Aberhart and Manning, captured in an array of their writings, speeches, radio broadcasts, letters, and interviews, within the context of the broader scholarship on the variant of premillennial Christianity popular in fundamentalist circles at the time. The chapter then considers the manner by which this particular Christian interpretation influenced the political goals of each of them while they respectively served as premier. In particular, it examines the relationship between this religious foundation and Aberhart's interest in social credit economics during the Depression and Manning's eventual turn to what he dubbed "social conservatism." The chapter closes by comparing the religious and political views of Wood with those of Aberhart and Manning, which helps to illuminate some of the more prominent differences between the two movements as well as highlight the broader implications of Aberhart's and Manning's religious-based thought and its impact on the direction of Alberta's politics.

ABERHART'S DISPENSATIONALISM

That Aberhart was a Christian fundamentalist who developed a particular fondness for premillennial dispensationalism is well known. As a child, Aberhart attended a Presbyterian Sunday school in the small southern Ontario town of Seaforth, but his family was largely indifferent to religion. As a high school student, he began to take Christianity more seriously, but it was not until he moved to Brantford in 1901 for his first teaching job that his religious views crystallized.[3] It was here that Aberhart became more fully aware of the broader fundamentalist-modernist religious controversy that had been raging in the Protestant churches of America, and to some extent Canada, in the previous decades. In reaction to both Darwin's theory of evolution and the application of new scholarly methods of historical interpretation (higher criticism) to the Bible in the late nineteenth century, many "modern" American Protestant clergymen had begun reinterpreting scripture in a way that questioned the doctrine of scriptural inerrancy. In turn, there was a subsequent reaction within American Protestantism against the growing popularity of these modern liberal interpretations of Christianity. Fundamentalism, a term derived from a series of pamphlets published between 1910 and 1915 that took aim at higher criticism and reaffirmed a conservative interpretation of scripture, would henceforth represent the Christian beliefs of those who rejected modernism, insisting on an entirely literal interpretation of the Bible. These beliefs included a recommitment to the doctrine of scriptural inerrancy and thus the historical reality of the virgin birth of Christ, His bodily resurrection, and all His miracles and literal pronouncements, in addition to those of the Old Testament prophets who had come before Him. Aberhart came of age in the heat of this controversy and had been groomed in his early days in Ontario by a staunchly fundamentalist preacher, Dr William Nichol. Indeed, as will become apparent throughout this chapter, it would be difficult to exaggerate how influential Aberhart's religious views, derived squarely from the fundamentalist side of this great religious controversy, would be on his political thought and action.

Reflecting upon his early encounter with this theological debate while attending university, Aberhart recalled his personal dissatisfaction with the popular modern interpretations of the Bible that took seriously passages that suited the interpreters taste while ignoring the rest, a practice that Aberhart found to be in direct contradiction to Paul's advice in 2 Timothy 3:16: "All Scripture is given by inspiration of God, and is profitable for doctrine, for reproof, for correction, for instruction in righteousness." Yet Aberhart's early attempts to take every word of the Bible literally quickly "came face to face with difficulties that bewildered [him] and seemed clear contradictions."[4] The solution, Aberhart would soon realize, lay in a radical reinterpretation of the scripture, founded on the belief that distinct passages were meant only for particular periods of human history:

> If we hope to understand the Bible, we must rightly divide the scripture, and as we discover the dispensations we shall find that each one of these passages refers to a different covenant of God with mankind. Hear me, please. Fail to get these proper divisions and you are bound to find bewilderment and contradiction. Here we stand at the parting of the ways. Will you take the right way?[5]

This passage refers to his eventual acceptance of the doctrine of dispensationalism, a theological understanding of history wherein the world progressed through a series of seven distinct "dispensations" within which God had a slightly different relationship with his followers. Dispensationalists believed humanity to be occupying the sixth dispensation, the Age of Grace, and were now awaiting the establishment of the seventh and final dispensation, the Millennium, which featured the Second Coming of Christ and the subsequent thousand-year period of peace on earth, as promised in biblical prophecies. Central to such a notion was a strong belief in biblical prophecy as a guide to understanding the arrival of the final dispensation. As noted in Chapter 2, dispensationalism originated in Ireland in the thought of John Nelson Darby, founder of the British Plymouth Brethren sect, before spreading to the United States in the last decades of the nineteenth century. It was eventually popularized by C.I. Scofield, whose infamous correspondence Bible study courses and eventual annotated Bible did much to instill dispensational thinking in the minds of American fundamentalists in the early twentieth century. Indeed, dispensationalism became a cornerstone of fundamentalist Christianity in that country. Dispensationalists, by and large, were also premillennialists. That is, they believed that Christ would return *before* the promised Millennium and that, in fact, the passage from the contemporary Age of Grace dispensation to the millennial dispensation would be solely God's doing.[6] In other words, humans are active in the world but significant change, like the movement from one dispensation to the next, occurs only through divine intervention. This outlook was diametrically opposed to the postmillennial view so prominent in social gospel circles that placed the onus on humanity to bring about the millennial reign of Christ's peace and righteousness.

As Elliott and Miller have clearly documented, premillennial dispensationalism became prominent for a time in southern Ontario owing to the popularity of the annual Niagara Bible Conference held in Niagara-on-the-Lake between 1883 and 1897, wherein several well-known American fundamentalist preachers would hold court. Although dispensationalism soon lost its lustre in the eyes of most church-going Protestants in the region, several prominent Ontario clergymen remained intrigued enough to invite a number of American dispensationalists, many associated with Chicago's Moody Bible Institute, a hotbed of dispensational theology, to speak in and around Brantford throughout the first few years of the twentieth century. Aberhart was often in attendance.[7] It was also around this time that Aberhart enrolled in C.I. Scofield's dispensational-based correspondence Bible study course, which, Aberhart noted, "placed me on a path that has proved more bright as the days go by."[8] Although Aberhart would work from a dispensationalist foundation in the early Bible study groups he led in Brantford, it was upon his arrival in Calgary in 1910 that Aberhart's involvement in prophetic Bible studies and teaching blossomed. In 1918, he began a Bible study group that steadily grew in popularity. By 1925, it had turned into a Sunday afternoon radio broadcast (*Back to the Bible Hour*) that, by the mid-1930s, would be regularly followed by hundreds of thousands. Although precise listenership estimates vary considerably, from 300,000 to 500,000 (the program's main audience was in Alberta, which had a population of roughly 730,000 in 1931, but also developed a following in portions of western Saskatchewan and even some northern American states), there is little doubt about its vast popularity in Alberta. Indeed, it is often repeated that, in the 1930s, "no one walking down the street in small-town Alberta would miss a word of what Aberhart said because every radio would be tuned in!"[9] Aberhart's radio program, wherein his impressive memorization of scripture was on full display, became his central outlet for spreading his premillennial dispensationalist views and attacking the growing modernist sentiment he sensed in the mainstream churches, which dared suggest that "some parts of the Word are not inspired," that "man is the product of evolution … and is an unfortunate victim of the environment … [and can be] justified by works of his own [rather than being] justified by faith in the atoning blood of Christ."[10] These would also be the central messages he instilled in his pupils attending the Calgary

Prophetic Bible Institute, which opened in 1927.[11] Importantly, Ernest Manning was one of the first students to enroll, and it was here that he received and internalized a heavy dose of Aberhart's particular interpretation of Christianity. It was upon this religious foundation that they would build a long-lasting radio ministry and a durable political movement, two activities that must be understood as complementary strategies motivated by their larger theological beliefs.

Aberhart outlined in significant detail his unique premillennial dispensational theology in a lecture series entitled *God's Great Prophecies*, published in 1924. These were a collection of dense and carefully argued expositions full of references to scriptural passages, especially those with a prophetic air that seemed to coincide with his belief in a foretold seven-year period of transition, or "Tribulation," that would end the present Age of Grace and lead the world to the Millennium and the establishment of the kingdom of God on earth. Included at the end of each lecture was a series of "Test Review Questions" to assist his lay followers with their retention of his views. According to Aberhart, the seven-year period of transition would begin with the Rapture, the point at which Christ returns briefly to earth to gather his true followers who had experienced a spiritual rebirth. Aberhart sums up the seven-year Tribulation that follows the Rapture as follows:

Immediately after the Appearing of Christ for His Church, we are told that the Antichrist will be revealed ... 250 days after the Rapture, the Antichrist will have ascended to the throne of the King of the North. The next great event will be the league of the Antichrist with the Jews. He promises the Jews their temple worship for seven years if they support his claim to the throne of the Kingdom of the North ...

... The last great event, with its accompanying horrors, is the "Battle of Armageddon."

... The armies shall besiege Jerusalem and then the immediate signs in the Heavens shall occur which precede the Lord's Coming. The stars will fall. The moon shall be turned to blood and the sun shall be darkened. On the earth a terrible earthquake shall shake its very foundations and the men's hearts shall fail through fear. They shall call upon the mountains to fall on them and hide them from the wrath to come.[12]

Inherent in this vision, and explained at length in the remaining lectures in this series, was Aberhart's rather grandiose prophetic understanding that, immediately following the Rapture and in the midst of a war between Japan and China on one side and the Western world on the other, an incredibly skilled diplomat (apparently a Turkish prince) would arrive on the world stage and gain international fame. This "superman" would in fact be the Antichrist, the Devil incarnate, who would assist in the rebuilding of the Jewish Temple and in return be allowed to claim the throne of Russia. A complicated serious of wars would break out in Europe and the Middle East before the Antichrist would eventually demand the Jews worship him, forcefully branding them with the number 666. Jewish reluctance would lead to another significant war, resulting in Jerusalem being sacked by the Antichrist. However, at this point Christ would return to meet the Antichrist in the great Battle of Armageddon, wherein Christ would be victorious and would subsequently usher in the final dispensation of history, the Millennium.[13] Aberhart described this period as follows:

> After the dreadful tribulation and the troublous days of the last days of the Law Dispensation, with its Anti-Christ and the Battle of the Armageddon, the Messiah, the Lord Jesus Christ will return again to earth in person and after purifying the earth, He will introduce His personal reign over all the earth for a thousand years. The seat of His power will be in Jerusalem and with him will be his Bride and Body, the Church of Grace.
>
> The Kingdom of God will cover the whole earth from the one end to the other. The Kingdom of heaven will constitute the enlarged land of Palestine promised to Abraham and his seed ...
>
> There will be universal peace under the beneficent rule of the Christ ...
>
> At the end of the thousand years, Satan who has been bound in the bottomless pit will be loosed again ... Satan finds the heart of the rebellious mankind as prone to evil as ever and easily gathers the nations together to Battle against the Lord and His saints and fire comes down to destroy them all. So the dispensation ends in the judgement of the Great White Throne.[14]

Interestingly, although the notion of the Rapture, the Tribulation, and the final Battle of Armageddon leading towards the millennial reign of Christ were derived squarely from the writings of Darby and were central to the interpretations of nearly all prominent premillennial dispensationalists, including the foundational American lay-theologians Dwight Moody and C.I. Scofield, certain aspects of Aberhart's detailed

Religion and Political Thought of Aberhart and Manning

exposition of biblical prophecy related to the seven-year Tribulation drew from distinct sources that went well beyond these mainstream purveyors. As Elliott and Miller note, Aberhart's conception of the Antichrist and his relation to world affairs drew from the works of popular apocalyptic author Sydney Watson (whose *The Mark of the Beast* provided a fictional account of the reign of the Antichrist during the Tribulation), the theory of British-Israelism (a rare belief system that understands the British to be a lost tribe of Israel and thus as having a certain manifest destiny foretold in scripture), and even his own "divine illumination."[15] Thus, at the foundation of Aberhart's premillennial dispensationalism was a unique interpretation of the events to transpire during the Tribulation. In separate works, Elliott has further revealed the unique propensity in Aberhart's thinking towards dispensationalist themes relating to the downward course of history, the depravity of man, and the coming Rapture and Tribulation prior to the Millennium.[16]

Elliott has also authored the most thorough assessment to date of the relationship between Aberhart's religious interpretation and his politics, ultimately arguing that Aberhart's eventual political pronouncements as leader of the Alberta Social Credit League were antithetical to his long-held premillennial dispensationalist Christian outlook.[17] More specifically, Elliott points to Aberhart's early disapproval of modernist Christian ministers who espoused a social gospel version of Christianity that understood man's salvation to lie in the good social works that would lead to a perfected society. From Aberhart's premillennial perspective, such efforts aimed at perfecting society were, in his own words, "as futile as a farmer hoping to purify a polluted well by painting the pump" because the world was to progressively deteriorate until God alone intervened to defeat the Antichrist and usher in the Millennium.[18] Elliott provides two great quotes from Aberhart's pre-Social Credit sermons that confirm his anti-social gospel views. Speaking to the notion of social reform, Aberhart stated: "God never intended us to reform the world. This world will never be fit for the everlasting habitations of the just. We are to seek and save the lost, pointing them to Jesus."[19] And to those eager for political change Aberhart answered: "The very best form of Government, democratic or otherwise, that man could ever establish upon this earth will not be sufficient to recover mankind, but will ultimately end in anarchy."[20] Yet Aberhart seemingly shifted gears entirely in 1932 by strenuously advocating economic reform by way of the social credit theory with which he promised to end "poverty in the midst of plenty." Thus, Elliott suggests that, by mid-1933, Aberhart's preaching "had become a kind of social gospel with emphasis on the 'brotherhood of man,' a theme that was repugnant to many fundamentalists." In adopting this viewpoint, "Aberhart departed from a long apolitical tradition which had characterized the adherents of dispensationalism."[21] In fact, Elliott suggests that Aberhart was implying that the Social Credit movement could actually usher in the Millennium, a direct refutation of his premillennialism.[22] That Aberhart himself did not see this seeming contradiction is, for Elliott, a case of Aberhart's having his basic humanitarian concerns awakened by the suffering he witnessed during the Depression, coupled with his tendency towards compartmentalized thinking and leadership ambitions that coalesced in a way that blinded him to the full implications of his thought.[23]

Elliott is quite right to suggest that the Depression and Aberhart's interest in social credit did bring about a significant shift in the tone and content of his sermons and speeches. His promotion of social credit was suddenly full of references to the "brotherhood of man" and the Christian duty to "end poverty in the midst of plenty." Indeed, much of Aberhart's Christian-based justification for the implementation of social credit to end the Depression was a near replication of the rhetoric employed by the postmillennialist UFA president Henry Wise Wood nearly two decades earlier. In April 1935, just months before he would become premier, Aberhart suggested to his radio audience that the philosophy of Social Credit was "based solely upon the Golden Rule, it teaches us to live and let live, it drives off the vultures that feast on humanity through its economic helplessness." Despite the greed and selfishness present in the world, he continues, "there is a group consciousness present in mankind ... Social Credit emphasizes this group concept." So, he would then ask his followers, are you still "favourable to the old capitalistic order of dog-eat-dog? The individuality concept of man must be secondary to the higher group concept. God's principle is to be your brother's keeper."[24] Social Credit embraced this principle, Aberhart would argue in a subsequent radio address, because "we are against the unfair and unethical practices in Canadian business. We are out to put our Christianity into practice, to show that the principles of Christ can and will cope with the unholy schemes of greedy financiers."[25] Indeed, he even went as far as to suggest that social credit was part of a "New Christianity" that was now appearing that represented a new era of "Christian Brotherhood."[26] Aberhart also regularly suggested that social credit was "practical or applied Christianity," that it was modelled after "God's Plan," that "God stood behind our crusade," and that "deliverance" was near should Alberta adopt the Douglas

Religion and Political Thought of Aberhart and Manning   113

plan.[27] And, as been noted by several scholars, such rhetoric confused and even angered many in Alberta's fundamentalist Christian community who had been groomed to view such attempts to improve the lot of humanity as interfering with "God's divine plan." Chief among Aberhart's critics in this regard was J. Fergus Kirk, president of the ultra-fundamentalist Prairie Bible Institute, who authored a lengthy critique of Aberhart's newfound interest in politics in early 1935 which defended a strict apolitical position and attacked the "false refuge" that was Social Credit, a movement that exhibited clear "communistic tendencies," a charge Aberhart quickly dismissed in a radio address in April of that year.[28] Yet it seems undeniable that the shift in emphasis towards the need to address the social conditions created by the Depression in Aberhart's radio addresses does indicate a commitment to a "worldly" position much closer to the social gospel than that of a premillennial dispensationalist.

Clearly, it is possible that Aberhart made an overt decision to utilize such antithetical rhetoric as an electoral ploy to appeal to former UFA supporters, who were very familiar with the Christian-based postmillennial political thought of Wood, but he certainly did not drop such rhetoric after becoming premier. Indeed, one can find similar references in his radio addresses and speeches up to his death in 1943, although it is also true that Aberhart continued to emphasize traditional dispensational themes related to the Rapture, Tribulation, and eventual passage into the millennial dispensation as well.[29] Thus, Elliott's suggestion that Aberhart's politics, akin as they were to those advocated by social gospel devotees, were antithetical to his long-held dispensationalist views seems plausible. However, the claim that Aberhart was unfaithful to this religious view by entering the political fray and demanding the introduction of social credit economics is, I argue, built upon a particularly narrow interpretation of premillennial dispensationalism that masks the way in which Aberhart's political activities were in fact very much in line with his broader religious perspective. That is not to say that contradictions cannot be found within the theological musings of Aberhart over his lifetime, for surely there are several. Nor would I dispute the charge that Aberhart occasionally borrowed rhetoric from social gospel practitioners in an effort to further popularize his movement. However, there remains a very important link between a fundamental component of his Christian theology and his eventual adoption of social credit economics that has thus far gone largely unnoticed.

Elliott's charge ultimately rests upon an understanding of dispensationalism that harkens back to early twentieth-century American liberal

Christians, who understood dispensationalism as a purely "other-worldly" theology that accepted the deteriorating conditions of the world as preordained and thereby rendering social efforts of any kind pointless. However, although American premillennial dispensational-ists did reject the notion of building a kingdom of God on earth, they also made a critically important distinction between the capacity of humanity to "save the world" and their capacity to "save souls," a task that did involve a particular social commitment.[30] For premillennial dispensationalists, the prime responsibility of Christians within the current dispensation was to accept the salvation that God freely offers to all by building up a personal relationship with God and being reborn in Him. This notion of Christian rebirth, central to American fundamentalism, was derived from a particular scriptural passage (John 3:3–5) wherein Christ warns Nicodemus that it would be impossible to see the kingdom of God without "being born again" of the "spirit." A rebirth in Christ came to represent a complete transformation of the individual, from a condition of spiritual emptiness to one full of the spirit of Christ. More importantly for premillennial dispensationalists, being born again in Christ was the action necessary to identify oneself as an authentic follower of Christ and thereby one of the lucky individuals that would be raised to Heaven by Christ during the Rapture and thus spared the terrors of the seven-year Tribulation. Yet God also gave His church a second task in this dispensation: evangelization, the dispensing of the gospel to those who have not yet experienced a spiritual rebirth in Christ so as to assist with their quest for salvation. Premillennial dispensationalists believed that those who died without having experienced this conversion were eternally damned. It was therefore the role of the church to reach these individuals before it was too late.

In other words, Christians in the present dispensation did have a worldly task to complete that was separate from the task of "saving the world through works." And that task was to work tirelessly to bring the message of Christ to as many people as possible and thus "save" them before the Rapture, the point at which Christ returns briefly to earth to gather his true followers who had experienced a spiritual rebirth. The remaining individuals, who had not experienced conversion, were left on earth to suffer under the rule of the Antichrist during the Tribulation. In fact, premillennial dispensationalists often utilized the metaphor of a sinking ship to describe the earthly conditions leading up to the Tribulation: although Christians could not keep the ship afloat, they could at least rescue a few of the passengers.[31] Thus, although the deterministic implications of dispensationalism seemed to

Religion and Political Thought of Aberhart and Manning   115

demand passivity when it came to social activism, many adherents also believed that humans did possess the agency in this dispensation to fulfill this call for evangelism, a belief that spurred a significant missionary effort on behalf of American dispensationalists in the twentieth century.[32] Religious historian George Marsden has taken this point further by demonstrating that many dispensationalists have, in certain cases, supported public and private social programs so long as they were "understood as complementary outgrowths of the regenerating work of Christ which saved souls for all eternity."[33] In fact, the desire to reach out to others and assist with their salvation was a central component of the larger "love thy neighbour" spirit that would, according to this religious outlook, naturally overcome individuals once they entered into a personal relationship with God and were reborn. Other, more worldly acts would also follow conversion, especially those related to feeding, clothing, and healing the needy. Such social acts were often understood as precursors to the conversion of the poor if poverty was perceived to be preventing them from properly nurturing their spiritual side. Importantly, however, these acts were never aimed at ushering in the Millennium or perfecting society. They were simply a means to the end of converting as many as possible prior to the Rapture. This is the fundamental difference with respect to social action between premillennial dispensationalism and the postmillennialism inherent in much of the broad social gospel movement as well as in the religious and political thought of Henry Wise Wood. And, as will be demonstrated in a more detailed examination of Aberhart and Manning's shared theology in the paragraphs below, Aberhart's sudden interest in political and economic reform in the 1930s was built upon a call to action within this world that fell squarely within this version of premillennial dispensationalism and its inherent commitment to saving the souls of one's fellows.

THE SHARED THEOLOGY
OF ABERHART AND MANNING

The basic points of the shared premillennial dispensationalist perspective of Aberhart and Manning were staples of the American fundamentalist movement that had emerged out of the revivalist traditions in the early twentieth century. The central tenets of this faith, encapsulated in the "Doctrinal Basis" of Aberhart's Prophetic Bible Institute, included a belief in the divine verbal inspiration of the entirety of the scriptures, the original "fall" of humanity and the subsequent "universal depravity of human nature," the atoning efficacy of the death of Christ, the necessity of spiritual rebirth as the initial step in one's salvation, "the everlasting happiness of the righteous and the awful and everlasting misery of the unbelieving wicked, in a literal lake of fire," and the literal Second Coming of Christ, first "at His appearing in the air for His Church" and second "at His coming to the Mount of Olives to establish the millennial reign of righteousness upon the earth."[34] The last point – Christ "appearing in the air for His Church" prior to returning again to establish the Millennium – was a direct reference to the Rapture. The Rapture and its implications were central themes within nearly all of the sermons delivered by Aberhart and Manning, but nowhere was the drama of its significance highlighted more than in *The Branding Irons of the Antichrist*, a play penned by the duo in 1931 that featured the story of a girl who had failed to seek a personal relationship with Christ and thus suffered terribly during the Tribulation, eventually being put to death by the army of the Antichrist for failing to worship him. The play ends with a voice behind the curtain offering the audience a rather dramatic warning: "Such shall be the tragic end of all those who learn too late that except a man be born again he will be left behind at the Rapture to face the branding irons of the Antichrist."[35] Not only did such a warning underline the consequences of failing to accept Christ before the coming Rapture, it also pointed to the motivation of Aberhart and Manning's ministry within this dispensation: to convince people to seek Christ and experience a spiritual rebirth. Indeed, Manning repeatedly warned his listeners of

the terrible importance of being ready when Jesus Christ appears, especially when you realize the appearing of Christ, the Rapture of the Church, can take place any day, any hour, any moment, and when it does, my friend, either you will be taken out of this world forever with the Lord, or you will be left behind to face the greatest time of trouble this world has ever known. Which will it be? It all depends on one thing … Have you the Son of God as your own personal Saviour today?[36]

It is this example of evangelism, which was repeated ad nauseam in the radio sermons of both Aberhart and Manning, that broadened the focus of dispensationalism beyond that of a pessimistic assessment of current social conditions towards a sense of mission on earth and is key to explaining the larger purpose of both Aberhart and Manning's actions in this world.

Religion and Political Thought of Aberhart and Manning 117

For dispensationalists, the present Age of Grace is a time wherein individuals are to develop a personal relationship with God in order to rectify their sinful nature and prepare themselves for the millennial reign of Christ. The individual was understood to be a fallen creature and therefore possessed inherent tendencies towards evil. Manning wrote to an inquisitive listener in 1946: "One of the great fallacies in so many modern religious philosophies is that they assume that man is inherently good at heart. [In fact,] Scripture declares that the exact opposite is true. That all men are born into this world spiritually dead ... with a heart that is deceitful above all things and desperately wicked."[37]

Importantly, men and women were incapable of altering this aspect of their nature independently. Change was possible through the power of Christ alone, and this could only occur through a spiritual rebirth in His name. In a letter exchange in 1932, Aberhart recalls the story of Nicodemus from the biblical Book of John, wherein Christ pointed to

[t]he absolute necessity of him being regenerated or Born Again by the Holy Spirit by which act he would receive a new and divine nature which would identify him with Christ and enable him to comprehend the things of God.

The Word of God declares that there is an atoning efficacy in the shed blood of Christ which cleanses the soul of the individual who personally appropriates the finished work on his behalf ... and makes him fit to enter into the presence of God Himself.[38]

Immediately, one notices in this theology a significantly different starting point than that of many of the mainstream social gospel versions of Christianity, which viewed man as essentially good and capable of attaining salvation by following the social teachings of Christ on earth. By stressing man's inherent depravity, Aberhart and Manning articulate a religious viewpoint that rejected any interpretation of eternal salvation through good works alone. It was rather by the divine grace of God that Christian individuals could find redemption by accepting His mercy and affirming Christ individually and thus being reborn. However, the notion of good works was not foreign to this interpretation of salvation. Rather, according to this outlook, good works on earth would be a direct result of this individual rebirth. In fact, Manning notes, "the spiritually regenerated individual thinks differently from the one who isn't. His attitude to his fellowmen is different. His attitude towards what he regards as his responsibilities to people is different. He inclines to love people instead of hating them."[39] It is this humanitarian concern, motivated by the Holy Spirit that resides in the individual who has experienced rebirth, that is to make a difference in the lives of others. Attempting to do good works without such regeneration is bound to fail because of the fallen nature of humanity. However good one's intentions, sin will eventually overcome the individual who has not had his or her soul cleansed by the grace of God through rebirth. The individual who has found Christ in this way is driven by "a love of Christ for what he'd done for us," and this is replicated in his or her dealings with fellow humans. "In other words," Manning says, "we express our Love for Him by being concerned about the people He was concerned about enough to die for."[40]

The expression of this love for others following individual regeneration was, for Manning, the single greatest factor explaining the actions of his mentor Aberhart, who, Manning suggests, "had a very, very deep sense of responsibility, and this grew from his Christian conviction that we were in this world to serve, that we are our brother's keeper, we have an obligation to others."[41] Surely it is this sense of obligation to their fellows, which Aberhart would mention on a number of occasions when promoting social credit doctrines, that encourages scholars to view Aberhart as akin to the progressive minister who preached the social gospel. Recall Elliott in particular, who found this emphasis on serving others so difficult to square with the "pre-social credit" Aberhart. Yet, in 1967 (thirty-five years after Aberhart took up the social credit cause), it was Manning, taking pains to repeatedly stress the "love for others" one would feel following rebirth. Furthermore, Manning would often reassert the essence of Aberhart's initial contention that the prime function of Christians within this world was not to solve social problems but to "bring people into a personal relationship with Christ."[42] This is a significant point in the theology of Aberhart and Manning that has been severely misunderstood. Their suggestion that the aim of Christians in this world should be to encourage others to develop a personal relationship with Christ is intimately tied to their broader belief in a deep love for others that motivates the regenerated individual to seek out and assist those who have not yet experienced rebirth and thus save them from eternal damnation. Therefore, the notion of "being thy brother's keeper" is a sentiment that demanded much more than simply providing those in need with physical handouts as required by social gospel theology. Rather, it required the Christian individual to work towards facilitating the personal rebirth of those in spiritual need and thus assist with the biggest prize of all, salvation in

Christ. As I will argue shortly, it is in the spirit of this facilitation, not in the hopes of building a perfect society, that Aberhart undertook his efforts to reform Alberta's economic system through politics, while Manning would eventually fight against the encroachment of socialism.

Despite rejecting outright the postmillennial notion that humans possessed the ability to usher in the Millennium, dispensationalists did, in theory at least, believe it to be possible to improve conditions slightly within each dispensation.[43] Speaking to the proper application of social credit economics, Aberhart argued that "it is the transformation of the individual's life and attitude of mind from this personal relationship with the living Christ that … is essential to the proper application of economics in order that the desired results may be realized."[44] Manning agreed that the best human efforts could not prevent social problems from deteriorating, but he believed that the root of the problem was not "the system" but rather the individual's alienation from God and the subsequent evil tendencies he or she suffered. Therefore, "the restoration of men to a right relationship with God is the first step towards an effective solution of our national problems."[45] In fact, the regenerated Christian has a duty in this world to alleviate the evil that lies at the root of present social problems. Manning writes: "While a Christian is in the world but not of the world he nevertheless has a responsibility to exert a maximum measure of influence to restrain the corruption in the world and to advance righteousness and whatsoever things are true."[46] He continues elsewhere:

> I have never been able to follow the reasoning of Christians who isolate themselves from public affairs then spend much time in deploring the fact that public life so often tends to materialism and unrighteousness.
>   In the realm of politics as in the realm of business [Christian] influence must always be toward righteousness and against evil.[47]

In fact, it will not be possible for the regenerated individual to avoid bringing his "love for others" into the social realm:

> Once a man is genuinely and supernaturally born again of the Holy Spirit the new nature he thereby acquires changes his attitude towards every issue of life, including those things that pertain to the government or management of the country of which he is a citizen.

It is his duty wherever he goes to leave behind the greatest impact possible by his Christian testimony and influence. There is no scriptural justification for excluding public affairs and other responsibilities of citizenship from the field of his influence.[48]

In these passages, one finds a distinct notion of Christian service *in this world*, with the intent of restraining evil and extending God's love. Such an interpretation surely contradicts the purely otherworldly interpretation of dispensationalism offered by Elliott, and there were certainly Alberta fundamentalist Christian sects, such as the Prairie Bible Institute, that would have loathed such attitudes towards earthly service. However, neither Aberhart nor Manning ever wavered from their foundational belief in the supreme aim of Christianity in this age: to bring others into a personal relationship with Christ before the Rapture occurred. Thus, any action in this world was, in the end, motivated by this concern and not by any desire to perfect society. Unlike Henry Wise Wood, who adhered to a particular postmillennial interpretation of history, neither Aberhart nor Manning suggested that all humans would eventually be converted and, consequently, all social problems solved. In fact, Aberhart argued that the Sermon on the Mount, the collection of Christ's social teachings that Wood interpreted as a guide to implementing the kingdom of God on earth, was meant for the Millennial Age, not the present Age of Grace.[49] What Christians could do was use their love for others to expand His influence in this world in a way that encouraged others to personally seek Christ and thus be saved prior to the Rapture. It is in this interpretation of the supreme duty of Christians in this age that one finds the key to understanding the social actions of both Aberhart and Manning.

As far back to the Second Great Awakening in the United States, American evangelical Protestants have understood personal spiritual conversion to require two things. First, the potential convert would obviously need some knowledge of Christ and the scriptures in order to comprehend the reasons why one should seek such rebirth. This "educational" requirement was met by the revivalists, who took it upon themselves to spread the Word of God in such a way that the plain people of the republic could understand and thus be enthused and overcome by the Holy Spirit contained within the Word. Second, the potential convert required a certain freedom to seek God's grace. As discussed in more detail in Chapter 2, American Protestantism evolved away from the Calvinistic notion of predestination and towards the Arminian notion that conversion, and thus salvation, was now con-

Religion and Political Thought of Aberhart and Manning   121

sidered to be an act of free individual choice. Therefore, individual
freedom in the religious and intellectual realms became a paramount
concern of nineteenth-century American Protestants. These prerequisite conditions for conversion were fully embraced by the Christian
fundamentalist movement that emerged out of the American revivalist tradition in the twentieth century. As Marsden has argued, "The
closest thing to a political principle that most fundamentalists seemed
to share was a profession of individualism that paralleled their theological dictum that the individual was the basic unit in the work of
salvation."[50] It was from this fundamentalist movement that Aberhart
derived much of his theology, so it should come as no surprise that
his actions in Alberta, like Manning's, were based on this principle of
individualism and aimed at fulfilling both of these conditions. The
first condition, education, was obviously undertaken through their
ministry, mostly over radio. It was in this service that Aberhart, and
then Manning, followed in the footsteps of the early American revivalists and brought, in plain language, the Word of God to the people of Alberta. The second condition, ensuring that the individual
possessed the freedom necessary to seek God's grace, was the primary
concern of their political and economic beliefs, and it is to this realm
of action that this chapter now turns.

ABERHART, CHRISTIANITY,
AND SOCIAL CREDIT ECONOMICS

As Alvin Finkel's detailed and perceptive history of Alberta Social Credit has demonstrated, the administration took to a more radical and left-
leaning path than often assumed upon attaining political power in
1935, with Aberhart in particular supporting a number of progressive
initiatives that went beyond the implementation of social credit economics.[51] Although the Social Credit government passed a myriad of
legislation pertaining to the early stages of social credit implementation in its first term, including taking steps towards the issuing of dividends and initiating wage and price controls, its more noteworthy
achievements are more accurately described as being social democratic in flavour. For instance, significant attention was paid to the conditions of labour in the province (such as new rules around minimum
wages, hours of work, safe working conditions, and employer–employ-
ee dispute-resolution mechanisms), the improvement of education (including improved working conditions for teachers and the creation of
more efficient schooling districts that were meant to enhance the edu-

cational experience of rural students), and, perhaps most surprisingly, health care (significant expansion of hospital capacity, enhanced funding for the fight against tuberculosis, polio, and cancer, maternity grants for needy mothers).[52] In fact, Aberhart himself, in both 1938 and 1939, confidently predicted that his government would march ahead "to the ultimate introduction of State Medicine."[53] This more "socially democratic" side of the Social Credit government was partly the result of the rather eclectic mix of supporters who became members of the broader Social Credit League. Although the league included a group of dedicated Social Credit devotees who single-mindedly sought implementation of the economic theories of Douglas, it also contained a larger grassroots contingent who, although supportive of Aberhart's plan to end the Depression by way of social credit "dividends," were less familiar with the technical aspects of the theory and more open to traditional styles of government intervention and even borderline socialist options in some cases. Myron Johnson has even argued that the failure of the Co-operative Commonwealth Federation (CCF) in Alberta was very much "an accident of history" given the large swath of potential CCF supporters who embraced the promises of Aberhart in 1935.[54] And it was the presence of these left-leaning citizens, and especially Aberhart's support for many of their proposals, that angered many within both the province's business community (which led a nearly successful attempt to unseat Social Credit in the 1940 election) and within certain fundamentalist Christian circles in Alberta (whose members accused Aberhart of abandoning his traditional dispensational theology and acting in concert with the dreaded social gospel crowd).

Surely it is true that Aberhart's theological and political thinking became somewhat muddled on occasion, and his lack of experience in the world of public policy was glaring at times. Yet Aberhart's support for certain state-initiated proposals aimed at relieving the suffering of citizens was, like his broader interest in social credit economics, not inherently antithetical to the logic of his broader premillennial dispensational Christian outlook. Rather, given the conditions of the Depression, such left-leaning proposals were understood by Aberhart as necessary steps in the larger battle to free the individual from poverty in order to allow the conditions necessary for personal spiritual conversion to take root. However, the nuanced focus on the individual's spiritual betterment inherent in this particular religious based political outlook was subtle enough to be overlooked not only by large swaths of Alberta's right-leaning fundamentalist Christian crowd, who charged Aberhart with religious hypocrisy for abandoning a focus on saving souls, but also by left-leaning Albertans who simply failed to notice the broader anti-collectivist implications of his overall vision. Indeed, the conditions of the Depression, which necessitated temporary action on the part of the state in the view of Aberhart, ultimately prevented the fundamental anti-collectivist logic of his premillennial outlook from unfolding into a full-blown individualistic and anti-statist conservatism until the tenure of Manning, who took control of the party upon the death of Aberhart in 1943. This section expands on this point by considering the relationship between Aberhart's religious interpretation, discussed above, and his approval of such worldly policies related to social credit economic theory and broader social democratic reforms. Not only will this help to dispel notions that his interest in such policies was antithetical to his religious outlook, it will also assist in setting the stage for an investigation into the policies pursued by his successor, Manning, who remained loyal to the same religious foundation as Aberhart's despite advocating quite distinct public policies.

The story of Aberhart's introduction to and eventual adoption of social credit economic theory, initially authored by Major Douglas, has been told in great detail many times over, and thus only a brief summary is included here. In short, the Depression that followed the great stock market crash of 1929 had a considerable impact on Aberhart, as it had on the vast majority of Albertans. The economy of the Prairie provinces was devastated by the culmination of high interest rates, mass unemployment, and a severe drought, and Aberhart was witness to a whole host of suffering, especially that of the students he taught in Calgary. In 1932, one of these students was driven to suicide because of his family's dire economic circumstances, an act that shook Aberhart considerably. That summer he was introduced to social credit economics by a fellow teacher who presented him with a book by Maurice Colbourne, *Unemployment or War*, which explained Douglas's theory in terms that spoke to Aberhart. After staying up through the night to read the book in its entirety, Aberhart reportedly exclaimed the following morning that he had found the solution to the Depression. By the fall of 1932, he was including an explanation of, and enthusiastic support for, social credit economics in his radio broadcasts.[55]

Social credit theory, in its simplest formulation, blamed the current economic conditions on a lack of purchasing power possessed by regular citizens, who were beholden to large financial institutions that controlled credit. Thus, despite the technological advances that had increased production, the economy was slowed to a halt because self-interested bankers refused to lend at reasonable rates, thus impeding regular patterns of consumption. The result was "poverty in the midst of plenty." To rectify this situation, the state was to take control of credit away from greedy financiers, who profited from high interest rates, and provide its citizens with a share or "dividend" of this "social credit" to allow them to buy goods. In doing so, the state would re-establish its citizens' purchasing power and the economy would be revived. However, Douglas was quick to note that such an action was not a charitable handout. In fact, because the technological advances that had increased production were the result of the culmination of all the people's efforts within the state, any production was part of their "cultural heritage." In other words, all citizens had a right to a share of that which was produced. Yet this was not a socialist vision aimed at redistributing wealth. Citizens were to receive a dividend but this was meant to enhance purchasing power to cover only the bare necessities of life. Douglas was a firm believer in the freedom of individuals, and he also believed that providing for them completely would wreak havoc on the market-based incentives that encourage individuals to continually improve their own lives. This would be a theme that would prove vitally important to Aberhart's own interpretation and attempted implementation of social credit economics in Alberta.[56]

Although considerable doubt has been cast on Aberhart's grasp of the more technical aspects of social credit theory, by 1933 he was eagerly trying to convince all who would listen that it was the key to ending poverty in Alberta. In a letter to an inquisitive listener who was confused as to why Aberhart sought significant economic reform but refused to endorse the CCF, Aberhart admitted his aversion to "our present capitalistic system" and his belief that there would be "no hope of recovery until it is abolished and a new system of economics introduced." Yet he was careful to add that "Red Socialism would prove, if anything, a greater disaster than even our present system." In defence of his preferred alternative, social credit economics, he noted:

> The Douglas System provides the bare necessities of life to every bona fide citizen of the Province, and forever frees our loyal citizens from the dread of poverty and starvation in the midst of plenty. At the same time it respects the personal rights and liberty of each individual citizen and has a definite policy for the encouragement and rewarding of his individual enterprise.
>
> One thing that appeals to me and I believe to every thinking Christian, in the Douglas System of Economics is the fact that from

beginning to end it is based on the great principles of God's great economy.[57]

Within this statement one finds three precise reasons why Aberhart favoured social credit theory, and although he never directly mentioned any religious motivation in his well-known *Social Credit Manual*, published in 1935, they were all strongly correlated with his theological position. First, social credit theory appealed to Aberhart's general Christian sense of duty towards his fellows by ensuring an end to the suffering associated with the Depression, although, as will be explained below, enhancing the freedom to develop spiritually rather than providing basic relief from material suffering represented the ultimate end. Second, social credit economics appealed to his premillennial dispensational perspective because it protected the freedom of the individual vital to personal spiritual development, whereas alternative plans, most especially socialistic ones, did not. Third, he was convinced that the structure of the social credit plan was actually modelled after the plan God had provided his followers to attain salvation. Each of these points will be expanded upon below.

Aberhart's defence of social credit was built first on his belief that a central demand of Christianity was to be "thy brother's keeper." To do nothing while your fellows suffered was simply not an option for the truly regenerated individual who was overwhelmed with a love for both God and His people. Preston Manning, son of Ernest and Muriel (who knew Aberhart even longer than Ernest had) Manning, argues that it was precisely this basic Christian dimension that initially drove Aberhart into politics. "According to my mother," Preston recalls,

the line-ups of discouraged, hungry, and even injured people in those soup-kitchen lines [at Aberhart's Bible Institute in Calgary during the Depression] increasingly drove Aberhart wild. The daily experience of seeing these line-ups, and the human waste and tragedy they represented, drove him to the point where he believed that something had to be done.

[The theory of social credit] happened to fit with Aberhart's preference for "reforming capitalism" rather than abolishing it as the socialists wanted to do. But what got him started on this whole strain of thought and action ... was a social consciousness informed by his Christian faith that simply couldn't abide the tragedy ... of those soup kitchen lines.[58]

According to Aberhart's theology, this sense of duty to those in need extended to all spheres of the regenerated individual's life, and the magnitude of the suffering he witnessed drew this social sentiment to the fore of his religious thought in the early 1930s. The Depression inflicted a wide-ranging poverty that could not be blamed on the laziness or ineptitude of the common folk. It was rather the economic system that allowed financiers to overcharge for credit that was to blame. As depicted above, Aberhart's speeches and sermons from 1933 onward referred much more often than they had previously to the importance of "the Golden Rule" and to the coming of "a new era of Christianity," one focused on "God's principle ... to be your brother's keeper." This shift in his tone demonstrates that a clear sense of Christian duty to his fellows had been awakened in him and now motivated his desire to reform the economic system, the goal being to eliminate the poverty that was crushing Albertans. Yet, as Elliott notes, this sudden interest in social action confused a certain segment of Christian fundamentalists in the province who had come to associate such action with the misguided social gospel tradition that Aberhart had long railed against. To a critic who had implied that the Depression was the cost Albertans must pay for their sins, Aberhart responded:

[Citizens] are suffering, not because God has failed to give but because the selfish, greedy, ungodly worshipers of the golden god and their henchmen have stolen the bounties from them. God hasn't punished mankind. He has poured out from his rich storehouse of heaven upon mankind but these grafters, these men who have confiscated the power are depriving people from their very living, starving them to death. Children are crying for bread. This man says you shouldn't try to relieve them?

It was the Lord Jesus Himself who took the whip of cords and drove the moneychangers out of the temple, wasn't it? He didn't stand at the door and pray that God would put them out. [59]

To those who further criticized his interest in worldly happenings, Aberhart replied with Psalm 41, which told of the blessings one would receive from God should one consider the poor.[60]

For Aberhart, social credit economics represented an attempt to put these Christian principles of brotherhood into practice. Of course, the Alberta CCF, heavily influenced by the major players in the Prairie social gospel movement and supported by a wide array of liberal-leaning church ministers, was pointing to the same Christian principles in its

Religion and Political Thought of Aberhart and Manning   127

demands for government intervention to end poverty. Yet, from Aberhart's perspective, social credit economics was built upon a significantly different, and more premillennial-friendly, intellectual foundation than the socialism favoured by the postmillennial social gospel crowd. Thus, the effort to differentiate the particular remedies offered by Alberta Social Credit from those associated with the CCF became a central occupation of Aberhart's. Responding to a letter that suggested Christ would support socialism, Aberhart was quick to revert to his Christian fundamentalist-based dislike of the social gospel and its promotion of socialism, arguing that "[o]ne of the weak points of socialism is its complete failure to recognize that a right relationship between man and man cannot exist until a right relationship between man and God is first established."[61] By focusing on "works" at the expense of "faith," the social gospel had overlooked the vital step of individual rebirth, from which good works would eventually follow. By paying little attention to such a necessity, left-leaning ministers were promoting an economic system (socialism) that failed to protect the freedom of the individual, that sacred pocket of liberty that was required for the individual to fully experience Christ and thus be born again. In a series of campaign-style radio addresses weeks before the 1935 election, Aberhart strove to make this point to his audience. At the heart of his message was the ever-repeated assertion that Social Credit, despite advocating state control of credit, was against traditional socialist ideas such as communal property or state ownership or confiscation of any kind.[62] Beyond this attempt to differentiate Social Credit policy from CCF policy, however, was a more fundamental distinction. In contrast to the "regimentation of the individual" experienced under socialism, Aberhart pleaded,

[s]ocial creditors believe in the freedom of the individual and provide for that freedom by guaranteeing to him the bare necessities of food, clothing and shelter ...
    This provision of the bare necessities of life will give the individual an economic freedom that he has never known before and must of necessity therefore give him a chance for self-development.

By providing such "bare necessities," Aberhart continued, "people would be able to prepare themselves in the sphere of life for which they have an aptitude and be better able to serve their fellows and their state through individual freedom." Ultimately, social credit would allow the citizenry to "find economic liberty so we can worship God as we please and live and let live knowing that our brothers will help us secure the bare necessities."[63] Be assured, Aberhart would add in a later campaign speech, that "God is behind our great crusade ... [and] we trust that there will sweep over this land a wave of reverence and adoration for God that was never previously known."[64]

Within these speeches one is provided with a glimpse into the overall goal of social credit as interpreted by Aberhart, and this in turn leads to the second, though strongly related, religious-based reason that he favoured as a remedy to the suffering he was witnessing. The poverty experienced during the Depression was not simply a case of human suffering that had to be rectified because God demanded charity for the poor. The poverty was, further, an impingement on the freedom of individuals and their development. Aberhart was adamant that the state had a central role to play in protecting this freedom:

> Modern liberty lies in the freedom of the individual from selfish control, duress, fear, or exploitation inflicted by another or others. If an autocrat, or a plutocrat, or a large corporation controls, directs, or regiments the actions of any individual or number of individuals without their consent, these latter have to that extent lost their liberty in the truest sense of the word.
>
> Intruders of liberty must be controlled by the state for the good of the community.[65]

As Manning would later explain, Social Credit's association with Christianity was based upon its recognition of "the supremacy of the individual as a divinely-created creature, possessing, as a result of divine creation, certain inalienable rights that must be respected and preserved."[66] Douglas had often mentioned the importance of individual development within the context of poverty elimination, and Maurice Colbourne, who popularized Douglas's theories, agreed, arguing that, because of the Depression, "man, although able to keep alive is unable to live fully, he exists but with bent back and brow weighted with anxiety and care."[67] However, it was Aberhart's particular interpretation of Christianity that led him and Manning to interpret this concern for individual development as primarily spiritual in nature. Aberhart touched on this theme initially in a series of radio lectures delivered in 1933, in the midst of the Depression and shortly after his conversion to social credit economics. God approaches us as individuals, Aberhart would note, and has given us "a right to choose our own destiny ... [and] it is on the basis of this right that our enlightenment places great responsibility on us."[68] "God always respects the individual and his

Religion and Political Thought of Aberhart and Manning   129

rights," Aberhart would continue in the next in the series of léctures, and "He makes no confiscation nor does he use compulsion."[69] Manning agreed, noting that "[t]he Bible speaks of the glorious liberty of the Children of God" and that "God intends people to be free." This is a vital recognition, he continues, because "the first stage of that liberty is to exercise your individual freedom to respond to Jesus Christ when he asks you to let Him be your Saviour and Lord."[70] In other words, protecting individual freedom was necessary because God insisted that individuals remain in a state of freedom, which thereby allowed them the possibility of freely pursuing a spiritual rebirth in Him. Therefore, Manning would argue, the goal of the Social Credit philosophy was "a free society in which the individual would have the maximum opportunity to develop himself." This required addressing the poverty of the Depression because the "attention to the cultural realm of life was limited by the economic conditions of that time."[71] In fact, Manning would continue,

[e]conomic insecurity is one of the things that circumscribes people and … [would be an area] where the government would assume responsibility. If we were going to put people in a position where this freedom of choice would be meaningful, then you had to do things which would … enable them to have economic conditions that wouldn't circumscribe them too much.

But one of the objectives of [government involvement] – sort of a new objective, in a way – was that that person, having some measure of economic security, whether he got it through government programs or greater development of the private sector – however he got it, would have that much more freedom to do the developing himself in these other lines.[72]

This is an absolutely crucial admission on the part of Manning if one is to grasp the true relationship between the shared theology of Aberhart and Manning and their support for social credit economics in general and their passage of social democratic legislation in particular in the heart of the Depression.

As an article from the *Alberta Social Credit Chronicle* argued, "Crushing and demoralizing poverty obscures men's spirituality." The goal of implementing social credit economics was to end this poverty and "only then would it be possible to appreciate completely the message of Him."[73] Aberhart alluded to this problem in his first electoral campaign when he suggested that "much of man's selfishness is produced today through the mad scramble to get the necessities of life. We have to trample one another down to do this." [74] By providing these necessities, the social credit system allowed individuals to cease this "mad scramble" and instead put their energies into cultural activities aimed at self-development, which for Aberhart clearly implied spiritual development. Upon encountering the constitutional roadblocks that prevented the implementation of social credit financial policies while he was in office, Aberhart complained: "The money monopolists will not issue the money tickets to enable the great clumsy, outworn financial system to work so the people must suffer privation and want. They must exist in undesirable depressing conditions that cannot improve their spiritual development." [75] In his admonishment of those who were thinking of abandoning the efforts of Social Credit to reform the economy, Aberhart told his followers that they required more tenacity and persistence "in our endeavor to help our friends and neighbours to find Christ in the supreme life." [76] And in 1939 he stated bluntly: "I am convinced that dire poverty and want makes people bitter and turn away from God." [77]

Thus, true to his dispensationalist interpretation of history, Aberhart, with Manning at his side, was attempting to fulfill his primary Christian duty within the Age of Grace by promoting social credit economics. The prime function of the Christian in this world was to bring individuals into a personal relationship with God. It was by way of his prophetic Bible and his radio ministry that he first sought to achieve this goal, but the poverty of the Depression was impeding individual Albertans' capacity to develop spiritually. Therefore, working out of his Christian-based "love for thy neighbour" spirit, Aberhart took up the cause of economic reform as a means of freeing the individual from an economic slavery that prevented spiritual rebirth. Social credit, rather than socialism, was the answer because, although socialism may be able to provide the individual with certain provisions, it also forced the individual into a certain bondage to the collective. The liberal-leaning ministry had little problem with this outcome, argued Aberhart, because it failed to appreciate the primary requirement of the Christian as individual spiritual rebirth. Instead, advocates of the social gospel understood themselves to be building the kingdom of God on earth. This was diametrically opposed to the religious goal of Aberhart, who sought to extend the Word of God to as many people as possible prior to the Rapture. By protecting the freedom of the individual, social credit economics could facilitate this evangelicalism. In fact, in his refutation of the socialist position on the basis of its failure to guarantee

Religion and Political Thought of Aberhart and Manning   131

individual liberty, one finds the reason why Aberhart was not interested in establishing a state religion based on his own fundamentalism, despite the claims of his critics.[78] Spiritual rebirth was a matter of free choice, and coercion on the part of the church or the state in this direction could never deliver God's salvation to the individual, just as the good works of socialism could not. It was the protection of the individual, not the establishment of the Millennium or a religious dictatorship, that stood behind his promotion of social credit as well as his broader interest in a free and democratic state rather than a theocracy.

Yet, despite such clear evidence that Aberhart did not act counter to his premillennial dispensational theology by endorsing social credit economics as a method of hastening the coming Millennium, a certain skepticism persists among scholars interested in Alberta Social Credit. A good deal of this skepticism with respect to Aberhart's goals can be attributed, I suspect, to the numerous references he made to social credit as being God's Plan or being based on the "great principles of God's great economy." As a series of lectures on the relationship between Christianity and economics that Aberhart delivered in 1933 indicates, he had convinced himself that social credit economics were in fact modelled after the plan God had provided for humanity to attain salvation, a third reason he favoured this approach over socialism. This connection is built upon Aberhart's interpretation of Isaiah 55:1–2, which reads:

[1] Ho, every one that thirsteth, come ye to the waters, and he that hath no money; come ye, buy, and eat; yea, come, buy wine and milk without money and without price. [2] Wherefore do ye spend money for that which is not bread? And your labour for that which satisfieth not? Hearken diligently unto me, and eat ye that which is good, and let your soul delight itself in fatness.[79]

In this passage, God is offering salvation to those who have no money. However, for Aberhart, the individual had to choose to seek God and thus accept this gift of salvation. In other words, the individual could not attain salvation on his or her own but only in co-operation with God. Aberhart writes: "Christ has done for you what you can never do yourself ... by association you get divine rights, forgiveness, mercy, peace." But, he continues, "people are the same in salvation as economics."[80] Individuals cannot free themselves from the oppression of the poverty experienced in the Depression on their own. Rather, such a task requires the co-operation of individuals in the form of state control over credit and the creation of purchasing power. Thus, Aberhart provided a justification for the group action required to put an end to the Depression by reminding listeners that spiritual salvation, too, requires a sort of co-operation, that between the individual and Christ.

However, the connection Aberhart drew between Christianity and social credit economics goes beyond this parallel with respect to co-operation and action. Aberhart argued that the only solution to the Depression that will work "must be fashioned along the system or plan that God has revealed."[81] Just as Isaiah 55:1–2 suggests that the salvation of the Lord is abundant but requires no money, the economic system should operate on the same principles. "Therefore," Aberhart writes, "if we are to pattern our economic system on God's Plan we must conduct our business without money and without profit. This is basic to the theory of social credit."[82] Remarkably, Aberhart essentially suggested that the technicalities of social credit theory, including the issuing of a dividend at no monetary cost to the citizen and the establishment of the "just price" to constrain profiteering, were sanctioned by God because they are in accordance with this passage in Isaiah that implies that the Lord's salvation is "without money and profit." Thus, just as "[r]ecognition and declaration of Jesus Christ as the all wise, all powerful son of God are essential to a full and complete deliverance, [the implementation of] social credit cuts off our dependence on financial credit and we are delivered economically."[83]

The attempt to link social credit to God's Plan in this manner represents surely one of Aberhart's more bizarre conclusions. It is difficult to know whether Aberhart really believed in this association or whether this effort was merely a way to provide social credit theory with a divine foundation in the eyes of his Christian audience, whose support he was actively seeking, although there is little evidence to suggest that he was being insincere. What can be gleaned from this attempted linkage is the ease with which listeners, and later academic commentators, could be seduced into believing that the Alberta Social Credit League was meant to usher in a new and perfect society within which citizens would acquire deliverance not only from poverty, but also from eternal damnation. Indeed, Irving quotes numerous followers of Aberhart who were convinced that the rise of the party represented the fulfillment of a divine plan that would result in eternal spiritual salvation for true followers of Christ.[84] Yet, from his broader theology and some specific comments he made with respect to social credit economics, we can be sure that Aberhart never interpreted the rise of his party or the promised end of the Depression to represent the foretold Millennium. In

Religion and Political Thought of Aberhart and Manning   133

fact, around the same time Aberhart was delivering his lecture series on Christianity and economics, he sent a letter to J.H. Coldwell that made explicit reference to his belief in distinct dispensations and, in the very next paragraph, he spoke of Douglas's system and its present application. There was absolutely no indication that the implementation of social credit economics was meant to bring about the next and final dispensation, the Millennial Age.[85] This point makes sense when set against the larger argument of this section that Aberhart's goal was to free the individual from poverty in order to allow the conditions necessary for personal conversion to take root. However, because such an argument has not yet been made in detail, it has been easy for scholars to overlook such comments and suggest that Aberhart's interpretation of social credit economics as a means to usher in the millennial reign of Christ was similar to the social gospel belief in building the kingdom of God on earth by way of good works on the part of its citizens. But this was not the case.

MANNING, CHRISTIANITY, AND THE DEFENCE OF THE FREE MARKET

Ernest Manning took control of Alberta Social Credit following the death of Aberhart in 1943 and led the party to a resounding electoral victory in 1944. He would remain the premier of Alberta until his retirement in 1968, leading Social Credit to an impressive seven consecutive majority electoral victories. Scholars have interpreted the leadership transition from Aberhart to Manning as a critical stage in the development of the party because it was under Manning that any serious attempts to implement the radical social credit economic reforms favoured by Aberhart were essentially abandoned and the party instead took a decisive right turn towards a full-fledged approval of free-market capitalism. To some, this shift indicated a return by Manning to the traditional fundamentalist Christian roots of the Calgary Prophetic Bible Institute, which rejected outright the social gospel and any related attempts to remake society in a way that could usher in the Millennium. Finkel in particular adopts Elliott's view of Aberhart as someone who abandoned his fundamentalist religious roots and embarked down a left-leaning political path and essentially became "a social gospeller." According to Finkel, it was not until its electoral victory of 1944 that the party took a decisive turn to the right, largely because Manning, given his fundamentalist Christian background, "does not appear to have embraced social gospel views comfortably."[86] Yet, as demonstrated above,

Aberhart's intentions were not in fact contrary to his fundamentalist dispensational Christian beliefs, and thus any interpretation of Manning's political motives as representing a clear shift away from Aberhart's religious perspective is misguided. Jared Wesley, on the other hand, offers a more nuanced appreciation of the differences between Aberhart and Manning, noting that both men remained committed to the protection of individual freedom but that Aberhart's individualism was tempered by a "communitarian notion of economic security," whereas Manning's was built atop a firmer commitment to self-reliance.[87] It is certainly true that Manning stressed self-reliance more often than his mentor, but this reading of the relationship between Aberhart and Manning overlooks the manner by which Manning remained faithful to the same basic religious outlook that sat at the foundation of Aberhart's political actions. In fact, as Dennis Groh has noted, "Christianity permeates [Manning's] whole system of thought."[88] Building upon this point, this section will demonstrate that, despite largely abandoning social credit economic theory, Manning retained a strong commitment to the same fundamental goal Aberhart had stressed: the facilitation of spiritual rebirth for as many individuals as possible. This can be seen first in his continuation of Aberhart's radio ministry, which brought the Word of God to hundreds of thousands, and second in his implementation, as premier, of political and economic policies that sought to protect and enhance the freedom of the individual, "a divinely-created creature possessing, as a result of divine creation, certain inalienable rights that must be respected and preserved."[89] Thus, the shift in policy direction from Aberhart to Manning was not the result of a differing religious perspective but rather the product of different legal and economic conditions.

Clearly Manning was not a clone of Aberhart. Beyond being less temperamental than his mentor, Manning quickly abandoned some of Aberhart's more bizarre doctrinal beliefs, including attempts to link scripture to social credit economics, and in doing so, he re-established a working relationship with much of Alberta's broader evangelical Christian crowd who had turned their back on Aberhart.[90] Yet the foundation of his thought rested upon the same premillennial dispensationalism as Aberhart's, with the foretold Rapture, Tribulation, and coming Millennial Age remaining the central focus of his radio sermons for the next several decades. In a summation of his dispensational outlook, Manning spoke of the Millennium as an age in which "there will be on this earth no more poverty or want, no more anxiety and fear, no more violence, crime, bloodshed or war," and reminded his lis-

Religion and Political Thought of Aberhart and Manning   135

teners that it would not be brought about by "the efforts of men," or by
"the building of world governments and world armies and world police forces." Rather,

[t]his future period of peace will be brought about by the literal,
bodily return of Jesus Christ to establish his long-promised kingdom of heaven on this earth. His future literal return, according to
the scriptures, will be accomplished by some momentous events
and performances. When He comes He will destroy the Anti-christ
at the great Battle of Armageddon. He will re-establish on this
earth the throne of David of old ...
     The Devil ... will be bound and cast into a pit for a thousand
years and the curse of sin will be checked on this earth ...
     Peace, security and prosperity will be the lot of all.[91]

Manning's interpretations of the prophetic scriptures central to dispensational eschatology – primarily the books of Ezekiel, Daniel, and
Revelation – and their relation to ongoing world events were the subject of dozens upon dozens of his radio addresses over the next decades.
The events of the Cold War were especially relevant for Manning given
the long-running dispensational assumption (shared by Aberhart) that,
following the Rapture, the Antichrist would emerge as the ruler of Russia, gain prominence as an unexpected diplomat, eventually launch a
destructive war on Israel, and finally be met and defeated by Christ at
the Battle of Armageddon. In the late 1940s and early 1950s Manning's
sermons were almost entirely focused on the news reports documenting the events related to Russia on the world stage and their relation to
the prophetic scriptures.[92] For Manning, there was little doubt that
world developments were pointing towards the coming Rapture and
the subsequent Tribulation under the rule of the Antichrist. In an early
1949 sermon, he bluntly stated: "God describes the world kingdom to
come in explicit terms. He says it will be a world tyranny, patterned
after the godless totalitarianism of Soviet Russia of our day, for whence
the Anti-christ of scripture, the product of atheistic communism, will
arise to head a world government that the peoples and nations of this
earth are preparing for so rapidly today."[93]
     Although Manning felt that developments related to the rise of Rus-
sia as a world superpower were part of a broad historical trend, foretold in the Bible, that would "end ultimately in the world-wide tyranny
under the coming Antichrist, after this Age of Grace has been brought
to its close by the personal appearing of Jesus Christ," his sermons re-

tained the broader evangelical concerns of his mentor.[94] That is, despite focusing so much of his energy attempting to distill world events through the filters of the prophetic scriptures and warning about conspiracies leading to a world-wide tyranny, Manning never lost sight of the larger mission that Christians in general and *Back to the Bible Hour* in particular were meant to serve. Manning observed that "the handwriting is on the wall today for all men to see ... the cumulative consequences of man's rejection of God's offer of mercy is catching up to us. We are mighty close to the final crisis stage," the coming Rapture and the terrible Tribulation for all those left behind.[95] Yet God, by His grace, has provided each individual with the opportunity to escape the foretold suffering:

Before human depravity reaches its climax, and God's certain judgment falls, He has offered mankind the Day of Grace. That is one of the great principles of God's dealing with man. Always before the judgment of God ultimately falls, He allows men and nations a period of time in which to recognize the folly of the course they are taking, and to yield themselves to His will, and to His Grace, and to His Mercy. That period of Grace is the individual's opportunity.[96]

That is, by turning directly to God and experiencing a rebirth through Christ, one could truly become one of His people and thus would be called up to heaven during the Rapture and spared the Tribulation. Indeed, God is "calling men and women individually to yield their hearts and souls and lives to Jesus Christ and a personal acceptance of their Saviour and Lord."[97] "My greatest concern for all our radio listeners," Manning would note, "is that they will not be guilty of the folly of procrastination," that they will not miss the opportunity "to make a personal decision for Jesus Christ." "Our hope and our prayer and our burden of soul for you," therefore is that "we make the appeal of Christ so real that you will be moved to say 'Yes' before it is too late."[98] This was of such importance for Manning that there was rarely a radio address that did not end without his pleading with listeners to recognize the seriousness of the situation, asking each one of them whether or not they had yet to make the personal decision to accept Christ as their personal saviour.

This is but a brief overview of a complex body of religious thought that Manning largely inherited from Aberhart and reinterpreted through the lens of world events in his day, especially pertaining to Russia, and their relation to the prophetic scriptures central to premillennial dispensationalism.[99] The more pressing task at this stage is to consider how this body of religious thought relates to his political thinking, which appears, on the surface, to deviate from that of Aberhart. It is widely agreed that, in essence, Manning's approach to governance while premier was characterized by a stern and unflinching defence of a free-market economy, something not found to the same degree in the rhetoric or policies of Aberhart. Lloyd Mackey has suggested that Manning's distaste for state-led collectivism that interfered with the market was derived from his broader dispensational-based distrust of communist Russia, given his assumption that the foretold Antichrist was to emerge as their leader.[100] In general, there was certainly a connection between Manning's free-market leanings and his dispensationalism, but it was more nuanced than Mackey allows.

Like Aberhart's, Manning's overall understanding of history was deterministic. Conditions in this world would continue to deteriorate until finally the Rapture would occur and thus usher in the final sequence of events leading to the terrible Tribulation and eventually the redeeming Millennial Age. Although the world's fate was already set, Manning was convinced that the fundamental cause of all social problems was humanity's alienation from God. Thus, it was only by way of individual spiritual regeneration that social conditions could get better, something that was theoretically possible in the short term but, given his dispensational outlook, something that would ultimately not occur on a scale large enough to save the world from its predetermined end.[101] This deterministic understanding did not, of course, turn Manning away from his evangelical crusade dedicated to convincing as many individuals as possible to "yield their hearts and souls and lives to Jesus Christ." But he was clear that the state, given its penchant for coercion and its distance from the activities of the church, could never take an active and direct role in this process. Rather, it was the job of evangelists such as himself or more broadly the church to deliver the Word of God to individuals who, in turn, would be responsible for addressing the problems of their community. "If the church is doing its job in building up people spiritually," argued Manning, "it's going to make them concerned for people; it's going to change their attitude toward people; and it's going to make them actively involved, I believe, as individuals."[102] The state, unable to ever fully reconcile humanity with God and thus address the root of all social problems, instead has as its responsibility the protection of the individual. This was essential given that, from Manning and Aberhart's religious perspective, God insisted

138   God's Province

that individuals remain in a state of freedom so as to have the opportunity to freely pursue a spiritual rebirth in Him. Fundamentally, this
required the state to ensure that individuals be as free as possible to
fully develop themselves, a goal that, for Manning as for Aberhart, implied a freedom to enhance their spirituality by pursuing a freely chosen relationship with God. And it is here that we can see the connection
between Manning's dispensational premillennial outlook, his particular distaste for the communist Soviet Union, and his strong preference
for public policy aimed at ensuring human freedom.

Speaking to the gradual spread of communism out of the Soviet
Union, Manning was clear: "It is about time that men and women woke
up to the fact that atheistic communism's infiltration is not merely a
political or economic issue. It is a satanic atheistic philosophy that sub-
tly induces men and nations further and further away from a sovereign
God, who alone is mighty to deliver and save."[103] In other words, given
communism's atheistic foundation, communist nations were bound to
inflame the innate depravity of its individual citizens. Yet encouraging
depravity was not communism's ultimate crime. Rather, the larger
problem was that "human depravity does not stop at rebellion against
God. Human depravity refuses to others the right to give God their allegiance and their worship."[104] For fundamentalist Christians such as
Aberhart and Manning, who understood humanity's God-given purpose in this present age as being the personal decision to turn towards
Christ and be reborn, religious freedom or "the right of individual worship" was the most sacred of all individual rights.[105] Thus, Soviet communism was not problematic simply because it had arisen in the land
of the foretold Antichrist (according to dispensational lore), but because it was an atheistic philosophy that overtly sought to restrict the
individual's right to make that all important personal decision to be
reborn. In fact, the Soviet Union's totalitarian character in this respect
gave dispensationalists such as Manning even more reason to suspect
that the Rapture was fast approaching, given that the foretold Tribulation was to feature a "world tyranny" controlled by the Antichrist.

Because of its overt atheistic and totalitarian nature, Manning identified Soviet communism as the most immediate and dangerous threat
to individual freedom. Yet less extreme versions of left-wing, state-di-
rected ideologies were also problematic given their potential to curb
individual freedom as well. In fact, on multiple occasions in his radio
broadcasts, Manning pointed to the story of Egypt's fiscal problems recounted in the Book of Genesis (Chapters 41–7) as a warning to those

who dared support leftist ideologies at home. According to Manning's interpretation, this particular narrative documented "the process by which the people of an entire nation lost their individual independence and freedom and were reduced to serfs of an all-powerful state bureaucracy."[106] In short, the biblical passage tells of the Egyptian pharaoh's dream that foretold seven years of bounty for the region followed by seven years of famine. The decision was subsequently made to commandeer significant portions of the country's produce in the following seven years as protection against the foretold famine. However, this action was ultimately not enough to prevent the citizens from being removed from their land and turned into serfs when economic conditions continued to spiral downward. For Manning, the moral of the story was the short-sightedness of the citizens:

The people didn't complain too much when the government commandeered one fifth of their entire food production and put it in storage ... It never seemed to occur to them that they could have laid the one fifth of their production in store for themselves and still owned it. Instead they were induced to turn it over to the state by the government's promise of social and economic security. It is a fact worth noting that when promise of social and economic security becomes society's first priority, two things usually happen. First, more and more people look to their government to provide the social and economic security they seek. Second, they become more and more willing to sacrifice individual freedom and independence in exchange for state-guaranteed security and ready to accept more and more regimentation of their individual and collective lives.

So insidious were the steps taken by which they lost their independence and freedom ...

Ladies and Gentlemen, that is not what God desires or intends for men and women. God intends people to be free.[107]

It is precisely here that one finds the vital connection between Manning's religious perspective and his strong aversion not only to the radical communism of the Soviet Union but also to the less extreme but perhaps more insidious left-leaning Prairie socialism of the CCF. Manning was adamant that, just as it was for the citizens of Egypt some 3,700 years ago, the larger the role played by government in the maintenance of the citizen's economic well-being today, the smaller the realm of authentic individual freedom would become. And, given His desire for each of us to freely turn toward Him, the increased regimentation of the individual was simply not God's wish for us. Therefore, the protection of individual freedom from an overreaching state, one derived from this particular religious interpretation, became the foundation from which Manning's political thinking derived in the same way it had for Aberhart's.

How did this outlook play out in a practical manner in Alberta under the premiership of Manning? As mentioned above, Aberhart had interpreted the devastating poverty caused by the Depression as a fundamental impediment to individual freedom and thus spiritual development. Manning entered the premiership facing a far different, far more positive, economic picture. The Depression had ended and Alberta was on the cusp of a general postwar boom, soon to be greatly expanded by the discovery of large pockets of oil and gas in Alberta in 1947. In addition, Manning had lived through the long string of constitutional roadblocks that had prevented Aberhart from implementing any serious social credit reforms in the late 1930s. By the time he was premier, Manning had been largely convinced that such reforms would be impossible under the current legal structure of Canada, but with the end of the Depression and the arrival of an economic boom, the party's implementation failures were essentially irrelevant. Now that the potential for mass poverty had subsided, the threat to individual freedom had become, in the eyes of Manning, the program of socialism promoted by the CCF, which had swept into power in Saskatchewan in 1944 and was gaining supporters in Alberta. The Saskatchewan CCF was led by the popular Baptist minister and social gospeller Tommy Douglas, whose modernist and liberal theological position put him at immediate odds with Manning. For Manning, the socialism of the CCF inevitably failed to protect individual freedom as a result of its association with the social gospel. Like Aberhart before him, Manning complained that people were "being misled into acceptance of a social gospel as being the key to personal salvation rather than supernatural regeneration performed by the Divine person of the Holy Spirit."[108] Therefore, citizens were missing the key point of true Christianity: to develop a personal relationship with Christ. If this personal relationship was devalued, then the individual freedom that it required would be devalued also. It would be this battle against the social gospel–infused socialism and the corresponding rigid defence of free enterprise that defined Manning's politics.

Religion and Political Thought of Aberhart and Manning   141

By the late 1940s and early 1950s, Manning had largely abandoned social credit economic doctrine and was advocating a political philosophy aimed at uniting the humanitarian concerns of socialism with the economic principle of free enterprise. This approach, which he dubbed "social conservatism," guided his entire premiership, although it was not fully articulated in writing until the 1960s, when he and his son Preston penned a treatise entitled *Political Realignment: A Challenge to Thoughtful Canadians* in an effort to alter the approach of mainstream conservative parties in Canada. When still second in command in Aberhart's government in the late 1930s, Manning had made clear that his preference for a state that would protect individual freedom was never meant to represent an extreme libertarian view wherein the state simply allowed the individual to operate freely in all situations. Rather, following Aberhart's adherence to the Christian principle of the brotherhood of man, Manning felt that it was the responsibility of the state to assist individuals in their quest to develop themselves by ensuring the facilitation of certain conditions that individuals could not create on their own. In fact, in defending legislation in 1939 meant to assist with the implementation of social credit economics, Manning defined the state's role as that of assuring "individual members of our society a greater measure of economic and social security and freedom than it would be possible for each individual to acquire for himself if left to his own resources."[109] This would entail the upholding of law and order to ensure the safety of the individual, mechanisms to assist the needy and the sick, and the maintenance of a stable economic system that provided the basic needs for citizens – hence Manning's early support for the state to take control of credit. Thus, it should come as no surprise that within *Political Realignment* Manning lauded the socialists' concern for poverty, disease, and underdevelopment. However, socialism's "insistence on collectivist approaches to the solution of public problems to a degree that seriously infringes upon individual liberties and freedom of action" was problematic.[110] Furthermore, Manning was convinced that the socialist economic doctrine, which favoured state control over the economy, created more long-term economic problems than it solved and thus failed to provide the resources needed to fund its humanitarian projects. However, free-market capitalism, he argued, "presents a highly practical and realistic system for the maximum development of physical resources through the utilization of human initiative and enterprise stimulated by the prospect of rewards," by stressing private resource development, supported appropriately by government.[111] Yet Manning admitted that despite preserving the freedom of the individual, this philosophy had "too often been lacking in positive commitment to social goals of a humanitarian nature."[112] This was a problem for Manning because of his Christian sense of duty to his neighbours. "Yet," Manning continued, "it is [this] economic system ... that has the definite capability to produce the goods and services required ... to adequately finance human resources development and social programs."[113] Thus, Manning stressed social conservatism, an approach that he believed would harness the humanitarian concerns of the socialist to the free enterprise system because it alone was capable of addressing them. However, Manning also made it clear that developing physical resources and addressing humanitarian concerns were means to a larger end: "The supreme objective in developing the physical resources of a nation should be to make possible the development of free and creative individuals."[114] Indeed, Manning consistently understood this to be the ultimate end of the state, a belief that can be traced back directly to his premillennial dispensationalist Christian outlook.

As Finkel has demonstrated, Manning's distaste for socialism, made apparent in *Political Realignment*, permeated his approach to governance over the course of his term as premier of Alberta. Despite significant levels of government spending on infrastructure, health care, and education that often well surpassed that of other provinces, due largely to increasingly high oil royalty revenues, Manning's government remained adamantly opposed to any collectivist meddling in the economy aimed at wealth redistribution. Perhaps most importantly for the long-term trajectory of Alberta's relationship with the petrochemical extraction sector, Manning's aversion to state-enforced collectivism strongly shaped the manner by which Social Credit responded to the development of the industry. Although the administrative intricacies of Alberta's complex regulatory regime are well beyond the scope of this section, scholars have left little doubt as to Manning's enthusiastic support, over his long reign in office, for privately funded projects rather than state ownership via crown corporations and the maintenance of a relatively business-friendly royalty-rate regime capable of attracting American capital.[115] No doubt this has set Alberta on a particular path from which it has been hesitant to deviate.[116] Although such policies tend to garner the most attention with respect to Manning's politics, his aversion to state-led collectivism bled through to many other areas as well. In the mid- and late 1940s, the Social Credit government widened the scope of a film censorship program and took stern anti-union measures in an effort to prevent "communist propaganda" from infiltrating the minds of the populace. Furthermore, Manning would continually stress self-reliance rather than government handouts to citizens in need, and this led to his support for the growth of voluntary welfare agencies. He also experimented with paying oil royalties directly to individuals rather than municipalities (a program that foreshadowed a similar ploy by Alberta premier Ralph Klein decades later), opposed federally sponsored regional economic development programs, protested against the public ownership of media outlets, most especially the CBC, and even opposed the sale of Canadian wheat to communist countries despite the clear benefit such sales offered to Alberta's farmers.[117]

Perhaps nowhere was this line of anti-statist thought more apparent, however, than in Manning's intense opposition to the proposed universal national medicare program that was being debated across Canada in the late 1950s and early 1960s. While Manning favoured the objective of the plan – that quality medical care be available to every citizen of the country regardless of income level – the notion of a "universal" program concerned him greatly:

> What is meant by the term "universal" is that the plan arbitrarily includes everybody whether they need the benefits and whether they wish to be included or not. It is a compulsory program in which participation is compelled by the state and not left to the voluntary choice of the citizen himself.
>
> This feature of the plan violates a fundamental principle of free society, namely the right of each citizen to exercise freedom of choice in matters relating to his own and his family's welfare. Welfare state advocates will scream that this is not so but no man can truthfully say he has freedom of choice if he is forced to participate in a compulsory state scheme for his medical services, whether he wishes or not.

For Manning, the logical outcome of adopting such a plan could not be clearer: "Canada is dangerously close to setting her feet on a path that can lead to but one ultimate end. That end will be a nation turned into a regimented socialistic welfare state." Thus, Manning championed an alternate system built around deterrent fees and a means-based system that ensured that low-income citizens would receive government assistance for their private insurance premiums:

God's Province

What I am advocating as a superior alternative to the federal proposal is a voluntary state-subsidized medical insurance program based on two sound fundamental principles.

1) That the individual has a responsibility to provide for his medical needs just as he has a responsibility to provide for his own needs in other areas affecting his welfare.
2) That society as a whole has a responsibility to ensure that such services are available at a cost to the individual within his ability to pay.

The alternative plan I have proposed does not require any element of compulsion and therefore does not do violence to the basic principles of a free society.[118]

Clearly, Manning's opposition to the universal medicare plan was, like his broader contempt for collectivism, rooted in his fundamental concern for individual freedom. One of the more interesting, although wholly underappreciated, aspects of the Canada-wide debate over this issue was that Manning's main rival in this struggle was none other than his CCF nemesis from Saskatchewan, the social gospeller Tommy Douglas. Approaching the issue from a fundamentally distinct religious foundation, Douglas anchored his defence of a universal program in a more collectivist Christian approach than Manning would allow. Indeed, from Manning's perspective, the social gospel roots of Douglas's plan were, at bottom, the precise reason why it was problematic. For Manning, the collectivist social gospel downplayed the importance of developing a personal relationship with Christ and therefore downplayed concerns with respect to the loss of individual freedom that this personal relationship required. Nevertheless, the universal plan was eventually accepted in Canada and the rest is history. Yet it is worth noting that one of the more striking aspects both of Manning's attack on a compulsory medical care program and of his broader treatise on social conservatism was that, despite his obvious religious background, neither contained any reference to religion save a brief mention of the need for religious liberty. In this way, both were modelled after Aberhart's *Social Credit Manual*, which also provided a purely secular description of, and justification for, social credit economics in 1935.[119] Yet, when one is provided with the appropriate contextual background, it is not difficult to see the connection between the broader political goals Aberhart and Manning shared – namely a fundamental defence of the individual and his or her inalienable right to be free – and their

Religion and Political Thought of Aberhart and Manning   145

particular Christian theological outlook. From this perspective, it is
clear that Manning's shift from social credit economics to free enterprise capitalism and a rejection of state-enforced collectivism originated in the religious interpretation initially espoused by Aberhart. Recall
Manning's emphatic argument that the prime function of Christians
within this world was not to solve social problems, but to "bring people into a personal relationship with Christ."[120] This task required a
combination of evangelicalism, which Manning provided in the form
of a radio ministry, and the construction of a political environment that
protected the individual's freedom, which Manning found in social
conservatism. Even the strong emphasis on human well-being that was
present in Aberhart's promotion of social credit reappeared in Manning's political views. This only makes sense given their shared belief in
the Christian notion of "love thy neighbour," a sentiment that would be
inescapably embraced by the spiritually regenerated individual. In other
words, while the endorsement of specific types of political and economic policy shifted from Aberhart to Manning, the end goal never
wavered. Indeed, Manning's defence of the free market was essentially
the logical unfolding of the individualism inherent in the religious
views they shared, although Aberhart's encounter with the Depression
delayed this "unfolding" for a time. Thus, commentators have produced
an inaccurate picture of Aberhart and Manning in depicting them as
significantly different political animals by applying "left-wing" and
"right-wing" tags on them. This misses the fact that, for both men, political policies were simply a means to a far greater end – eternal salvation for as many individuals as possible prior to the Rapture – and thus
could and should be changed if the social conditions affecting the individual's freedom required it.

Despite the fact that Manning's thinking about the state, the role of
the market, and the importance of the individual was clearly derived
from his Christian theology, it has been broadly assumed, especially
among Alberta journalists, that the influence of religion upon Manning's political thought was most apparent with respect to his positions
on specific social issues, such as laws around liquor consumption or
regulations on businesses on the Sabbath. In other words, critics pegged
Manning as an early social conservative who used biblical arguments to
decide specific "moral" policy issues. Yet, as former Social Credit cabinet minister Ray Speaker argues, "there was no direct religious influence in cabinet decisions with Ernest Manning. The only question we
asked ourselves when a decision had to be made was 'where is society
at on this?' If it was clear they wanted something, that is what they

146   God's Province

got."[121] This description seems to hold true when one recalls Manning's commitment to holding a province-wide plebiscite and allowing the citizens to decide on the controversial demand to loosen regulatory restrictions on liquor in 1957. Of course, to suggest that religious motivation was never discussed within the confines of cabinet is not to say that Manning would not have developed strong policy preferences on certain social issues that were influenced by his faith. In fact, Manning believed that a certain collective responsibility for morality fell to the government. Thinking back to his time as premier, Manning recalled: "I don't depreciate one bit the prime responsibility of the individual; he has to assume responsibility for his own morality standards. But I think the state has a legitimate and inescapable responsibility in the field of morality."[122] However, as Speaker has noted and author John Barr has argued elsewhere, Manning did not seek to impose his particular religious-based values on others through specific social policies, at least consciously.[123] Instead, he approached his responsibility as premier for society's collective morality in a more nuanced manner, one that, unsurprisingly, also derived from his Christian beliefs.

When his government faced a situation that demanded a "collective moral response," Manning drew inspiration from a particular passage in the Old Testament. This was the story of the ancient nation of Israel's request for a king despite the earlier commandment by God that it was to be different from all other nations and follow the leadership of God rather than a human king, recounted in 1 Samuel. Samuel, the spiritual leader of Israel at the time, remembered God's initial commandment and thus asked God to intercede on his behalf to ensure that the people did not turn their back on the earlier demand of God. However, Manning notes, God would not comply with Samuel's request. Instead,

[he] went on to say [to Samuel], "Do what they say, but before you do it, tell them (and he stressed this repeatedly) what the consequences will be." I think the expression is "vehemently protest unto them" what will be the consequences of choosing this materialistic society of the nations round about them, versus their society which had the powerful spiritual background of their close personal relationship with Deity. It always seemed to me there's a great lesson there for governments and leaders in a democracy. You can't refuse … the ultimate will of the people. But you do have a responsibility to say, "Look, before we do this, stop and realize this is going to be the ultimate consequence."[124]

Religion and Political Thought of Aberhart and Manning   147

It was for this reason that Manning was willing to make his case on certain issues, liquor laws for example, but in the end was willing to, in the words of Speaker, ask, "Where is society at on this?" Despite his belief that God would most likely prefer humanity to pursue certain policies as opposed to others, Manning felt that it would be against God's larger edict for governments to impose them on the people. Indeed, there is something incredibly democratic in the ultimate demand that individuals should remain free in the hope that they would eventually turn to God on their own free will. Thus, Manning's democratic commitment to follow the will of the people coincided with his and Aberhart's more fundamental concern with the role of the state. Its purpose was not the creation of a Christian society governed by biblical laws. In fact, throughout their premierships, both Aberhart and Manning routinely dismissed calls from Christian citizens to enforce Christian lessons in the school curriculum.[125] The purpose of the state, rather, was to protect the freedom of the individual, who had been created and granted free will by God and must therefore be allowed the room to develop to his or her fullest potential. By ensuring that this freedom was protected and working to spread God's Word outside the state apparatus (such as through their radio ministry), Aberhart and Manning would provide the two conditions necessary for individuals to pursue spiritual regeneration on their own prior to the Rapture foretold within premillennial dispensational theology. Thus, both Manning's preference for the free market and his respect for the people's political will would derive squarely from his religious beliefs.

CONCLUSION:
THE POLITICAL THOUGHT OF ABERHART AND MANNING
AND THE TRAJECTORY OF ALBERTA POLITICS

Like Henry Wise Wood, Aberhart and Manning considered keeping religion out of the political realm an impossible notion. As Manning noted, genuine Christianity provides one with an outlook on life that cannot be divorced from anything: "It isn't a matter of 'should [politics and religion] be mixed.' You can't separate them."[126] In fact, as the above sections have demonstrated, the political thought of both of these men was founded directly upon their particular Christian interpretation. Of course, Wood drew from the more progressive postmillennial religious outlook, and this produced a much more optimistic account of the possibilities contained within political action than that of Aberhart or Manning, who were stern premillennialists. Because they interpreted the coming Millennium to reside completely outside the realm of human agency, their understanding of the aims of "post-conversion" Christians on earth was far different from that of Wood, who had suggested that mankind was to usher in the Millennium by way of good works that followed the teachings of Christ. Instead, Aberhart and Manning argued that action in this world must be part of the larger goal of facilitating the spiritual conversion of as many individuals as possible prior to the Rapture. Obviously, this difference committed the UFA and Social Credit to favour different political policies with distinct political goals. Essentially, this was a difference between "saving the world" and "saving souls."

More generally, because the religious outlook of Wood, on the one hand, and Aberhart and Manning, on the other, drew from the same broad tradition of American evangelical Protestantism, certain similarities were bound to appear. Of course, neither Aberhart nor Manning was American (as was Wood), nor had they spent any significant chunk of time in the United States. In fact, Aberhart was introduced to premillennial dispensationalism in southern Ontario, the very bosom of Canadian Protestantism. Yet, as I argue extensively in Chapter 2, premillennial dispensationalism, although it originated in Great Britain and found sympathetic ears in Canada, encountered incredibly fertile soil in America and grew to become an essential component of the Protestant fundamentalism of America to a degree far more intense than was found in Britain or Canada. Indeed, the individuals most responsible for fanning the flames of premillennial dispensationalism after its arrival on the North American continent were American preachers W.L. Moody and C.I. Scofield, the very figures Aberhart openly credited with his particular religious development. In addition, Aberhart developed friendships with several prominent American dispensationalist preachers, chief among them Norman Camp of Chicago's Moody Bible Institute, after which Aberhart would model his Calgary Prophetic Bible Institute.[127] In the early years of his institute and radio program, Aberhart even used course lessons drawn from American sources before getting around to creating his own.[128] It is true that premillennial dispensationalism enjoyed a period of popularity in Ontario in the late nineteenth and early twentieth centuries, but its arrival was greeted coldly by the mainstream churches. Today it only survives in small pockets throughout Protestant Canada, although it remains central to the faith of millions upon millions of Americans. It is in this sense that I claim that Aberhart and subsequently Manning were influenced by a particular stream of American evangelical Protestantism, a claim that is further substantiated by the fact that the same unique tensions between conservative and radical tendencies present within America's broader evangelical tradition (and in the religiously inspired thought of Wood) would reappear in the thought of Aberhart and Manning. In other words, the populist conservative sentiment inherent in the political thought of Wood was reaffirmed in the thought of Aberhart and then Manning.

At a basic level, Wood's, Aberhart's, and Manning's theology was founded upon the evangelical Protestant assumption that human nature was inherently evil and it was only through spiritual regeneration, or rebirth, in Christ that individuals could cleanse their soul of selfishness and sin. This obviously placed a significant responsibility on the individual citizen and generated a particularly conservative emphasis on individual behaviour in both the private and public realms. This conservative element is not difficult to see in Alberta Social Credit. The intense devotion to biblical literalism that characterized the Christian fundamentalism of Aberhart and Manning encouraged a strong conservatism based upon the moral laws of God. Although they agreed with Wood's insistence that the individual citizen must be a disciplined and hard worker, Aberhart and Manning went beyond Wood in this regard, continually lamenting the declining morality of society, expressing their distaste for alcohol, cards, dancing, and commercial or sporting events on Sundays, and even attacking journalists for daring to question an organization as divinely inspired as Social Credit. However, the emphasis they placed on the common individual's intellectual and spiritual capacity for rebirth, and especially the conditions such conversion required, committed Aberhart and Manning to an equally intense devotion to individual liberty not typical of Tory conservatism. Thus, a certain radical anti-establishmentarianism and a corresponding commitment to grassroots democracy grew out of their opposition to any institution that impinged on the freedom that the individual required to pursue spiritual rebirth.

For Aberhart, this meant attacking the "Fifty Big Shots" whom he understood to be withholding credit and thus causing "Poverty in the Midst of Plenty." For Manning, who would preside over far more prosperous economic conditions in Alberta, this meant supporting the free market in the face of an emerging socialism that threatened to subdue the individual to the collective. Of course, Manning's shift away from social credit economics and towards an uninhibited capitalism has garnered suggestions that he and Aberhart were, ideologically, distinct political animals. However, from the perspective of their shared religious foundation that exalted common individuals and their liberty, we see that their divergent economic policies were simply circumstantial means towards the same end. Nevertheless, Aberhart and Manning followed the general path groomed by the political thought of Wood and maintained both the conservative religious-based demand for individual moral responsibility and the populist egalitarian and anti-establishmentarian orientation that blossomed in post-revolution evangelical America, an orientation largely foreign to the more Tory strains of conservatism in the rest of the country.

Despite this similar commitment to a populist conservative sentiment, however, the defeat of Wood's postmillennial religious interpretation by Aberhart's premillennial version did have a significant impact on the precise direction of Alberta politics from 1935 onward. On the whole, Aberhart and Manning shared Wood's antipathy towards the socialistic economic arrangements advocated by Prairie social gospellers in the first half of the twentieth century. As discussed in Chapter 3, Wood understood commerce to be a "natural" institution, and the notion of centralizing more economic control in government went against Wood's evangelical populist impulses, which stressed the problem-solving capacity of ordinary people. More fundamentally, he felt that the economic oppression of the farmer was due, not to the structure of the system itself, but to the depravity of unreformed individuals operating within the market system. And thus only large-scale individual spiritual regeneration, not the abolishment of capitalism, could lead to a society wherein trade became a more just enterprise, conducted on the basis of Christ's moral laws. This was the view that ultimately underlined Wood's opposition to the radicals within the UFA who went on to support the CCF after his retirement.

No doubt Aberhart and Manning would have agreed that economic oppression was rooted in the depravity of man and that society's only hope to fully rectify the situation was wide-scale religious conversion, or rebirth, at an individual level. However, because of their premillennial Christian interpretation that held that God rather than humanity would usher in a millennial period of perfect justice on earth, the notion that men could succeed in converting the whole world and thus build their own perfected social system was perceived as fantasy. Thus, despite the fact that Aberhart and Manning referred to the virtue of co-operation on a number of occasions, the building of a perfect co-operative economic or political system demanded by Wood was never a goal they shared. In fact, from their premillennial perspective, even at-

Religion and Political Thought of Aberhart and Manning

tempting to construct such a system was considered beyond the proper aim of the state, that of simply ensuring that the freedom of the individual was protected. It is true that Aberhart generated a scathing critique of aspects of the political and economic system, especially pertaining to the power possessed by the large economic and financial interests that were in a position to exploit the farmers and business people of Alberta. Yet, he never offered more than a general demand to "reform" such institutions, and even that amounted to a state-sponsored credit provision proposal designed to enhance the agency of individuals by increasing their purchasing power and thereby ending the poverty that was impeding their freedom. When the oil boom changed the economic dynamics of the province under Manning, all notions of significant reform were abandoned. By allowing the market to operate in a largely unregulated manner, the government was now in a position to ensure that a condition of individual freedom and opportunity prevailed. Thus, although Wood's initial antipathy towards socialism helped set Alberta on a particular ideological path, it was the intense devotion to individual freedom stressed by Aberhart and Manning that led to the vilification of any form of economic collectivism that might jeopardize the freedom of the individual. It is here that one finds some significant roots of contemporary Alberta's strongly pro-market, anti-redistribution sentiment.

Speaking to this sentiment, Finkel begins his authoritative history of Alberta Social Credit with a notion largely shared by scholars of Alberta history and politics: "The Social Credit League dominated political life from 1935 to 1971 and shaped a political culture that is unique in Canada." He elaborates by pointing to a shift in Alberta's political culture, suggesting that while open to "radical ideas of all sorts" in the 1930s, the province would eventually be dominated by "a visceral anti-socialism." Tying this shift to Manning's social conservative outlook, Finkel concludes that "this philosophy gradually became that of the party as well and ... deeply influenced political thinking among Albertans as a whole."[129] I agree with Finkel's conclusion and want to expand upon it within the context of this larger study. If, as I argued in Chapter 1, one is prepared to allow that strong leaders possess a certain agency with respect to guiding political communities in one direction or another (even when broader contextual facts are accounted for), it seems clear that Manning in particular was quite influential when considering the trajectory of Alberta politics. Not only was he premier for some twenty-five years (and the most powerful cabinet minister for eight years prior), he approached his governance responsibilities from a clear anti-statist direction, which meant that several of his government's policies were built atop this foundation. Perhaps none were as important for the long-term trajectory of Alberta politics as those related to oil and gas extraction. Although various governments since 1971 have introduced slight changes, the basic foundation of the largely anti-statist model initiated by Manning in the late 1940s remains essentially intact and largely governs the province's approach towards its most important asset. Not only have contemporary Alberta governments shied away from large-scale government investment in the sector (let alone the kind of crown corporations found in neighbouring Saskatchewan), low royalty rates and, most recently, a reluctance to regulate the industry significantly in response to environmental concerns undergird the province's approach to the sector.[130] That is not to say that every provincial government since Manning has been a carbon copy in this regard. As will be discussed in more detail in Chapter 5, the Lougheed administration stands out as one that was far more open than others to state-led economic development with respect to this sector, although it is also true that such efforts were still a considerable distance from the degree of collectivism demanded by those on the left at the time. Similarly, recent Alberta governments have tended to shy away from such direct involvement, especially since the neo-liberal–inspired administration of Ralph Klein.

More broadly, recent governments have maintained low personal and corporate tax levels, resisted overt state meddling in the economy, taken strong stands against labour unions, implemented social programs that emphasize self-reliance, and even experimented with private health-care options that potentially violate the "universal access" model Manning argued so sternly against in the 1950s.[131] Of course, Alberta governments have rarely shied away from government spending. In fact, Alberta's per capita spending levels on health, education, and infrastructure have, from the time of Manning until today, consistently ranked well above Canadian provincial averages.[132] Yet such spending tends not to disrupt the broader commitment to resist collectivist meddling in the economy. This is especially true when one considers the continuity found with respect to the dominant forms of political discourse utilized by successful parties. Wesley in particular has noted that, since the Depression, Alberta's most successful leaders have consistently "preached individualism, stressing the importance of personal responsibility, free enterprise, private-sector development, entrepreneurship, a strong work ethic, the evils of socialism, and the protection of individual rights and liberties" in defending these types of policies.[133]

Religion and Political Thought of Aberhart and Manning   153

As this chapter has made clear, despite refusing to include religious reasoning within their political campaign literature, Aberhart's and Manning's motivation with respect to this type of rhetoric was derived directly from their premillennial dispensationalist Christianity and the subsequent concerns for individual freedom that emerged from it. Indeed, as Manning told his followers, "God intends people to be free."[134] However, this type of political discourse, founded upon a blatantly religious conception of the role of the state vis-à-vis the individual, did not dissipate in Alberta with the sudden decline of Social Credit in the early 1970s. In fact, as Wesley demonstrates, the less overtly religious Progressive Conservatives "rose to prominence in Alberta by speaking in the code that the Socreds had cultivated for nearly two generations."[135] Central to such a code was the ongoing rhetorical commitment, which would be present in all PC administrations from Peter Lougheed to Ralph Klein and beyond, to protect individual rights, encourage individual self-reliance, and avidly support free enterprise over state-led collectivist approaches to economic development. Surely not all of the policies enacted by PC governments have perfectly coalesced with such a commitment, a reality captured nicely by Roger Gibbons's quip that the overall approach of Lougheed's administration demonstrated "a strong belief in the spirit if not necessarily the practice of free enterprise."[136] Yet the perpetual reliance on such rhetoric by the dominant political party in Alberta says something important about Alberta's political culture and its relationship to a form of political discourse that was essentially introduced into the province by Aberhart and, more importantly, constantly emphasized and repeated by Manning during his twenty-five-year reign as premier. Indeed, it seems clear that in this respect Manning, working from a clear religious foundation, strongly influenced the political trajectory of the province. That is not to say that broader contextual factors were unimportant. Certainly Alberta's initial socio-economic conditions, including its initial class composition, its quasi-colonial status, its unique inheritance of American agrarian settlers, and its precise religious makeup, as well as more contemporary factors related to its reliance on specific resource staples and the subsequent political power possessed by corporations involved in these industries, on the one hand, and the economic prosperity this resource base has created, on the other, have all conspired to push Alberta politics in this anti-collectivist direction. Yet, just as it was for Henry Wise Wood in the 1920s and 1930s, contextual factors can help explain why figures such as Aberhart and Manning were successful politically, but such factors cannot wholly account for their success or wholly explain

154   God's Province

the precise direction in which each man guided the province via political discourse and public policy. In fact, it is not entirely clear that, given
the broad popularity of Aberhart's more interventionist policies in the
midst of the Depression, the Alberta citizenry would not have embraced
a similarly charismatic and interventionist leader in the 1940s, 1950s, or
beyond had Manning not essentially been anointed premier and gained
the people's trust by way of his leadership capabilities thereafter. To pursue this question more thoroughly is beyond the scope of this study,
but the broader point remains: working from a distinctly religious position that guided their thinking about politics, Aberhart and especially Manning did much to guide Alberta on an anti-collectivist trajectory
that is largely unique among Canadian provinces.

   Beyond the generation of this particular anti-collectivist, pro-free-
market sentiment in Alberta, the difference between Wood's postmillennial approach and the premillennialism of Aberhart and
Manning helped to ensure an equally important distinction between
the approach to politics stressed by the UFA and Social Credit. As C.B.
Macpherson and later David Laycock have noted, although both parties were clearly committed to the principle of populist democracy,
Social Credit essentially abandoned the grassroots deliberation insisted upon by the UFA in favour of a top-heavy "plebiscitarian" populism built around the authoritarian personality of Aberhart and his
faith in the complex workings of social credit economic theory.[137]
Local groups (Social Credit "study groups") throughout the province
still formed the foundation of the movement, and thousands of supporters continued to spread the message of social credit economics
to the unconverted, but as Laycock argues, that participation was restricted to mass education and organizational tasks and did not extend to more meaningful avenues wherein participants could
"critically assess their problems, or develop their own solutions within a general ideological framework."[138]

   In fact, Aberhart, who followed Major Douglas in this regard, had insisted that the role of the people within a functioning democracy was
to "demand results," and the role of the democratic leader was to respond to this general demand by enlisting the services of the necessary
experts to "deliver the results." As Aberhart notoriously argued,

   You don't have to know all about Social Credit before you vote for
   it; you don't have to understand electricity to use it, for you know
   that experts have put the system in, and all you have to do is push
   the button and you get light. So all you have to do about Social

Credit is to cast your vote for it, and we will get experts to put the system in.[139]

Manning, ten years after his retirement from politics and over thirty years after Aberhart made the above claim, similarly defined democracy as "people expressing a general will for general results and leaving experts to work out the details." This approach, Manning continued, "is probably a little more realistic even than participatory democracy. In participatory democracy we have tended, I think, to ask people to make decisions which they are not in a position to make for the simple reason that they haven't the technical knowledge or background, or information, to make that decision." Douglas's social credit theory, however, avoided the problem posed by an ignorant citizenry because it did not require that the "rank-and-file" needed to "know how." Rather, "what they need to worry about is the results they want. The government's job is to respect that expression of public will, and to assume the responsibility of obtaining the technical experts ... to develop programs which will give the results the people want."[140]

Similarly, Aberhart relegated "the people's" representatives within the legislature to the sidelines. Social Credit MLAs were tasked with facilitating delivery of the results demanded by the people by simply allowing the non-elected social credit "experts" to install social credit legislation while the MLAs focused their energies on maintaining support for the party within their local constituencies. Indeed, Macpherson long ago documented the many ways in which Aberhart refused to partake in legislative debates and circumvented Social Credit MLAs – and even his own cabinet – in his effort to implement social credit reforms in conjunction with those of the social credit experts.[141] Of course, Aberhart did strive to maintain an ongoing connection with "the people," but this was done not through the legislature, in which he rarely spoke, or through the mainstream press, which he despised, but rather through his incredibly popular weekly religious-based radio program, which permitted him to take his message directly to the people while simultaneously allowing them to feel part of the process when he responded to their letters and comments on air. The result was a technocratic and non-participatory form of plebiscitarian populism that attempted to meet the demands of the people, articulated as a "general will" captured by the general election, but was devoid of both the level of citizen involvement stressed by the UFA as well as the more traditional methods of interest articulation that were meant to be used within the legislatures of representative democracies.

156   God's Province

The implications of this plebiscitarian model of democracy, according to Laycock, was an adherence to a "model of benevolent technocracy" that insisted the deliberative political life stressed by Wood and the UFA was largely unnecessary. "Why would people need or want to concern themselves with other people's business," asks Laycock, "when it is apparent that all are well attended to in the scientifically arranged land of abundance?"[142] Indeed, the certainty with which Aberhart explained the "purely scientific" nature of social credit economics that would undoubtedly end the Depression made the type of grassroots deliberation that took root in the UFA locals seem inefficient. However, this clear lack of concern for the input of the common citizen was not only a product of Aberhart's confidence in Douglas's technocratic theories or of his own authoritarian leadership style. In addition to these variables, Aberhart's premillennial interpretation of Christianity was an important factor in this approach to democracy.

The broader religious goal of Aberhart's involvement in politics was, again, the facilitation of spiritual rebirth for those individuals not yet saved. For Wood, whose goal was the perfection of society, the notion of intense grassroots co-operation was an absolute requirement for the successful implementation of the "co-operative spirit" in society at large. Surely Wood's American populist agrarian background encouraged in him a certain sympathy towards populist, ground-level co-operation, but beyond this, his religious-political goal of societal perfection called for the type of deliberative participation that occurred in the UFA locals. Aberhart's religious perspective, on the other hand, ensured that he had no interest in perfecting society or the grassroots deliberation this apparently required. He did support the notion of the "spirit of Christ" filling as many as possible, but this would not require deliberation, only a personal commitment to God and the scriptures. Similarly, citizens were expected to support Social Credit, but extensive debate or co-operation beyond this support was unnecessary and, in fact, might even impede the individual's spiritual self-development by placing restrictions on his or her time and energy, which was to be spent investing in his or her personal relationship with Christ. In other words, scholars have been correct to point out the apolitical mentality and corresponding lack of concern that Social Credit displayed for local deliberation when compared to the UFA, but they have failed to see the manner by which this difference is partly derived from the larger premillennial religious vision of Aberhart when compared to the postmillennial vision of Wood.

This is a vitally important point if one hopes to understand more fully contemporary Alberta's paradoxical populist, yet apolitical, culture given Laycock's argument that this dimension of Social Credit discourse "was central to the process within Alberta that eviscerated popular democracy and undermined opportunities for its future rebirth."[143] Yet the development of this apolitical or plebiscitarian populist political culture, like the province's strong rhetorical commitment to an unregulated market economy, is a product of the broader emphasis on individual freedom stressed by Aberhart and Manning, an emphasis that was largely absent from the postmillennial thought of Wood. Indeed, since 1935, Alberta politics have been defined by an emphasis on individual freedom that both encourages a pro-market/anti-redistribution sentiment and questions the need for traditional deliberative politics. Folk wisdom seems content to associate this emphasis on individual freedom with Alberta's "rugged frontier" or "cowboy" heritage. However, as this chapter has demonstrated, this emphasis on individual freedom has very strong roots in the fundamentalist premillennial Christian religious interpretation of Aberhart and Manning and their long and influential reign over Alberta's politics.

5

Religion, Political Thought, and Public Policy in Contemporary Alberta

Social Conservatism vs the Anti-Statist Religious Perspective of Preston Manning

In 1971, only three years after Ernest Manning retired from the premiership of Alberta, Social Credit's thirty-six-year rule came to an end at the hands of Peter Lougheed and the Alberta Progressive Conservative (PC) party. The province was growing increasingly urban, secular, and dependent on the oil and gas sector, and the accession of the young, Harvard-trained Lougheed seemed an appropriate antithesis to Social Credit and their general agrarian and conservative Christian-based platform. For many, especially the growing contingent of non-religious in the province, who were more inclined to bracket religious considerations from political debates, the rise of Lougheed and the PCs represented the final nail in the coffin for Christian-based public policy in Alberta. Yet Manning's retirement in 1968 and the PCs' victory in 1971 did not come to represent the end of religious influence in Alberta's politics as many had predicted. In fact, despite the province growing more secular as a whole and Lougheed or his successors never displaying any overt dedication to religious concerns, religious-based political thought in Alberta would enjoy a resurgence of sorts in the late 1980s and early 1990s. As a plethora of political commentators have noted, a clear strain of religious-based social conservatism emerged in both the federal Reform Party of Canada, largely based in Alberta, and the contemporary provincial PC party under premiers Ralph Klein and Ed Stelmach, culminating in what essentially amounted to a fifteen-year battle waged by the governing provincial PC party against the extension of a variety of rights for homosexuals. However, the focus by political observers on this strain of social conservatism in contemporary Alberta politics has caused many to overlook a more important, although some-

Religion and Political Thought in Contemporary Alberta   159

what subtler, instance of religious influence in the political thought of Preston Manning, founder of the federal Reform Party, Alberta MP from 1993 to 2002, and son of long-time Social Credit premier Ernest Manning. In fact, this chapter will argue that, despite Manning being a federal rather than a provincial politician, it was his religiously motivated political thought, not the socially conservative strain, that has most influenced contemporary Alberta politics.

This chapter is somewhat distinct from the previous two in that it offers a broader consideration of the role played by religion in the province's contemporary politics by examining the influence of these two distinct strains of thought. The first half of this chapter provides a detailed exploration of the nature of the strain of religious-based social conservative political thought found in contemporary Alberta and its particular influence on the province's politics in the 1990s and early 2000s. This exploration begins with an investigation into the religiously motivated thought of Ted Byfield, probably the most influential purveyor of social conservative sentiment in Alberta in the 1980s and 1990s, before turning to a consideration of the social conservatism within the Alberta PCs, who have dominated Alberta politics since 1971. Although religious-based social conservatism was popular in certain circles of Alberta and undeniably influential with respect to the PC stance on homosexual rights in the 1990s and early 2000s, this section notes that neither Alberta in general nor the PC party in particular was, in fact, dominated by conservative Christians. Rather, socially conservative arguments were influential largely because of a set of unique political circumstances, and as those circumstances changed, the influence of social conservatism within the province's politics declined.

That is not to say that religious-based arguments have not influenced politics in contemporary Alberta. Indeed, after discussing social conservatism, this chapter turns to the religiously inspired and highly influential political thought of Preston Manning. Despite being a federal politician, Manning had a strong influence on the direction of Alberta politics in the early 1990s, As leader of the federal Reform party, he demanded a fairer deal for western Canada within Confederation, the reform of Canadian political institutions to ensure that the "common sense of the common people" was given more weight, and, above all, a hasty end to high taxes and out-of-control spending at the federal level. Yet, it was partly in response to this call for increased fiscal responsibility on the part of the federal government that the Alberta PCs changed course and embraced a program of sharp reductions in government expenditures under the premiership of Ralph Klein in the

160   God's Province

early 1990s. Although scholars have previously noted Manning's influence in this regard, they have largely failed to grasp the religious interpretation upon which his influential political thought was built.
Manning's demand for a smaller, fiscally conservative, and democratic
state that was more responsive to the wishes of "the common people"
was built upon a premillennial Christian perspective that he largely
shared with his father, Ernest Manning, and Social Credit founder
William Aberhart. In other words, his strong pro-market leanings were
not derived from the wave of "new right" economic and political
thought that was emanating out of the Thatcher and Reagan administrations of Britain and the United States. Instead, they were rooted in a
decidedly anti-collectivist sentiment that originated with the belief that
the divine purpose of the state was to ensure the freedom of the individual citizen. To overlook this connection is not only to miss a vitally
important point of continuity between Ernest and Preston Manning,
but also to miss the continuing presence of a particular individualistic
religious interpretation within the elite political circles of Alberta that
continued to influence the province's trajectory well after Ernest Manning had retired. And this particular religious interpretation can be
traced back through the thought of Ernest Manning, William Aberhart, and Henry Wise Wood and into the broader American evangelical Protestant tradition articulated earlier. The second half of this
chapter systematically explores the connection between Preston Manning's religion and his politics, focusing on his Christian-based approach to politics, his religiously infused understanding of the state and
its relationship to the market, and his biblically inspired conception of
democracy. The chapter concludes with a discussion on the broader political implications of the religious-based political thought of Manning
in the province and the manner by which his thought represents an
important bridge between historical and contemporary Alberta and its
dominant parties' continued adherence to both an anti-statist and fiscally conservative trajectory and a populist yet non-deliberative or apolitical democratic sentiment.

UNDERSTANDING RELIGIOUS-BASED SOCIAL CONSERVATISM
        IN CONTEMPORARY ALBERTA POLITICS

Social conservative sentiment has traditionally been strong in pockets
of Alberta, especially rural pockets outside Edmonton and Calgary, but
its popularity broadened to a degree in the late 1980s and early 1990s
largely in response to the Charter of Rights and Freedoms and the

Religion and Political Thought in Contemporary Alberta   161

doors it opened for those groups who had previously been denied certain rights because the larger, Christian-based public perceived their behaviour to be immoral. Easily the most elegant and widely read spokesperson on behalf of this particular strand of faith-based thought in the wake of the Charter was Edmonton-based magazine publisher and early Reform Party advocate Ted Byfield. Born in Toronto, Byfield began his journalism career in Washington DC before moving to Ottawa, then Winnipeg, before finally settling in Edmonton in 1968. It was here, in 1973, that Byfield began the *St John's Edmonton Report*, which in 1980 joined with the *St John's Calgary Report* to form the legendary *Alberta Report* newsmagazine. *Alberta Report* enjoyed immediate success on the back of its strident opposition to Trudeau's National Energy Program (NEP), which forced Alberta to sell oil to the rest of Canada at rates much below market. By the mid-1980s, the magazine's strong pro-Albertan political perspective propelled its circulation to over 50,000, with an estimated readership eclipsing 250,000.[1] Ted Morton, the Alberta-based academic, politician, and early supporter of a new Alberta-based conservative party, recalled that "Alberta Report was our Internet, it was our website, Facebook and Twitter ... in those early years [of conservative activism], almost all roads passed through Alberta Report."[2] Yet, although Byfield was one of the earliest advocates of a "western interests party" and a key early Reform Party activist, his influence on Alberta politics extended well beyond his initial involvement in the political movement. The popularity of *Alberta Report*, due primarily to its anti-Ottawa political stance, allowed Byfield and eventually his son, Link Byfield, to spread widely an articulate and often passionate defence of conservative Christian values in a language that spoke to the average citizen. In an odd parallel to the influence of William Aberhart's *Back to the Bible Hour* radio program in the 1920s and 1930s, Byfield's message in *Alberta Report* helped to focus a way of thinking for thousands of politically interested and religiously inclined Albertans whose political frustrations had been, before Byfield, largely undefined and unable to coalesce in a useful direction.[3]

The essence of Byfield's social thought – the message that most easily resonated with readers – was the notion that the vast majority of the ills of contemporary society, including crime, domestic abuse, family breakup, and even rampant government spending leading to chronic deficits, could be traced back to the declining influence of traditional Christian values, especially as they pertained to the norms governing sexual behaviour.[4] For Byfield, contemporary society's acceptance of pornography, adultery, feminism, and homosexuality was rooted in an increasingly secularized public school system, one that, in turn, was rooted in the widespread but gradual acceptance of the secular humanist ideas of American philosopher and educational reformer John Dewey. In the late 1800s and early 1900s, Dewey, suggests Byfield, set about to eradicate from public education curriculums traditional religious understandings of human nature and of good and evil.[5] In Byfield's opinion, the ultimate product of this lengthy progression towards secular education was a rejection of the traditional family, the natural institution that exists to provide children with the initial love, support, and, most importantly, moral foundations upon which they could grow into upstanding Christian citizens. The approach of contemporary governments, dominated by the "liberal left" that had come of age in the notorious 1960s, was one of complicity. The embrace of secular public schools, easier divorce laws, the legalization and funding of abortion, feminism and the devaluing of the "home-keeping function," generous welfare programs that eliminated natural incentives to work, the homosexual "lifestyle," and most recently, the potential for universal daycare, all reeked of an attack on the traditional family by a generation who had abandoned traditional Christian teachings.[6] In place of behaviour guided by traditional Christian moral barriers within society, Byfield now saw a rampant increase in crime, neglect, abuse, and reckless government spending, the latter an effort to rectify this crisis. In short, society was reaping what it had sown.

Byfield's columns also contained a multi-faceted program of reform, though rarely articulated in a systematic manner. Responding to "the systematic attempt to abolish religious influence on the law and society," Byfield utilized *Alberta Report* as a vital tool within the larger battle to gradually re-establish traditional Christian morality in the minds of citizens.[7] The universal values encapsulated in the Christian message were essential to a healthy society, and the most crucial task was to repeal the secular educational reforms inspired by the thought of Dewey. In the long run, Byfield implied that this change in educational philosophy would gradually set society back on its Christian moorings and that the collective ills of neglect, crime, and abuse would eventually cease to be problems on the magnitude that he understood them to be in the late twentieth century. However, this education-based solution did not prevent Byfield from demanding additional legislative changes in the here-and-now to prevent society from descending even further. The most obvious of these demands was the immediate prohibition of abortion, an act, in the eyes of Byfield, that violated the right to life of an innocent child. Non-traditional sexual practices were also an area of

Religion and Political Thought in Contemporary Alberta   163

particular concern. Homosexuality was clearly wrong in the eyes of Byfield, but it was the demands of what he called the "homosexual lobby," who openly advocated homosexuality as "a lifestyle, something all children should be familiar with and encouraged to investigate," that most infuriated him.[8] The open embrace of homosexuality, alongside the social acceptance of adultery, was seen as a threat to the traditional family, and *Alberta Report* therefore came out very strongly against any proposed advances in the rights of homosexuals, including rights to be free from discrimination based upon their sexual orientation, to adopt children and, of course, to marry.

Secular education, abortion, and same-sex rights were often the most controversial issues raised by the magazine, but Byfield also targeted a legal system that imposed lax punishments for violent crimes, state funding for the arts (which tended towards anti-religious expression), the dissemination of pornography, state support for multiculturalism and the endorsement of cultural relativism, the promotion of universal daycare programs (which would further encourage mothers to be away from their children), and, overall, the overbearing size of a contemporary liberal welfare state that devoted billions of tax dollars to social programs required simply because society had abandoned the very moral foundations that would make such services superfluous. Public policy, Byfield argued, had to be constructed in a way that reversed such initiatives, not because law in itself could make humanity "good," but because law could prevent certain aspects of society from getting worse. Yet he remained steadfast in his overarching belief that pornography, feminism, abortion, same-sex marriage, the legal system, and all other threats to the stability of society were peripheral, simply extensions of an education system that had failed generations of students by abandoning the universal moral message of Christianity and replacing it with a moral relativism that reinforced rather than challenged the darker aspects of our inner natures. "To change society, you must preach the gospel," noted Byfield, but this can only seriously begin once we ask ourselves the crucial question: "What are we teaching our children about right and wrong?"[9]

Of course, the story of society's demise constructed by Byfield was simplistic and lacking causal rigour. Yet the simplicity of the story was precisely why it connected so clearly with conservative readers in Alberta, most of whom had come of age within the confines of a Christian-based code of personal and societal norms and were now increasingly bewildered by the direction their society had taken. Older citizens, who played a significant role within the Reform Party movement, had witnessed first-hand the rapid changes that seemed to accompany the anti-Christian sentiment of the "Sixties," and Byfield's attempt to draw a causal link between such sentiment and the problems of contemporary society hit home with force. From their perspective, it was undeniable that schools were now secular, that churches were less full, that single-parent homes were more prevalent, and that the social acceptance of sexual permissiveness and non-traditional sexual unions were on the rise. It also seemed true that society's youth were more violent, more prone to drug use and theft, and less eager to work hard or serve their fellows than previous generations had been. Although it is doubtful that all readers traced these problems back to Dewey, the notion that the traditional family was under attack from anti-Christian forces was popular among certain segments of Alberta conservatives in the 1980s and 1990s.

That this message appeared in *Alberta Report* alongside dozens of articles that emphasized the political and economic injustices done to Alberta and the larger Canadian West by central Canada simply added to the indignation of readers. No doubt the social conservative message became entangled with the western alienation issue in the minds of many readers and they turned *en masse* to the Reform Party in the hope of solving both at once. Not only did Reform offer a potentially powerful voice for the economic and political concerns of the West, it could also play a leading role in the struggle against the anti-Christian forces present within left-wing parties that seemed to advocate feminism, abortion, "value-free" education, multiculturalism, "soft" punishments, and gay rights. As will become clearer shortly, this battle to restore Christian morality within society was never the intention of Reform leader Preston Manning, nor was it the central objective of most of the senior policy analysts or political strategists within the upper echelons on the party. But it was a central goal for many of the grassroots members of the party as well as for a number of Alberta-based Reform MPs, and a good deal of this sentiment was originally articulated in a coherent and helpful way by Byfield and his *Alberta Report* newsmagazine.[10]

In addition to Manning and Byfield, five former Reform MPs from Alberta constituencies agreed to be interviewed for this study. Each of these participants self-identified as Christian, was part of the 1993 electoral breakthrough, and spent several years in the House of Commons. Although most of those interviewed had difficulty stating with much precision how their faith influenced their political thinking, all five exhibited clear religious-based social conservative positions with respect

Religion and Political Thought in Contemporary Alberta   165

to such issues as abortion, homosexual rights, and secular public education. Indeed, their thinking closely followed the concerns initially expressed by Byfield. The decline of Christian values and the corresponding growth of moral relativism were particularly troublesome. Common laments included the loss of "our moral compass," "our religious heritage," and "our freedom to publicly celebrate our faith." Surveying the growing societal acceptance of abortion, divorce, pornography, and same-sex relations as a result of this growing "moral relativism," one MP stated: "It is clear that we are not adhering to biblical principles. When a country turns its back on God there are repercussions." With respect to more specific policy, the MPs left little doubt as to their distaste for legalized abortion and same-sex marriage, although two of the respondents were open to the notion of same-sex civil unions because, as one stated, "homosexuals are a part of society and should be treated as regular citizens." Despite this slight disagreement around homosexuality and the state, the MPs' anger tended to coalesce around a shared distaste for the Charter of Rights and Freedoms and those "special interest groups" who relied on it to push their anti-Christian agenda with respect to abortion or homosexual rights, or even the rights of criminals, through the court system. Indeed, this was a very common sentiment in the broader Reform Party, as it brought together social conservatives with secular democrats upset with the "anti-democratic" nature of Charter-based social policy decisions.[11]

In the mid- and late 1990s, the Alberta PC party gained a reputation for harbouring a large contingent of socially conservative members who played an important role in the political and policy decisions of the party in a way clearly unparalleled in the rest of Canada. To be sure, the Klein government's central goal coming out of the 1993 provincial election was to reduce public spending significantly in an effort to eliminate the deficit. In addition, Klein himself was not an evangelical conservative and neither his previous actions as mayor of Calgary nor the bulk of his statements as premier suggest he was a stern social conservative. In fact, it is generally well known that Klein held some attachment to aspects of Aboriginal spirituality rather than to traditional Christianity and was generally more tolerant of non-traditional lifestyles than many in his party.[12] Yet, in the earlier years of Klein's tenure as premier, the PCs found themselves waging a battle against an unexpected enemy, a gay man named Delwin Vriend who was suing the provincial government for failing to protect him when his employer, an Edmonton Christian college, fired him because of his sexual orientation. This was not a battle on which the PCs had campaigned.

166   God's Province

In fact, a number of MLAs complained to the author that this issue distracted the party from their central purpose, the elimination of the
province's deficit. Yet, the fight against Vriend engulfed the party and
would come to represent the key starting point in what essentially
amounted to a fifteen-year battle against the progression of homosexual rights in Alberta.[13] Relying on media reports, secondary academic literature, and, most importantly, semi-structured one-on-one
interviews with twelve current or recently retired Alberta PC MLAs, the
following paragraphs recount and analyse this period of socially conservative influence within the PC party before providing some broader conclusions with respect to social conservatism's overall influence
on contemporary Alberta politics.

    Although the types of concerns initially raised by Byfield – the secu-
lar nature of the education system, the prevalence of single-family
homes, and the increased reliance on daycare – were occasionally raised
by socially conservative PCs in the mid-1990s, they did not come close
to matching the intensity with which the issue of publicly funded abortions or the progression of homosexual rights was met by certain members of the PC caucus between 1994 and 2009. With respect to abortion,
which was roundly condemned within the interviews conducted for
this study, a group of Christian social conservatives within the PC caucus waged a particular battle to place restrictions on the public funding
of abortion in 1995, which ultimately led to a successful vote within
the legislature whereby funding would be restricted to "medically necessary" abortions only. However, the Alberta Medical Association balked
at having to provide a more narrow definition of "medically necessary,"
and the PC caucus, to the dismay of evangelical Christians such as Lorne
Taylor and Victor Doerksen, voted against forcing the association to do
so and the debate around restricting access to publicly funded abortions was subsequently dropped.[14] Debates around homosexual rights,
on the other hand, did not end so quickly.

    Although suspicion of homosexual behaviour was not unusual in
large segments of Alberta's and Canada's population in the late 1980s
and early 1990s, it was the case of Vriend, an Edmonton lab instructor
who, in 1991, attempted to file a complaint with the Alberta Human
Rights Commission after being fired from his job at a Christian college
after admitting he was gay, that sparked significant debate and, ultimately, the governing PC party's long history of anti-gay pronouncements and policy proposals. After having his complaint refused on the
grounds that "sexual orientation" was not included as protected ground
under the province's existing human rights legislation, Vriend took the

Religion and Political Thought in Contemporary Alberta   167

Alberta government to court on the charge that this exclusion breached his right to such protection guaranteed by the Charter of Rights and Freedoms. In 1994, the Alberta Court of Queen's bench agreed with Vriend that the failure to include sexual orientation as protected ground violated section 15 of the Charter. The government immediately appealed the decision and was rewarded with a ruling in its favour by the Alberta Court of Appeal in 1996. The case was subsequently appealed to the Supreme Court of Canada, which, in 1998, ruled that the province was indeed in violation of the Charter by failing to include sexual orientation as protected ground in its human rights legislation.

Prior to the initial 1994 ruling, there were scattered comments made by prominent PC cabinet ministers that ridiculed the homosexual lobby and the province's own human rights commission for potentially providing such "anti-family" groups a public forum.[15] However, it was on the heels of the 1994 ruling and the government's subsequent decision to appeal that socially conservative PC MLAs were given an unexpected platform from which to publicly express their antipathy towards the prospect of providing homosexuals with "special" rights and a steady stream of such sentiment quickly followed.[16] In 1996, Klein himself admitted that homosexuality was an "individual's choice of lifestyle" and that he felt that providing them "extra" rights was wrong. Lorne Taylor, a stern evangelical Christian, agreed but went further by noting that homosexuality, unlike race, reveals a person's character and morality. "It's not normal behavior," continued Taylor, "sexuality is probably one of the most important issues in society in terms of morality and behavior."[17] That same year, Social Services Minister and evangelical Christian Stockwell Day broadened the PC government's anti-homosexual stance beyond the contours of the ongoing *Vriend* case and the debate about the protection of homosexuals in the workplace by insisting that his department would avoid placing foster children in the care of gays, preferring instead to "look for that placement which puts kids into the most normative societal situation possible."[18] Day, alongside fellow evangelical Christian MLA Victor Doerksen, then attempted to block a $10,000 government grant to the Red Deer Museum in 1997 that was to be used to study and document the lives and contributions of homosexuals in central Alberta. Day, who was clear in his belief that homosexuality was morally wrong in the eyes of God, admitted that "lifestyle is a matter of personal choice" but that the use of tax dollars "to promote a particular lifestyle is where I have problems."[19]

Upon learning that the Supreme Court had ruled against Alberta in the *Vriend* case in April 1998, a strong contingent of MLAs urged Klein to utilize the notwithstanding clause, but a closely contested vote by caucus was won by those eager to accept the court's ruling and move on. The government, however, refused to follow through on the largely symbolic act of changing the wording of its human rights legislation to ensure it was in agreement with the court's ruling, preferring instead that sexual orientation simply be "read into" its existing law. In addition, Klein subsequently appointed a ministerial task force on gay rights to investigate the larger ramifications of the Supreme Court decision and suggest "legislative fences" to limit the ruling's impact on other provincial laws. One of the task force's direct recommendations was the Domestic Relations Act, which explicitly defined a common-law union as "a relationship between two people of the opposite sex."[20] Similarly, in 1999, Victor Doerksen put forth a private member's bill that reaffirmed the definition of marriage as that "between one man and one woman" and included further provisions to utilize the notwithstanding clause should the courts attempt to impose same-sex marriage on the province. Despite the protests of Justice Minister Dave Hancock, who correctly argued that marriage was a federal responsibility, the bill was loudly supported by evangelical Christians Taylor and Day and was easily passed as the Marriage Act by the PC-dominated legislature in March 2000.[21]

Despite the best efforts of social conservatives, however, the Alberta government's fight against homosexual rights faced additional legal obstacles with the Supreme Court's landmark *M vs H* decision in 1999, which found Ontario's refusal to offer common-law benefits to same-sex couples unconstitutional. The Alberta government thus had little choice but to amend its common-law legislation, and in 2003, it finally passed the Adult Interdependent Relationships Act, which granted same-sex couples the opportunity to claim common-law status and the benefits that accompanied that designation. Yet, for PC social conservatives who had attempted to proactively block the legalization of same-sex marriage in Alberta in 2000, the devastating blow was landed in 2005 when the federal government responded to instruction from the Supreme Court to legalize same-sex marriage in Canada. As one MLA lamented to me, "I think it's absolutely wrong, but we really had no choice because marriage is federal jurisdiction. Same-sex marriage was shoved down our throats by the federal government."

Having finally lost the decisive battle against same-sex marriage, however, social conservatives within caucus were not ready to abandon their cause. In 2006, MLA Ted Morton sponsored a private member's bill that would have protected the right of those opposed to homosexuality to

Religion and Political Thought in Contemporary Alberta   169

speak out against the practice, provided parents the right to prevent their kids from learning about it in public schools, and allowed marriage commissioners to refuse to perform gay marriages. Although the bill was quashed by the ending of a legislative session, the notion of "parental rights" in public schools would become an important bargaining chip shortly thereafter. In June 2009, the Alberta PCs utilized their overwhelming majority within the legislature to pass Bill 44, the Human Rights, Citizenship and Multiculturalism Amendment Act. Although this bill clarified certain operational procedures for the province's existing Human Rights Commissions, the centrepiece of the Act was the written inclusion of "sexual orientation" as protected ground from discrimination under Alberta's human rights legislation. The decision, some eleven years after the landmark *Vriend* ruling, to reverse course and formally include sexual orientation within the province's human rights legislation was meant to represent a long-overdue act of recognition for the province's homosexual community. However, praise from sexual diversity activists was quickly muted when it became clear that the bill contained a further change in section 11. Building upon the province's School Act, Bill 44 reaffirmed the right of parents to pull their children from any course of study or educational program that dealt explicitly with religion or sexuality and added sexual orientation to that list. By including such a clause in the Human Rights Act, the government essentially banned mandatory "gay-friendly" courses in public schools and placed teachers within the crosshairs of the province's Human Rights Commission should they fail to properly notify parents that such topics would be discussed.

The striking contrast within Bill 44, which contained both a symbolic recognition of sexual orientation and a clause that strengthened the right of concerned parents to prevent their children from learning about sexual orientation, along with sexuality and religion, was not lost on commentators. Indeed, there was immediate suspicion that the religious conservatives within the PC caucus had insisted on the inclusion of the "parental rights" clause as a trade-off of sorts, in exchange for consenting to the symbolic recognition of sexual orientation as protected ground within the human rights legislation.[22] For socially conservative MLAs who championed the clause within caucus, a sense of immediacy was provided by a groundbreaking decision in British Columbia in 2006. Faced with the prospect of a lengthy battle before the BC Human Rights Tribunal against Murray and Peter Corren, who argued that public schools were guilty of discrimination because they failed to include sexual orientation within the curriculum, the BC government agreed to revise public education courses to ensure that homosexuality was presented in a respectful manner. More importantly, the BC government simultaneously placed tougher restrictions on the right of parents to remove their children from such lessons.[23] The prospect of an Alberta Human Rights Commission eventually forcing the provincial government to revise its curriculum in a similar manner while preventing parents from removing their children from such "gay-positive" instruction was "maddening" to religiously conservative MLAs suspicious of homosexual behaviour and eager to protect the right of citizens to oppose it, based on the Charter's promise of freedom of religion.[24] The PC caucus's inclusion of parental rights in Bill 44 was therefore a necessary compromise with such MLAs, who were opposed to the broader purpose of the bill – the symbolic recognition of sexual orientation as protected ground from discrimination.[25]

Thus, as the preceding paragraphs have demonstrated, religious-based social conservatism certainly did influence the agenda of the Alberta PC party throughout the 1990s and early 2000s. Given the province's political history, especially the long and influential premierships of notorious fundamentalist Christians William Aberhart and Ernest Manning, commentators have tended to assume that Alberta is ultimately a province dominated by conservative Christian ideas and the long fight against gay rights on the part of the PCs was simply a by-product of this. The popularity of a writer like Byfield and the relatively large number of socially conservative comments emanating from both Alberta-based Reform MPs and PC MLAs in the 1990s seem to confirm this thesis. However, there is a lack of scholarly literature that considers the influence of religion on the politics of contemporary Alberta, and the result has been a general acceptance of the broad assumption, especially in media circles, that Albertans and their politicians are quite religious and socially conservative compared to Canadians in the rest of the country. Yet a brief look at the numbers provided by Statistics Canada suggests that the "Alberta as a Bible-Belt" theory does not hold water.

As demonstrated by the compilation of four different surveys in Table 5.1, Alberta was second only to British Columbia among all provinces with respect to the percentage of citizens who declared that they had no religious affiliation whatsoever in 2001. In addition, two separate surveys note that only British Columbia and Quebec contained a smaller percentage of citizens who regularly attended religious services either weekly or monthly than Alberta.[26] Similarly, only British Columbia and Quebec contained a smaller percentage of citizens who declared

Religion and Political Thought in Contemporary Alberta   171

Table 5.1
Religiosity in Canada, by province and region, as percentage of population

% of population that:	Canada	AB	BC	SK	MB	ON	QC	Atl
Declares no religious affiliation (2001)	16	23	35	15	18	16	6	8
Attends religious service weekly (2005)	25	27	17	36	36	28	15	39
Attends religious service monthly (1999–2001)	32	31	25	39	36	36	25	41
Declares they are "very committed to religion" (1997)	19	18	13	23	23	22	17	26

Sources: Row 1 data represent calculations by the author based on statistics drawn from "Religions in Canada," 2001 Census, Statistics Canada, http://www12.statcan.ca/english/census01/products/highlight /Religion/PR_Menu2.cfm?Lang=E. Row 2 data taken from Bibby, *Beyond the Gods and Back: Religion's Demise and Rise and Why It Matters*, 53. Row 3 data taken from Clark, "Pockets of Belief: Religious Attendance Patterns in Canada." Row 4 data taken from Bowen, *Christians in a Secular World: The Canadian Experience*, 53–5. A special thanks to David Rayside who shared some of his ongoing work, which included reference to some of these statistics.

they were "very committed" to religion in 1997 than Alberta. Obviously, such statistics do not provide a conclusive picture of religious activity in Alberta in the mid- to late 1990s, but they certainly contradict the general thesis that Alberta is a Canadian outlier when it comes to religious participation among the electorate. Alberta is not, it seems, a province dominated by the religious.

Of course, one might argue that it is not that Alberta contained an unusually large number of religious adherents among its population, but rather that those who were religious practise a distinctly conservative or fundamentalist brand of religion that differentiates the citizenry from that of the rest of Canada.[27] As Table 5.2 demonstrates, the religious makeup of Alberta in 2001 was somewhat different from that of the other provinces in a way that speaks to its broader populist religious heritage, discussed in Chapter 2. For instance, Alberta contained a smaller percentage of Roman Catholics and Anglicans than the Canadian average, two congregations with deep European roots that are traditionally understood to be more hierarchical in their organization, more communal in their theology, and more open towards the insights of scholarship. Alberta also had the highest percentage of "Other Protestants" in Canada. This is significant because this category contains members of the Pentecostal, Christian Reformed, Evangelical Mission-

172   God's Province

Table 5.2
Religious identification across Canada as percentage of population, 2001

Country/province (total population)	Canada 29,639,030	Alberta 2,941,150	Saskatchewan 963,150	Ontario 11,285,550	Nova Scotia 897,570
No religion	16.2	23.1	15.4	16.0	11.6
Roman Catholic	43.2	25.7	29.8	34.3	36.5
United Church	9.6	13.5	19.5	11.8	15.9
Anglican	6.9	5.9	6.8	8.7	13.4
Baptist	2.5	2.5	1.7	2.6	10.6
Lutheran	2.0	4.8	8.2	1.9	12.3
Presbyterian	1.4	1.0	0.1	2.5	2.5
Methodist	0.1	0.06	0.01	1.5	.003
Other Protestant	6.7	10.4	7.5	7.4	4.1
Muslim	2.0	1.7	0.2	3.1	0.4
Jewish	1.1	0.4	0.09	1.7	0.2
Sikh	1.0	0.8	0.05	0.9	0.03
Church of Latter Day Saints (Mormon)	0.3	1.7	0.03	0.2	0.3

Sources: Calculations are the author's own based on data drawn from "Religions in Canada," 2001 Census, Statistics Canada, http://www12.statcan.ca/english/census01/products/highlight/Religion /PR_Menu2.cfm?Lang=E. Also, the category "Other Protestant" includes those belonging to the Pentecostal, Christian Reformed, Evangelical Missionary, Christian and Missionary Alliance churches, and those identified as "Born Again," "Evangelical," "Apostolic," and "Protestant."

ary, Christian and Missionary Alliance churches, and those who, on the 2001 census, identified themselves as "Born Again," "Evangelical," "Apostolic," and "Protestant." In other words, it seems that Alberta had a higher percentage of "evangelical" or "conservative Protestant" individuals than the rest of Canada. Granted, this is not a perfect measurement. In fact, measuring evangelicals has been notoriously difficult across North America, given the contested meaning of the term among both scholars and religious adherents. It is worth noting, however, that in 1997 Kurt Bowen found that, of those citizens who declared that they were "very committed to religion," roughly 38 per cent of those from Alberta belonged to "Conservative Protestant" churches, whereas the percentage was 27 per cent in the remainder of the Prairies and only 17 per cent in Ontario.[28] Although not entirely conclusive, this finding does suggest the existence of a certain continuity in Alberta with respect to the larger proportion of Protestant fundamentalists in Alberta measured by W.M. Mann in the 1930s. Yet it is important to remember that, despite Alberta appearing to contain a higher proportion of "conserv-

Religion and Political Thought in Contemporary Alberta   173

ative Protestants" than the rest of Canada, the total number in contemporary Alberta is not overwhelming. Indeed, returning to Table 5.2, one finds that the percentage of Albertans who are not religious, in addition to those who declare themselves to be members of the Roman Catholic, United, Presbyterian, Methodist, or Anglican churches – five groups that are generally not considered to be "conservative Protestant" – totals roughly 69 per cent of the population. The same categories in Ontario add up to roughly 75 per cent. Again, these statistics do not fully describe the nature of religious activity in either province, but they do suggest that although the religious makeup of Alberta is different than the rest of Canada (slightly more evangelical or conservative), it is not a significant outlier.

Related to this conclusion is the broader point that social conservative sentiment is not as widespread in Alberta as one might expect. Certainly significant pockets of Albertans are outright opposed to the advancement of homosexual rights, especially in areas outside Edmonton and Calgary, but the notion that there is province-wide agreement on this is fiction. In the late 1990s, in the heat of the debate over homosexual rights in Alberta, the provincial government's own research demonstrated significant variation with respect to views towards the definition of a family and the advancement of homosexual rights within the province. Views on gay adoption, spousal benefits, marriage, and even whether homosexuality should be a topic of discussion within public school curriculums were canvassed, and the findings revealed a polarized electorate with only a very slight majority in opposition to the advancement of the homosexual cause.[29] Doreen Barrie has since pointed to a number of polls conducted in the late 1990s and early 2000s that sought to measure Canadian attitudes towards issues such as abortion and same-sex rights, and these also suggested a polarized Alberta electorate that was not significantly out of step with the rest of the country. For instance, asked whether they favoured abortion in a 2001 poll, 39 per cent of Alberta citizens said "Yes," a percentage that placed the province in between British Columbia, Quebec, and Ontario, which tended to be more favourable to abortion, and Saskatchewan, Manitoba, and Atlantic Canada, which tended to view abortion less favourably than Albertans. Similarly, surveying a variety of polls on same-sex rights, Barrie notes that although Albertans tended to be slightly less favourable to the legalization of same-sex marriage than the Canadian average (which was an essential deadlock in 2003), several polls demonstrated a solid majority of Albertans expressing support for equal rights for same-sex individuals.[30]

174   God's Province

Given the above evidence with respect to religious adherence in general and social conservative attitudes in particular within the Alberta citizenry in the late 1990s and early 2000s, it should come as no surprise that the provincial PC caucus was not dominated by conservative Christians espousing a message akin to that of Byfield. In fact, in the interviews conducted for this project, religious MLAs from the PC party tended to fall within three distinct groupings that, for the sake of simplicity, I label as "progressive," "outright rejection," and "compromise." The first, and easily the smallest, group was that of "progressive" Christian MLAs who claimed to have no problem with the extension of same-sex rights or the legalization of same-sex marriage. In general, these MLAs interpreted the message of Christ as one of tolerance, love, and non-judgment. The second group of Christian MLAs was larger than the "progressive" group but still represented, as a less-rigid MLA noted, "a noisy minority" within the general collection of Christian MLAs. This was the "outright rejection" crowd, who, as the label suggests, wanted absolutely no movement on the gay rights issue. Homosexuality was clearly against the will of God and, given its implicit attack on the structure of the traditional family, was also detrimental to the health of society. The religious-based political thought of this group most closely resembled that of Byfield. Although those MLAs who adopted this view were careful to avoid hateful language in the interviews conducted, it was clear that homosexuality itself, let alone same-sex marriage, troubled them on a personal level owing to their religious beliefs. It was precisely this type of sentiment that operated behind the comments and policy proposals of hard-right social conservative Christians like Taylor, Doerksen, and Day, each of whom issued numerous anti-gay statements in the press while simultaneously working in caucus to block the inclusion of same-sex rights in the province's human rights legislation, prevent homosexuals from taking on foster children, disallow pro-gay museum grants, and outright refuse any kind of compromise on the legalization of same-sex marriage. Yet, despite the significant amount of press coverage that the comments and policy proposals of this group received, it is important to reiterate that this collection of MLAs represented only a minority of caucus members.

The third group, the "compromisers," was comprised of Christian MLAs who found the issue of same-sex rights problematic because of the tension between their commitment to serve all citizens and their own personal sense that homosexuality was morally wrong. The majority of those interviewed for this project belonged to this group, and all the MLAs who participated generally agreed that such "compromis-

Religion and Political Thought in Contemporary Alberta   175

ers" made up the majority of the entire PC caucus as well. Essentially, the
members of this group were okay with the granting of same-sex "civil
unions" and the benefits that would accrue from such a designation
but were opposed to the legalization of same-sex marriage. This sense
of hesitation and eventual compromise was captured in the thoughts of
one MLA:

> I really believe that God loves all people equally and because of
> their sexual preference or disposition, I should not hold myself in
> judgment of them. I should deal with them as people who have
> every bit as much right as I have to be here and to live safe and free
> lives. [Yet] I still feel it isn't following God's law to be homosexual,
> and so I find it difficult ...
> I did vote for them to be able to form legal relationships to get
> benefits. I don't believe in marriage for those people because mar-
> riage to me is in God's law a sacrament. And why would they go
> for that? I haven't really understood why they want that sacrament
> if they want a different kind of relationship. If we don't believe it's
> natural or in God's law to have male couples and female couples,
> why do they want to have marriage? It doesn't make any sense
> to me.

A second Christian MLA largely agreed with this sentiment, recalling
the personal angst he had felt during the debates over same-sex rights
within caucus because homosexuals "are people like everyone else and
we were there to serve everybody. But, was same-sex marriage best for
society? I found it very difficult." A third MLA agreed that marriage was
clearly meant for a man and a woman but added, "I respect the agency
of homosexual couples to live together but please don't force it on me
or don't ask me, as a believer, to perform their marriage. This is my fear,
that we evolve to a situation where pastors are forced to marry them."
    Thus, when taken together, the data on religious adherence and at-
titudes towards homosexual rights in Alberta seem to disprove the general assumption that Albertans are unusually religious or socially
conservative. In addition, despite what amounted to a fifteen-year battle against homosexual rights waged by the Alberta PC government,
the majority of Christian MLAs were personally open to a certain degree
of compromise. Although unwilling to support same-sex marriage,
which had a clear religious connotation and brought up issues related
to the freedom of religious expression, they were largely okay with the
extension of other rights, including the inclusion of sexual orientation

as protected ground in the province's human rights legislation and the provision that same-sex couples could be eligible for common-law spousal benefits. Although it is obvious that the vast majority of Christian MLAs opposed same-sex marriage for religious reasons, the impetus behind the more general fight against basic homosexual rights that was waged by the PC government over a fifteen-year period is not as clear. In other words, if a solid majority of Christian MLAs within the PC caucus were not the avid "homophobic" characters that the press sometimes depicted them as being, why was the PC government, as a whole, so adamant in its fight against the inclusion of sexual orientation in its human rights legislation or the extension of common-law benefits to same-sex couples? An important piece to this puzzle, and this was stressed by nearly all MLAs interviewed, was that Premier Klein and other senior leaders of the party interpreted their primary policy goal as being to reduce government spending. They did not enter the political realm with any preconceived agenda related to same-sex issues; nor did they campaign on any promises to block the advancement of same-sex rights. When the *Vriend* issue flared up in the early 1990s, Klein allowed a simple caucus vote to be determinant with respect to the government's response. According to those MLAs interviewed, the power of caucus over issues related to social policy largely continued unabated under the Stelmach government, which passed the controversial Bill 44. Yet, given the makeup of caucus described above, it still seems surprising that the government would tend so strongly towards an anti–homosexual rights position. The broader reasons for this response were twofold.

First, further complicating the "religious makeup of caucus" line of inquiry is the existence of a small contingent of MLAs who shared many of the views towards same-sex rights with the hard-right "outright rejection" Christian group, yet were working from a secular libertarian approach rather than a religious background. Conservative academic and former PC MLA and two-time leadership candidate Ted Morton was a key member of this group. Morton has been a long-time critic of "judicial activism" and the anti-democratic nature of court-made law in Canada, and he has combined these concerns with his broader contention that any social policies that fail to support the traditional family are detrimental to society. Despite being one of the more outspoken social conservatives in recent PC caucuses, Morton has never alluded to any particular religious beliefs as the foundation for his position. Rather, he seems to have been motivated by a more general republican belief that a proper democracy can only be sustained by way of instill-

Religion and Political Thought in Contemporary Alberta   177

ing proper "moral character" into its citizens. In a speech delivered prior
to becoming an MLA, Morton reminded the audience of "the role of the
natural family in producing public morality" and the "moral foundations of freedom" before ridiculing the "new egalitarians ... represented primarily by the gender feminists and the gay rights movement –
that target the natural family as public enemy number one." Such
groups "like to present themselves as the party of freedom ... [but] the
constant recourse to non-democratic institutions – courts and other
non-accountable bureaucracies – discloses their true authoritarian
bend." The only way to avoid the "soft despotism" implicit within this
group's approach is to "make enlightened family policy a cornerstone
of the democratic state."[31] As an MLA, Morton has put his concerns regarding the necessity of the traditional family at the forefront of his
agenda and has made clear his stern opposition to same-sex marriage
and the general advancement of homosexual rights.[32] Yet, it is important to understand that, despite being very popular in religious-based
social conservative circles, the sentiment expressed by Morton is derived largely from his republican and libertarian leanings as opposed to
a particular religious interpretation. Thus, it is a mistake to simply assume that all social conservatives in the PC caucus were working from
a religious foundation. That Morton drew much support from conservative religious groups for his anti-gay stance tends to cloud this fact
for a number of commentators eager to paint the PCs with a conservative Christian brush.[33] However, the existence of MLAs such as Morton
within the PC caucus helps to provide part of the answer to the larger
question related to the specific source of the stern social conservatism
inherent in many PC policies and proposals if the Christian "outright
rejection" group made up only a small minority of the caucus. Essentially, they were not the only social conservatives at work within the
PC party.

Second, and more importantly, the 1993 provincial election produced
a unique PC caucus. The opposition Liberals essentially swept the Edmonton and area seats, leaving the PC caucus full of business-minded
Calgary MLAs alongside representatives of the more socially conservative
rural areas of the province. The result was a far more conservative caucus, both fiscally and socially, than had been the norm under Peter
Lougheed or Don Getty.[34] The initial court ruling on the *Vriend* case in
1994 suddenly placed this caucus in the middle of a debate that the
Klein government had not sought out, but it was one that stirred up
passions in the province, especially among the religiously conservative.
In fact, a number of MLAs admitted in interviews that by leaving the

government's stance with respect to homosexual rights open to a caucus vote, Klein inadvertently opened the door for a small minority of
extreme, religiously inspired social conservatives to expound their views
in a way that riled up many conservative-minded people in the province
who had already been immersed in the socially conservative message of
Byfield and his popular *Alberta Report* newsmagazine. As the government's own polling showed, although there was essentially an even split
among Albertans between those in favour and those opposed to extending certain rights to homosexuals, there was a significant difference between the views of those living in larger urban centres and the
views of those living in rural locations. Unsurprisingly, opposition to
the advancement of gay rights was far stronger outside larger cities, a
finding that correlates nicely with the fact that citizens residing outside Edmonton and Calgary were far more likely to attend religious
services on a regular basis.[35] Given the results of the 1993 provincial
election, the PCs suddenly found themselves in a position where a solid
segment of their electoral support, especially in areas outside Calgary,
was dependent on their strong stand against the advancement of gay
rights.[36] In other words, a large contingent of rural MLAs in caucus,
whether they were personally opposed to gay rights or not, had little
choice but to back the religiously conservative position because of the
views of their largely socially conservative rural constituents. Indeed,
eight of those MLAs who participated in this study admitted to feeling
significant pressure from those opposed to homosexual rights within
their constituency, which was located outside Edmonton or Calgary. In
fact, as one former PC cabinet minister and outspoken evangelical Christian admitted, the press tended to give the "religious right" in caucus far
too much credit for the PC government's stance towards gay rights.
Rather, it was the "rural right," driven by political calculation based on
constituents' socially conservative beliefs, that successfully pushed the
Klein government towards an anti-gay position.[37]

What emerges from the above section on social policy in contemporary Alberta is a somewhat muddled picture of just how religion influenced the PC government from 1993 until 2009. As the polling data
indicates, the population of Alberta was not unusually religious or overwhelmingly socially conservative. However, the heavy rural presence
within the governing caucus ensured that socially conservative views
were given significant attention. The result was a PC government head-
ed largely by fiscal conservatives, many of them secular, eager to tackle
the provinces deficit, yet having to broker compromises with a strong
contingent of MLAs who had little choice but to advocate a socially con-

servative agenda, especially in the face of the *Vriend* case and eventually the issue of same-sex marriage itself. There are certainly examples of overtly religious PC MLAs speaking out against homosexuality, but these individuals were a small part of a larger coalition of caucus members who were largely responding to the popularity of Byfield's message in their own constituencies. But this suggests a rather indirect role for religion in the overall "social conservatism" story in Alberta provincial politics. Religious considerations were very important to the hard-right conservative Christians within caucus, who took the most extreme socially conservative positions, but religion was only one of two or three significant influences for the more numerous moderate Christian MLAs whom I dubbed "compromisers." Rather than simply abiding by their Christian interpretation, which tended to be suspicious of homosexuality, they balanced their approach by considering their commitment to "represent everybody" and their own electoral self-interest together with the corresponding views of their constituents. However, the religious-based social conservatism of rural Albertans, who were essentially overrepresented within the PC caucus, had a significant influence on a number of those middle-of-the-road MLAs who were most likely Christian but, more importantly, were most interested in adhering to the will of their constituents for fear of losing their electoral support.

Nevertheless, religiously motivated social conservatism has declined significantly in Alberta and elsewhere in Canada since its height surrounding the *Vriend* case and the subsequent debate around same-sex marriage in the early 2000s, a fact that suggests its influence on the province's politics in this regard has largely subsided. In fact, social conservative fears with respect to the advance of homosexual rights via the courts have generally declined across Canada, including in Alberta, as citizens have become more accustomed to the notion of homosexuals being individuals who deserve adequate protection from discrimination. A recent poll confirms this trend, demonstrating that province-wide opposition to the legal recognition of same-sex marriages in Alberta stood at 28 per cent in 2011, down from 59 per cent in 1996.[38] In a more anecdotal testament to this shift in attitude in Alberta, it is widely held that the anti-homosexual comments of a religiously motivated Wildrose Party candidate that emerged during the 2012 provincial election campaign helped to derail the party and allowed the governing PCs to escape with yet another electoral victory.[39] Of course, religious-based social conservative sentiment has not disappeared entirely from the province (a fact confirmed by recent debates over both the rights of religious schools and home-schooling

180   God's Province

parents to teach their children about homosexuality from their religious perspective and the issue of mandatory Gay-Straight Alliance
clubs in provincial schools), but on the whole, the influence of religious-based social conservatism has declined significantly from its
height in the 1990s and early 2000s. Given continuing trends towards
increased secularization within the citizenry, it is difficult to imagine
it attaining such influence again.[40]

PRESTON MANNING'S CHRISTIAN APPROACH
TO POLITICS

When Preston Manning admitted in the early 1990s that he was an
evangelical Christian who attended a particularly conservative church
in Calgary, he added to the speculation that he was, like Byfield, a strident social conservative who sought the opportunity to impose his religiously based views of a properly ordered Christian society upon an
unsuspecting public. Indeed, this view was encouraged by the publication of two journalistic books and an influential news article that argued that Manning was a stern social conservative who was eager to
rewrite Canadian social policy according to his religious views should
he attain power in the federal 1993 election.[41] However, political sci-
entist Tom Flanagan, who worked closely with Manning while serving
as Reform's director of policy, strategy, and communications in the early
1990s, has convincingly challenged this depiction of Manning as a hard-
core Christian fundamentalist eager to impose a socially conservative
agenda upon Canada. Speaking to the influence of religion on the political thought of Manning, Flanagan argues that he is best understood
not as an evangelical moral crusader intent on "storming Babylon," but
rather as one seeking to bring the Christian principles of mediation,
reconciliation, and self-sacrifice to bear on federal politics.[42]

As the remainder of this chapter will demonstrate, Flanagan is quite
correct to dispel the argument that Manning's politics were driven by
religious-based social conservatism. Although he worked from a conservative Christian foundation similar to Byfield's, Manning generally
followed the religious perspective of his father, insisting that the divine
purpose of the state was to protect the freedom of the individual rather
than to legislate "righteousness" by way of socially conservative policy.
However, despite acknowledging Manning's loose adherence to the social conservative philosophy espoused by his father, Ernest Manning, in
the 1960s, which promised to unite the humanitarian concerns of the
left with the free-enterprise philosophy of the right, Flanagan com-

Religion and Political Thought in Contemporary Alberta   181

pletely overlooks the religiously based logic that operated behind
Ernest's socially conservative position and that subsequently informed
the political thought of Preston.[43] In fact, despite acknowledging Manning's desire to import a Christian-based approach to mediation and
reconciliation into the political sphere, Flanagan concludes that Christianity "is the personal motivation for Manning's political career but
does not determine his political positions."[44] The remainder of this
chapter takes direct aim at this conclusion, arguing that Flanagan, along
with most commentators on Manning and the Reform Party, has overlooked a more subtle yet incredibly significant aspect of Manning's
thinking, a characteristic that emerged directly out of his religious perspective and connects with his broad political ideology along more
than one dimension. Thus, I argue that Manning's thought represents
a distinct, religiously motivated conservative strain that differed from
both the secular, urban conservatism of Peter Lougheed or Ralph Klein
and the religious-based social conservatism of Ted Byfield and a number of Reform MPs and PC MLAs. Utilizing both political and religious
addresses by Manning, entries in his personal journal housed at the
University of Calgary Archives, and two lengthy one-on-one interviews
conducted by the author, this chapter now turns to a detailed exploration of the political thought of Preston Manning, with particular emphasis on the role played by his religious perspective.

Largely in response to the negative attention his religious background was receiving from the national media, Manning included a
chapter on his spirituality in his 1992 book *The New Canada*, which set
forth his broader political vision. Beginning with a description of the
two most prevalent historical streams of Protestantism on the Canadian Prairies, the left-leaning social gospel and the right-leaning evangelical traditions, Manning suggested that at the heart of both is the
Christian principle of reconciliation. In fact, compared to Ernest Manning and William Aberhart, Manning was far less dismissive of the social gospel. In an interview with the author, Manning noted: "I see the
social gospel and caring for others in the name of Christ as one dimension of the Christian faith, a legitimate and important one. Jesus
provided the example of the Good Samaritan and said 'go and do
likewise.' Social concern and social action is part of the Christian
gospel."[45] In other words, the great divide within evangelical Protestantism in North America between those advocating a Christianity
build solely around personal spiritual development and those advocating a Christianity based solely upon "good works" was largely misguided. Indeed, Manning understood these competing extremes as

actually being two dimensions of Christianity, "perfectly balanced in the life of Jesus."[46] Yet, while he acknowledged the value in reconciling the broken relationships of diverse groups of people on earth (what the social gospel tradition calls "social justice" and what Manning himself refers to as the "horizontal" dimension of Christianity), he followed his father in asserting that it is reconciliation with God, or the "vertical" dimension, that we first require before we can turn with appropriate care to the needs of our neighbour.[47] Drawing directly from the broader Protestant fundamentalist tradition, Manning noted the story of Nicodemus in the biblical Book of John to make this point:

Unless a man is born again – transformed spiritually inside – he can't enter into a relationship with God that changes his behaviour and enables God to strengthen and purify and direct his horizontal activities. And how does that come about, how is one born again spiritually? By believing, is what Jesus told Nicodemus. Not by going to church, or trying harder, but by believing.[48]

Building upon this notion in his personal journals, Manning noted that "love of one another is the principal effect of receiving the gospel," but this first requires a response on the part of the individual to the initiative God has taken, through Christ, to reach out to each of us.[49] Although "strained or broken relationships are the principal sources of frustration, pain, and despair in our modern world," it is in building our relationship with God, rather than developing any particular social program, that will eventually lead to improved relationships on earth.[50] Speaking to the individual's role in improving relationships on earth, Manning was clear:

I think it's most important to get one's relationship to God right and see what service obligations follow from that, than to make your relationship to God secondary and launch into saving the world with your own strength. That doesn't mean that you abandon trying to achieve a better society, but I think you approach it on a more realistic basis if you first recognize and address the reality of evil – in your own life and in the world – which requires some sort of divine intervention because it can't be fixed by social engineering.[51]

Yet, despite sharing this broad evangelical notion of the necessity of spiritual renewal in Christ with both Aberhart and his father, as well as

Religion and Political Thought in Contemporary Alberta   183

a traditional premillennial Christian understanding of the "end of days," complete with the Rapture, Battle of Armageddon and the final return of Christ that will occur at the bequest of God alone, the potential immediacy of such an occurrence did not push Manning towards the prophetic scriptures that Aberhart and Manning had emphasized.[52] Asked whether he believed in the fundamentalist Christian understanding of the Second Coming of Christ, Manning replied:

> Yes, but with this emphasis: Not employing such understanding to try to predict the when and the where of end-time events or who's going to be fighting whom at the Battle of Armageddon. I feel that there's been so much abuse and perversion of the prophetic scriptures on these points that I tend to shy away from that type of interpretation or proclamation. I prefer to emphasize what the Apostle Peter emphasized in his second epistle when, speaking of the end times, he says, "Seeing that all these destructive things are going to happen, what manner of persons ought you to be?" He then brings the discussion and the emphasis back to living a Christ-like life no matter what the times or circumstances.[53]

Such a description corresponds well with the observations of journalist Lloyd Mackey, a long-time associate of Manning's, who argues that Preston is a mainstream evangelical Christian interested in the "relational aspects of faith," whereas his father, Ernest, invested much time in the unique eschatological theories associated with early twentieth century Christian fundamentalism.[54] In fact, Preston rejects much of the dispensationalism so central to Aberhart's and Ernest Manning's theology, an interest he chalks up to the "cataclysmic times" they governed in comparison to the contemporary landscape. In fact, Manning conceives the kingdom of God as "a sphere in which one is rightly related to God and that God is genuinely supreme," rather than as a precise political order that one should expect to find on earth.[55] Yet Manning does believe there are major epochs in history in which God deals with "his own people" differently than in other periods.[56] The primary example of this difference is found in comparisons between the actions of God in the Old and New Testaments of the Bible, a distinction that strongly influences the direction of Manning's Christianity. Manning interprets much of the Old Testament as an account of God's "legal initiative," the record of God providing a set of laws to Moses that, if obeyed, would restore the Hebrews' relationship with God. However, this attempt at reconciliation through the application of "the rule of law" was unsuccessful, leading the latter-day prophets to realize that "unless laws can be inscribed on the human heart, and not merely written on parchment or tablets of stone, law by itself is insufficient to restore or regulate relationships between people and God or among themselves."[57]

This realization was confirmed by God's second initiative, which comprises the bulk of the New Testament. This is the "mediation initiative," the arrival on earth of Christ, "a unique and divine mediator" sent by God "to restore our relationship to him and to one another."[58] Christ's life was one dedicated to reconciling people with God by way of his teachings. Motivated by a selfless love, Christ eventually makes the ultimate sacrifice in the interests of reconciling humanity with God. The resurrection of Christ, according to Manning, is to be interpreted as a sign that God accepts this mediation effort and that humanity is now free to accept the self-sacrifice of Christ as well as His accompanying promise to free us from our sins so long as we follow His teachings, seek forgiveness, and make restitution for our sinful behaviour. The suggestion that we are "free" to do so, however, is of supreme importance. The essence of Christianity is, for Manning, making the free choice to follow or not follow the teachings of Christ, to accept His offer of reconciliation or reject it and continue to fall short in our relationship with God and others. One cannot be coerced into righteousness.

Although this choice represents the fundamental turning point in the life of a Christian, it is not the end point. Believers, argues Manning, possess "an obligation to have a Christian influence on everything – from bringing Christian ethics to bear, to practicing reconciliation, to trying to introduce people to Christ in whatever sphere we're in."[59] Clearly influenced by his father's long involvement in both Christian evangelism and Alberta politics, Manning is quick to conclude that the scriptures did not support arguments made by certain Christian fundamentalists in favour of political non-involvement. In fact, in an undated address he gave over his father's radio program in the 1970s, Manning provided a number of examples from the Bible that, in his view, demonstrated that God intended Christians to be involved in the political world.[60] Indeed, given the enormous impact the state can have on the lives of its citizens, in addition to its potential for constraining evil, Manning concluded that it would be foolish to abandon this institution to the non-religious. This is especially important when one considers the divine purpose of the nation, an understanding that Man-

Religion and Political Thought in Contemporary Alberta   185

ning draws from the seventeenth Book of Acts, wherein Paul explains
to the Athenians that nations were created by God. For Manning, this
implies that nations must necessarily possess a particular spiritual purpose envisioned by the creator. Thus, he reasoned, nations are "the context in which man seeks for God."[61] Therefore, although the process of
law-making can never fully reconcile humanity with God and lead to
completely harmonious relations on earth, as evidenced by the experience of the Hebrews in the Old Testament, the political realm is of
supreme importance nonetheless. The nation is a creation of God that
must be governed in a particular manner so as to allow it to serve its
purpose: facilitating humanity's search for God. By facilitating this
search, the state can indirectly assist citizens in their quest to improve
social relations on earth as more and more individuals turn towards
God. The implications of this conclusion with respect to the proper
arrangement of the state will be explored in the following section.

Confident that Christians were meant to have influence in the political sphere, Manning delivered a speech in 1988 that outlined his preferred approach.[62] Despite the allegations made against Manning in
the early 1990s with respect to his possessing a "secret social agenda," he
distanced himself from any attempt to utilize the legislative and administrative machinery of government to implement a Christian agenda based upon the laws of God.[63] Not only would such a coercive
approach turn many ordinary Canadians away from Christianity, it
would also further distance Christians from the actions of Jesus, who
was clearly a non-coercive figure: "I think that the greatest fear of most
secular people with respect to the religious person in politics is that
they will use the tools of the state to make laws that coerce people into
the religious person's positions. I have never advocated that because
Jesus never did, and God Himself doesn't use that kind of coercion."[64]

On a more practical level, Manning was convinced that the strategies of those social conservatives who sought to utilize the state in the
manner preferred by Ted Byfield, for instance, were doomed to fail:

To Ted [Byfield] and the more militant Christians who want to legislate people into righteousness, I argue that that doesn't work.
That is the lesson of the Old Testament. You have this 400-year-old
experiment of an attempt to achieve a just and righteous society by
the imposition of the rule of law, and to a degree far greater than
anything Ted or anyone else would ever advocate today. But the
conclusion of the latter-day prophets was that there are limits to

186 God's Province

law – that unless those laws can be written not on tablets of stone or in the statute books, but the tablets of the heart, internalized, true righteousness is not achievable.[65]

In fact, speaking to a group of politically active social conservatives after he retired from politics, Manning suggested that they "rely less on urging government interventions with respect to abortion, same-sex marriage, and euthanasia prevention and much more on proposing non-governmental initiatives to advance their causes."[66] Furthermore, he would note in a separate speech:

If the Christian community wants to be heard and influential on this issue in the public square ... our entry point ... should not be first and foremost the enunciation of a position – the usual starting point for most moralists and legalists.
  Rather our initial starting point should be to first identify with the suffering of those embroiled in the issue ...
  Is this not God's way? – Incarnation preceding proclamation – Jesus living and identifying with the suffering of humanity for thirty years before he ever gave the Sermon on the Mount with its moral principles and declarations.[67]

Such an outlook leads to Manning's alternative method of political involvement for Christians. Rather than pursuing the "coercive approach," Manning developed an approach based upon his deep faith in the actions of Jesus, which he dubbed "Working Christianly with Someone Else's Political Agenda." This method drew inspiration from biblical situations wherein followers of God were a minority living within pagan kingdoms but eventually managed to have a significant impact. Following the example of Jesus, who rejected the idea of pursuing a direct political agenda, "this approach leads Christians to play more of a servant role, and mediating role, in the political process, rather than an advocate or interest-group role."[68] Indeed, Manning continues elsewhere, "[t]he heart of practicing Christianity is the sacrifice of self-interest in the interest of reconciliation, unity, and the bringing into being of a new creation."[69] As Flanagan has rightly noted, it was upon this interpretation of the life of Christ – the ultimate example of self-sacrifice in the interests of reconciliation between God and humanity – that Manning modelled his approach to politics in general and his role as leader of the Reform Party in particular. In an interview with the author, he noted:

Religion and Political Thought in Contemporary Alberta 187

There is a sense in which the "reconciliation of conflicting interests" is what politics and government at its highest level is all
about. I was never in government so had no opportunity to practise
this approach to reconciliation from that position. But I did have
some opportunities to practise it to some extent in relation to
party politics.

The one occasion where I did try particularly to apply my Christian concept of reconciliation – and I think Tom [Flanagan] perceived this – was when we were trying to transform Reform into
the Canadian Alliance and build a bigger, broader tent ...

I really did believe that you couldn't be the mediator between
two groups alienated from each other like the Reformers and the
Progressive Conservatives without at least being willing to sacrifice
some of your own interests and position.[70]

It is a mistake, however, to assume that this was the only way in which
religion influenced Manning's politics. Despite Flanagan's suggestion
to the contrary, Manning's faith did impact his thinking on questions
related to both the role of the state and his conception of democracy,
although it did so in a more nuanced manner than most commentators
have understood. It is to these dimensions of his political thought that
we now turn.

MANNING'S RELIGIOUS PERSPECTIVE
AND HIS CONCEPTION OF THE STATE

In a landmark 1987 speech, Manning clearly articulated a political position that would largely form the backbone of Reform Party policy for
the next thirteen years.[71] Drawing from his interpretation of "the West's
Conservative heritage," Manning outlined four basic conservative principles to which the new party must commit itself:

1. Firstly, it would mean a new and deeper commitment to the
individual person and family as the primary units of Canadian
society ...
2. Secondly ... we are prepared to rely heavily on the exercise of responsible individual and corporate enterprise, and the operations
of the marketplace, as the primary engine for guiding economic development ...
3. Thirdly ... we view government as an institution whose primary
mission is to enable free and responsible individuals and organiza-

tions to pursue their own interests and aspirations within a framework of law, rather than governments telling individuals and organizations what to do, or doing for them what they ought to do for themselves, or imposing enormous financial and legal constraints on their activity. This means we would express a distinct preference for a modest and fiscally responsible government at the federal level ...

4. Finally ... while we uphold freedom of conscience for all citizens, we also acknowledge Canada's Judeo-Christian heritage and its value as a source of moral and ethical guidance ...

Thus, in rejecting any form of political collectivism that jeopardizes the primacy of the individual in society (or the family that sustains it) and in similarly relying upon a largely unregulated economic market and a scaled-back federal government, one that is not afraid to acknowledge Canada's religious heritage, Manning offered a vision of a "New Canada" that clearly moved away from the liberal-based secular welfare-state model of governance that had emerged in the post–World War II period. In fact, many commentators have suggested that a good deal of Reform's sudden electoral support was due to the general breakdown of consensus in developed countries around the welfare-state model in the face of mounting fiscal and social problems.[72] Yet, although decreasing confidence in the welfare-state model in the 1970s and 1980s may help to explain certain segments of Reform's electoral support, it is a mistake to assume that Manning's interest in reducing the size of government and freeing individuals and corporations in the marketplace was a product of this new wave of neo-liberal thought that was gaining followers in the intellectual and political circles of the United States, Britain, and Canada. Rather, as the first principle enunciated above suggests, his broad political principles were built first and foremost around the recognition and protection of the individual as the "primary unit of Canadian society," a point that highlights the central continuity of his political thinking with that of his father, stretching back to the 1940s, and is most clearly articulated as a "socially conservative" position in *Political Realignment*, a book Preston co-authored with Ernest in 1967.[73] And, just as it was for Ernest Manning, this primary commitment to the individual, as well as eventual support for a pro-market, small-government ideology, was derived at a fundamental level from Preston's Christian perspective.

Having concluded from his study of Chapter 17 of the Book of Acts that the purpose of the nation is to provide a context in which man seeks God, Manning noted that the apostle Paul

> presents God as the God of history and politics – he forms the nations, governs their history and their boundaries – with a purpose – "that they might seek God and find him" (17:22–3). Do our national institutions, ways of life, facilitate a seeking after the God of history and politics? What might do this? Freedom! Believers ought to be in the forefront of advocating, safeguarding freedoms ...
> A nation will be judged on the extent to which it fulfills God's purpose for it – the freedom it gives to seek (or not seek) God.[74]

Thus, reasoned Manning, if one accepts that the boundaries of nations were set by God, one could conclude that He understood nations to have a particular purpose and therefore a nation may be judged, in the end, "not just on its economic performance or political structure but did it serve some bigger, broader purpose ... did it honour the freedom that God seemed to value or did it not?"[75] This emphasis on freedom within the nation is tied directly to humanity's condition as determined by God. Men and women, Manning argued, have been equipped by God with certain reasoning capacities but

> [God] also seems to attach enormous value to their freedom to exercise it one way or the other, including negatively. I mean, He didn't create pre-programmed robots; He made human beings with reasoning capabilities and the freedom to exercise those capabilities. What I find awe-inspiring is the fact that He gave humans freedom even knowing that they would abuse it.

Thus, Manning continued,

> I think God values freedom because of the relationship it makes possible when people freely choose to follow Him.
> [Because] God himself seems to attach an inordinate value to freedom – evidenced by the fact that He gave people free will, including the freedom to reject him ... we too should attach a high value to personal freedom.[76]

190   God's Province

Individual freedom, in the same way it was for his father before him, is
therefore a foundational component of Manning's Christianity and
subsequently becomes the driving force of his politics. Indeed, freedom
becomes an absolute requirement within the nation, which, in Manning's view, has as its divine purpose the facilitation of humanity's
search for God. Thus, the central political question that emanates from
this view is, as Manning asked in his personal journal, "What laws, institutional arrangements, [or] public policies facilitate the seeking after
or not seeking after God?"[77] In answering this question, Manning was
adamant that there are strict limits to what the state can actually
achieve: "I don't think the institutions of the state are as well suited to
achieving positive goals as they are to constraining evil, including constraining restrictions on personal freedoms." This conclusion is related
in important ways to Manning's broader contention that, although "ex-
tremely important," government and politics "are not the ultimate an-
swers to human needs."[78] Indeed, echoing his father's contentions,
Manning noted in his personal journal that "God's Love for the world,
as displayed in Jesus, is the ultimate answer to suffering and pain" – a
belief that coincided with his broader reflections on the need for individual spiritual renewal on a mass scale if one hoped for a significantly reformed society.[79] And Manning, along with most conservative
Christians, was clear that no authority, be it church or state, can coerce
someone into accepting Christ by way of a spiritual conversion. This
can only occur through a personal decision by the individual to respond to the offer of salvation made to us by Christ. So what is the
state's role? Manning returned to the foundational concept of personal freedom:

> The state can facilitate spiritual transformation – at least the oppor-
> tunity for it to occur – by maintaining liberty, the freedom to
> choose. Even freedom to choose in the area of faith itself requires
> a political climate that facilitates or accommodates such freedom
> of choice ...
>   Thus, one of the biggest things a state can do is to make sure it
> itself is not a coercive force restricting people's liberty and to do all
> it can to create an environment where freedom of choice and per-
> sonal freedom of conscience is respected and protected.[80]

Just as it was for his father several decades earlier, it was at this point
that the connection between Manning's religiously inspired focus on
individual freedom and his distinct preference for a "modest and fis-

Religion and Political Thought in Contemporary Alberta   191

cally responsible government" came into view. Manning clearly reject-ed "the concept that Mother Government and universal social programs run by bureaucrats are the best and only way to care for the sick, the poor, the old, and the young."[81] This liberal welfare-state model, although obviously preferable to outright totalitarianism, was prob-lematic for Manning because it relied on a large interventionist gov-ernment that built barriers between individual citizens and the freedom to which they were entitled. Certainly, the Canadian welfare state that Manning railed against in the late 1980s and early 1990s was not overtly restricting the freedom to worship, but by imposing hefty personal taxes to fund a myriad of secular social programs that were administered by an army of secular bureaucrats, the Canadian state was placing undue restrictions on the individual and failing to offer com-passionate care to those in need. Not only would individuals be re-quired to work longer hours to earn the cash required to support their family because of high taxes, they would also often find themselves en-tangled in the cold and inefficient web of secular government bureau-cracy when accessing services. Furthermore, individuals would be targeted by government programs that sought to direct their behaviour in certain areas. Even more problematic, however, was the potential power and size of the secular state relative to the individual should the collectivist logic operating behind the welfare-state model be followed to its conclusion. As government services grow, the corresponding agency and responsibility of individuals, families, and even community-level organizations are eroded. To continue down such a path would not only further impede basic political and economic freedoms, it would also jeopardize the individual's ultimate freedom, that of reli-gious worship and expression. Of course, Manning also routinely men-tioned his contention that the free-market system was most suitable system for generating jobs and wealth for ordinary Canadians.[82] Yet his emphasis on overall individual freedom in the political and economic realms, together with the corresponding demand for a small govern-ment that respects freedom of conscience (identified in his 1987 polit-ical speech and eventually solidified within much of the Reform Party's policy platform), was derived directly from his Christian perspective. In fact, in addition to his broader concerns surrounding individual free-dom, Manning's preference for a largely unregulated economic market as the chief distributer of resources as opposed to a state-led socialistic system had even more precise biblical roots. The biblical view of human nature, Manning suggested, is accurate in that it recognizes the human disposition towards evil and greed. More interesting, however, is the

192   God's Province

fact that the Bible "doesn't denounce self-interest outright but rather tries to turn it into good." Manning continued:

For example, the old Jewish law about loving your neighbour could have stopped right there – "Love your neighbour. Period." But it doesn't. It says: "Love your neighbour as yourself." There's some sense in which appreciation of your own self-interest is necessary to know what it is you can do and should do for others. And the same principle is found in Jesus' Sermon on the Mount ... He said "Do unto others as you would have them do unto you." There's a subordinate clause, which follows the altruistic clause, which is tied to self-interest. Again the implication is that unless you have an appreciation of your own self-interest, you won't be able to understand the interests of others and therefore be able to respect and serve them.[83]

It is the capitalist rather than the socialistic economic system that allows people the freedom to both follow their self-interest, a desire inherent in our natures, and to follow or reject the teachings of Christ which compel us to overcome extreme selfishness and act charitably towards others. Manning returns to the Book of Acts to provide an early example of the dangers a community faces should it fail to take the presence of human self-interest seriously. Chapter 2 of Acts depicts an early group of Christians living in a socialistic arrangement wherein an attempt was made to hold all possessions in common and provide to anyone as he had need. However, this community failed to account for self-interest and quickly broke down. Manning notes:

The principle of "from each according to his ability" was almost immediately violated by Ananias and Sapphira (Acts 5:1–11) who sold a piece of land ostensibly to support the church but withheld a portion of the revenues for themselves. And the principle of "to each according to his needs" began to break down (Acts 6:1) when the Gentile widows claimed they were receiving less charity than their Jewish counterparts. Ananias and Sapphira paid with their lives for the violation of the principle "from each according to his ability" – that's the degree of coercion (the death penalty) that you would have to have to fully enforce that principle.[84]

Of course, even a cursory glance through the Gospels of the New Testament clearly demonstrates that God wants humanity to act charitably

Religion and Political Thought in Contemporary Alberta   193

towards those in need, but, Manning argued, such behaviour will only happen consistently if the individual freely chooses to follow this command. Only the freedom inherent in a market economy allows for this choice. Forced charity, or social justice, within a strongly regulated market is bound to entail immense impediments on the freedom of the individual, as was the case in the story recounted above from the Book of Acts. Any potential gains in terms of addressing pressing social inequalities by way of socialism are simply not worth the steep decline in personal liberty experienced by citizens. The nation's purpose is to safeguard the freedoms citizens require in order to choose to follow or reject God. Poverty is a very real problem from a Christian perspective, but any meaningful solution must grow from voluntary charity on the part of individuals, individuals who have chosen to build a relationship with God and therefore freely follow the commands of Jesus to act honestly and with compassion and service towards the needy. This Christian-based behaviour represents the height of what Manning, in his 1987 speech, labelled "the exercise of responsible individual and corporate enterprise." We should always, added Manning, "stress the importance of accepting responsibility whenever we talk about the importance of freedom itself."[85] However, a policy advocating that the state should step in to enforce this responsibility, beyond some general laws that protect citizens from particularly heinous acts, is bound to fail and is contrary to God's wishes for a free nation.

This did not mean that Manning was outright opposed to all government services, much to the chagrin of stern neo-conservative Tom Flanagan. In fact, in noting that Manning showed little interest in academic "neo-conservatism," that he failed to exhibit strong policy preferences with respect to common conservative issues like the crown or the military, and that he dared propose both clear pro-market/anti-statist initiatives *and* plans for government-led programs that would fund various scientific research, assist with job retraining, and encourage "green" industry, Flanagan concludes that Manning was an "eclectic" thinker akin to American Democrat Bill Clinton rather than an authentic conservative.[86] Indeed, Manning did call for certain government initiatives to ensure that those most in need would be taken care of, and he did favour certain regulations that could help prevent some of the negative environmental consequences of economic activity.[87] Yet to imply that Manning's thought was somewhat eclectic is to misunderstand the philosophical foundations from which this thought grew.

Manning worked from a particular Christian perspective rather than from a neo-conservative intellectual foundation. The protection of in-

194   God's Province

dividual liberty through reductions to government services and the encouragement of less regulated market activity were of immense importance to him, but the embrace of such public policy could not overlook the Christian-based responsibilities that followers had for their fellows or even the natural environment. Speaking specifically to the issue of environmental protection Manning noted:

> Our faith teaches us that God supremely values relationships – our relationship to Him, our relationships with each other, and our relationship to His creation – the Biblical word for what others may call nature or the environment.
>
> There is such a thing as the Christian concept of Environmental Stewardship – that we are called to care for the environment, not only as an obligation to ourselves and our children, but as an obligation to God.[88]

Yet in the same address Manning was careful to stress the importance of the voluntary role to be played by individuals as opposed to a reliance solely upon government-led regulations. In fact, he urged his Christian audience to practise environmental stewardship in their own lives and, once this action earns them the credibility to speak on the issue publicly, to focus on the "demand side" of the problem:

> [We must focus] on reducing in absolute terms the insatiable appetite, the "greed" of modern consumers and societies for more of everything and the pressure that such demands put on all the ecosystems. Is this not a task that the Christian community should focus on – by both example and advocacy – our faith long ago identifying greed as one of the most deadly of sins?[89]

Similarly with respect to all charitable activity, the ideal solution would rely solely on voluntary organizations motivated by Christian principles, but in the conditions Manning found himself in (a secular world that had largely turned its back on God), the requirement to "be thy brother's keeper" demanded a place for certain state-led programs.[90] The trick, however, was to limit such activity as much as possible and certainly not to let it grow to a level that severely limited the individual's liberty by way of burdensome taxes and excessive restrictions. Whether or not a primary reliance on voluntary organizations, in conjunction with a few government regulations on an otherwise unregulated market economy, could really have much of an impact on environmental protection or poverty alleviation is, of course, debatable, but this was the logic behind Manning's "eclectic" political thought nonetheless.

MANNING'S RELIGIOUS PERSPECTIVE
AND HIS DEDICATION TO DEMOCRACY

Overall, Manning's political thinking with respect to the purpose of the state and its corresponding relationship to the free market derived from his Christian perspective and was translated into the more general "anti–big government" and "pro-free-market" stance that subsequently formed much of Reform's policy backbone. However, it is important to recognize that his thought was translated into policy not simply because it was favoured by Manning, but also because Manning perceived this type of policy to represent the wishes of the majority of western Canadians.[91] In fact, Flanagan bases his contention that Manning's political thought was not strongly influenced by his religious beliefs on his observation that, at a foundational level, Manning's ultimate goal was not the promotion of small government/pro-market policy but rather the introduction of democratic reforms that would ensure the political demands of the majority of citizens were respected and acted upon.[92] This coincides with Manning's admission that he was largely driven by his "personal conviction that there is a need to restore 'the common sense of the common people' to a more central position in federal politics," a desire that resulted in the continual demand for the implementation of a number of mechanisms designed to enhance direct democracy.[93]

Admittedly, this desire for a more representative democratic system that gives more political weight to the views of a potentially secular majority than to the particular policy positions developed by Manning in accordance with his Christian views seems counterintuitive. Yet Manning's overall approach to politics clearly rejected any attempt to impose public policy based upon Christian values on others. Of course, this emphasis on democracy is most certainly related to Manning's broader understanding of individual freedom as the highest goal of political action. In what other political system are individuals more free than in the most democratic? Indeed, in a journal entry in 1997, Manning confided that he viewed the growing call for democracy around the world as the "work of God."[94]

Manning, following his father, drew additional inspiration with respect to the value of the common will of a potentially secular citizen-

196 God's Province

ry from the Old Testament's Book of 1 Samuel.[95] This was the historical account of ancient Israel's response to God's initial commandment
that they were not to follow the lead of neighbouring nations that had
kings but were to be governed solely by God. However, Israelites began
clamouring for a king of their own, and Samuel, their spiritual leader,
was forced to ask God for a king despite his own view that the people
were acting wrongly in making this demand. Upon hearing this request, God instructed Samuel to "protest solemnly unto them [the citizens of Israel], and shew [sic] them the manner of the king that shall
reign over them." Samuel subsequently delivered a lengthy speech to
the people of Israel, listing the many ways in which a king would abuse
them, but to no avail. The Israelites maintained their wish for a king,
and God complied and ended His divine reign over them. Preston took
from this account three lessons for Christians who find themselves in
political office: first, such individuals should pray for God's counsel as
Samuel did; second, they should "protest solemnly unto the electorate
and endeavour to show them where their demands may eventually
lead" should they desire something contrary to the will of God; and, finally, they should be prepared to accept the demands of the masses but
also to interpret the masses' decision as a rejection of God rather than
a rejection of their political leadership.[96] Both Ernest and Preston Manning followed these lessons in their political lives, and so long as they
possessed the opportunity to explain why certain public policies were
unwise, they were prepared to accept the will of the majority despite the
knowledge that such an action could be against the will of God. Again,
the freedom to reject God is paramount.

Perhaps most interestingly, the method of ruling described in 1
Samuel was the precise approach Manning devised for Reform MPs (including himself) who were faced with a vote on a contentious moral
issue wherein their own personal views might differ from the will of
their constituents. Rather than instructing MPs to vote their conscience
on contentious issues, Manning told them to make their preferences
known to their constituents, to engage constituents in debate with the
hope of demonstrating why the MPs' view was more appropriate than
the other option, but, in the end, to vote in accordance with the wishes of the majority:

I used to tell the people of Calgary Southwest that if they had a position – even on moral issues – and it could be clearly determined
that it was the position of the majority, I would reluctantly represent it in the House of Commons with my vote. I wouldn't be able

Religion and Political Thought in Contemporary Alberta   197

to argue for it, because I wouldn't believe it to be right. But I could and would vote for it.

Of course, I would get a lot of flack on this position from Christian people. They would say "you should be exercising leadership on these moral issues ..." I would reply that my idea of democratic leadership was to employ all my leadership skills to try to change my constituents' views, but not to vote against them if I could not do so.[97]

In other words, the decisions made by a majority may be wrong in the eyes of God but such a method ensures an element of transparency: it will be the majority of citizens rather than the individual politician who will be held morally accountable, just as the Israelites, not Samuel, were held accountable by God. Thus, the democratic will of the majority, regardless of the wisdom inherent in their position, was to prevail over Manning's or his MPs' own preferences in the political realm.[98]

Yet, as the quote above regarding his desire to "restore 'the common sense of the common people' to a more central position in federal politics" attests, Manning was not simply a democrat. He was a radical democrat who believed in the moral and intellectual capacities of the ordinary citizen and sought to bring the demands of such "common people" to bear on a political system. This demanded a party structure that welcomed and engaged ordinary grassroots citizens in a series of open meetings wherein their judgments could be heard and incorporated into the very policy proposals that would eventually be put to a vote. Despite the strong influence that Manning's Christian faith had on so much of his thinking with respect to engaging in politics and developing particular public policy, he noted that his appreciation of the "common sense of the common people" and the righteousness of populist movements that were built on this sentiment came "first and foremost from my study of western Canadian political history and from my father's long involvement in one such movement."[99]

Of course, he was correct to point to the decidedly populist nature of western Canada's political history, and it is not a stretch to suggest that a politically aware individual growing up in the midst of this culture, especially as the son of Alberta's premier, would tend towards a favourable impression of "the common sense of the common people" and the corresponding argument that this "common sense" should carry significant political weight. Yet even this argument for populist politics – one based on political culture rather than explicit religious interpretation – has a religious dimension to it. As discussed in more detail in previous chapters, given the strong influence that the American evangelical Protestant strain had on the political thought of Henry Wise Wood, William Aberhart, and Ernest Manning, not to mention the broader religious and political culture of the province in the first half of the twentieth century, it is easy to see how the individualistic and anti-establishmentarian populist sentiment inherent in this religious tradition was transposed onto the early Alberta political scene. Yet, even though Manning seems to have been unaware of this connection between the American evangelical Protestantism tradition and the populist sentiment in early Alberta politics, there is no doubt that his reading of the life of Jesus strongly reinforced his belief in the righteousness of populism. The ministry of Jesus was clearly built around the common people rather than around the spiritual and political elite. However, Jesus was not simply taking advantage of those most easily manipulated. Manning noted:

[Jesus] respected the capacities of ordinary people – some of His most profound statements, like in John 4 about "God is a spirit," were made to humble ordinary people like that Samaritan woman at the well. He must have believed, not only that she could understand what he was talking about, but also that she could act on it and communicate it to others.[100]

In a series of personal journal entries in the fall of 1996, Manning further noted the various ways in which the actions of Jesus recorded in the Book of Matthew reinforce a populist approach to democratic politics. Jesus showed compassion for the physical and spiritual needs of the ordinary people, He believed them to be more receptive to spiritual truths than elites, and He responded to them emotionally rather than intellectually so as to truly meet their needs. Yet Jesus also condemned the people for living wicked and godless lives, although, Manning noted, He actually blamed the spiritual and political leaders of the people for leading them down this sinful path. In placing blame on the elites, Jesus provided the people with an assessment and condemnation of their leaders.[101] Such reflections on the part of Manning point to the parallels he perceived between the actions of Jesus in relation to the common people, to whom He hoped to deliver spiritual salvation, and Manning's favoured populist approach to federal politics, which was meant to deliver democratic justice to the masses. In fact, Manning followed his reflections on the populist nature of the actions of Jesus with a message of condemnation aimed at the political elites,

Religion and Political Thought in Contemporary Alberta   199

a message inspired by the language Jesus used when addressing the spiritual leaders of His time:

By your preoccupation with partisan interests and your excessive discipline you have stifled the voice of the people and subverted the public interest.

... because you have banished the spirit and the will of the people from your deliberations, the people have forsaken you.

Because you have taken this House of the People, and turned it into the House of the Parties, because you have subjected the will of the voters to the will of the whips, because you have turned this temple of democracy into a den of patronage and partisanship, the will and spirit of the people has departed this place.

And it will be so, until enough Reformers are elected to restore the spirit of democracy to this place.[102]

Despite this parallel, however, Manning never wavered from his broader contention: politics could never deliver the spiritual salvation that humanity ultimately desires. This was available only by way of a personal relationship with God made possible by the sacrifice of Christ. Thus, he approached politics in precisely the same way both his father and Aberhart had done before him – instrumentally. The overarching purpose of the nation was simply the facilitation of the individual's freedom to pursue this spiritual relationship. Manning, like his father, understood limited government and a free economic market as the best way to ensure such freedom, and they each favoured particular political policies accordingly. However, to impose such policies on an unwilling public would be self-defeating. The citizenry might require instruction from time to time, as the common people did from Jesus, but ultimately, it was their freedom to choose the appropriate policies that mattered. Thus, despite making extensive mental effort devising political positions that ensured individual freedom, Manning had little choice but to allow grassroots citizens the opportunity to be the final arbiters after he presented his political vision. This must have been a difficult position to accept at times, and as Flanagan has argued, Manning was not always able to overcome his personal preferences when policy decisions were made, but this was the logic behind Manning's emphasis on democracy in general and populism in particular.[103] This logic,

200   God's Province

like his general pro-market, anti-state ideology, was derived largely from
his religious perspective. To overlook this is to misunderstand a great
deal of Manning's political thought.

CONCLUSION:
THE POLITICAL THOUGHT OF MANNING AND
THE TRAJECTORY OF CONTEMPORARY ALBERTA POLITICS

Between 1971 and 1985, Alberta PC premier Peter Lougheed largely
abandoned Social Credit's long-running laissez-faire approach towards
economic development and utilized the province's substantial oil and
natural gas royalties to pursue an aggressive strategy of government-led
economic diversification that required extensive infrastructure im-
provements and state resources to assist Alberta-based businesses.[104]
However, the implementation of the National Energy Program (NEP) in
1980, combined with a worldwide oil price bust in the mid-1980s, dramatically changed the fiscal picture in Alberta. Despite a variety of
measures implemented by Lougheed's successor, Don Getty, major Alberta businesses subsequently began to crumble and the government's
deficit ballooned. Consequently, confidence in the "state-led" economic strategy quickly eroded and, under new premier Ralph Klein in the
early 1990s, a more blatant "pro-market" sentiment began to re-emerge,
ultimately pushing the PCs to embrace a neo-liberal economic agenda,
complete with a significant reduction in government expenditures.[105]
Yet, in a remarkable testament to the popularity of this fiscally conservative approach, the PCs were able to maintain, and perhaps even enhance, their support among the electorate after unleashing a painful
round of cuts.[106]

The less than rosy economic situation Alberta suddenly found itself
in during the mid- and late 1980s had a significant impact on the public's appetite for smaller government and state interference in the market. Indeed, the opposition Liberals led by Laurence Decore essentially
outflanked the PCs on the right in the early 1990s by campaigning on
the promise to rectify the fiscal mismanagement of the government
and to address the province's rapidly rising debt by way of significant
spending cuts should they be elected. In a testament to the popularity of this view at the time, the Liberals temporarily soared ahead
of the PCs in the polls. However, Ralph Klein's accession to the leadership of the PCs (1992) and subsequent provincial election as premier
(1993), largely by following Decore's lead by promising drastic spending cuts, would ultimately undermine the Liberals' electoral hopes. In

Religion and Political Thought in Contemporary Alberta   201

addition to the pressure applied by Decore and the Liberals, the anxiety around public deficits in Alberta was encouraged, especially in elite academic and business circles, by the neo-liberal economic arguments emanating out of the Reagan and Thatcher governments of America and Britain respectively.

However, for the grassroots Albertans who embraced government frugality in the early 1990s, it was often the arguments made by the soft-spoken orator with the familiar last name that most influenced their way of thinking. As David Taras and Allan Tupper have argued, it is difficult to overstate the important role played by Manning's Reform Party in shaping the public mood in the province and subsequently capturing the attention of provincial PC MLAs.[107] Similarly, Jared Wesley has noted the impact on the mood of Alberta citizens of the significant "redefinition of Western Canadian conservatism" orchestrated by the emerging Reform Party in the late 1980s that took direct aim at the Red Tory vision of conservatism open to significant state interventions that had guided the Lougheed administration.[108] In fact, the PCs were beginning to fear the potential for a provincial wing of the Reform Party that, according to polls at the time, would have easily defeated them in the early 1990s had it existed.[109] As it turned out, a provincial Reform Party was not created, but it is important to note that a strong contingent of Alberta's Reform members voted in the provincial PCs 1992 leadership contest and, it is assumed, strongly supported the candidacy of the anti-statist Klein over that of his chief opponent, Nancy Betkowski, a long-time cabinet minister who seemed more comfortable with the state intervention–friendly Red Toryism of Lougheed.[110] Clearly, the causal forces behind the PCs' policy shifts were more nuanced than the above brief description allows. It remains, however, that as the Alberta economy waned and the provincial deficit grew, Reform's initial crusade against high taxes and government spending, led most forcefully by Manning, became awfully appealing to working-class Albertans. Loudly encouraged by the wealthy business class based largely in Calgary, Klein won the PC leadership and his government subsequently responded with a program of deep cutbacks aimed at substantially reducing the size and scope of the provincial government. In other words, Reform played a significant role in the articulation and re-popularization of a strong pro-market, anti-state sentiment that had long been part of Alberta's dominant political rhetoric but had gone somewhat dormant during the 1970s oil boom and the subsequent explosion of state expenditures under the premiership of Lougheed. This is not so say that Preston Manning was as influential on Alberta's long-term political trajectory as leaders such as Wood, Aberhart, or Ernest Manning. However, he and his party did intervene at a critical juncture in contemporary Alberta's political history, and it is undeniable that he played a role in the province's sharp turn right in the 1990s. And as has been demonstrated above, Reform's fiscally conservative message owed much to the political thought of Manning, who, in turn, drew from a familiar religious foundation.

Despite emphasizing the relational principles of reconciliation and self-sacrifice rather than the dispensationalism and "end of days" biblical prophecy of Aberhart and Ernest Manning, Preston Manning's Christianity was largely a continuation of their premillennial interpretation. Society's ills were the result of humanity's distance from God and only by way of an individual effort on each of our parts to seek spiritual renewal and build our relationship with Him could we rectify the pain in our personal and social lives. The chief product of this individual renewal with God, or "rebirth," would be a new-found love for others and a desire to bring this love to bear in the various spheres of life within which one operates. However, the notion that society could be perfected was fantasy, for it was inconceivable that all people would actually seek a spiritual rebirth. Societal perfection would come from God alone. Thus, the divine purpose of the state was not to seek a perfected society but rather to ensure that individuals were free and thus granted the potential to seek out God without undue restriction. This obviously led Manning to stress the right to religious freedom, but as with his father, this emphasis on individual freedom also carried with it a strong aversion to economic collectivism and excessive state interference in the lives of its citizens. The result was a clear commitment in the late 1980s and early 1990s to the market economy and a less active state, a stance that would ultimately help reposition the Alberta electorate away from Lougheed's state-led model and towards the program of state reduction embraced by Klein and the governing PCs.

Beyond this demand that the state's size and scope be reduced was Manning's fundamental commitment to democracy in general and populism in particular. Both the Christian-based commitment to the freedom of individuals, including the freedom of citizens to make poor political choices, and the broader anti-establishmentarianism inherent in the American evangelical Protestant tradition that, by way of his father, he was groomed in lie behind Manning's thinking with respect to democracy and populism. Similarly, this Christian-based preference for democracy also lies behind his rejection of the notion that the state ought to impose traditional Christian morality upon its citizens, a stand

Religion and Political Thought in Contemporary Alberta   203

that clearly distinguished his thought from that of Ted Byfield and other social conservatives active in Alberta in the late 1980s and early 1990s. Manning's conservative Christian background ensured that he most likely agreed with Byfield that abortion and same-sex marriage were contrary to God's moral laws, but his overall commitment to democracy, derived from his broader conception of the divine role of the state as being the guarantor of individual freedom, meant that imposing Christian morality on its citizens was of greater harm.

Beyond this general commitment to democracy, however, was Manning's oft-cited desire to increase and enhance the avenues available for direct citizen participation in the democratic process. Indeed, his continual calls for the implementation of populist mechanisms, such as citizen initiatives, nation-wide referenda, and the ability to "recall" MPs, placed him well outside the distinctly anti-participatory conception of populist democracy adhered to by William Aberhart and Ernest Manning, who defined democracy as "people expressing a general will for general results and leaving experts to work out the details."[111] As discussed in Chapter 4, this amounted to a model of benevolent technocracy that sought to ascertain the people's will but was devoid of the type of meaningful citizen involvement stressed by the UFA in the 1920s and 1930s. Preston Manning, for his part, completely disavowed the notion, implicit in Social Credit's view of democracy, that ordinary citizens were incapable of making vital political decisions. Instead, Manning argued that so long as they were provided the proper information, society would be better off if the "people" rather than the "elites" were charting its political course.[112] More importantly, Manning understood the exercise of political freedom through active political participation as a necessary requirement to maintain political freedom itself, a view that clearly differed from the implicit suspicion of political participation that one finds in the strong premillennial perspective of William Aberhart and Ernest Manning, discussed in Chapter 4.[113] Thus, whereas Henry Wise Wood encouraged participatory and deliberative populist politics in part because such activity was required to bring about the kingdom of God on earth, and Aberhart and Ernest Manning placed less emphasis on such participation as they distanced themselves from any notion that humanity could, in fact, build a kingdom of God on earth, Preston Manning reaffirmed the importance of political participation because, ultimately, he understood such action as mandatory if one hoped to ensure that individual freedom was to be protected from a potentially oppressive state. In other words, Manning's interest in participatory politics is rooted, paradoxically, in a foundational anti-statism that itself is derived from his insistence that God wants individuals to be free. This was an important point of contention between Aberhart and Ernest Manning on the one hand and Preston Manning on the other, who together shared both a certain Christian-based anti-statism and a strong commitment to democracy, yet differed with respect to the value they placed on political participation. However, it is worth raising a certain qualification here. Yes, Preston was more outwardly committed to participatory democracy than Ernest was, but as mentioned above, Preston did seem to simultaneously emphasize the role that experts should play with respect to providing "proper information" to citizens prior to their involvement. In fact, one needs only to recall his Christian-based approach to handling situations wherein the populist politician's constituents feel differently on any given issue. His advice to Reform politicians in such situations was essentially to engage the people and attempt to explain why they were "wrong" but, ultimately, to vote in the House of Commons according to their wishes. It is difficult to pursue this potential conflict further without completing additional research on this point, but suffice it to say, Preston's belief in the capacity of ordinary people might not have been quite so distant from the conception inherent in Social Credit's more blatant anti-participatory approach as is often assumed. In fact, pursuing the relationship between these two conceptions of democracy from a different angle, David Laycock has argued that the strong anti-statist/pro-market message inherent in Manning's political thought and in the platform of Reform amounted to an indirect commitment to significantly contract the parameters of democratic life in a way that shadowed that found in Social Credit.

It is undeniable that Manning was motivated by a genuine desire to increase the political influence of grassroots citizens, and early Reform membership conventions did include vigorous participation from "common people" that well surpassed levels of meaningful participation found in Alberta Social Credit study groups, but his strong opposition to an active state and the "special interest" groups that fed off its public subsidies inadvertently committed Reform to a "plebiscitarian" conception of populist democracy akin to the one adhered to more explicitly by Aberhart and Ernest Manning. This conception, argues Laycock, holds that

[the] mediation of citizens' policy preferences through deliberation in and among traditional political parties and organized interests

harms the body politic because such processes are too easily captured by a closed circle of "special interests" and their benefactors. The only way to avoid such harm is to minimize the influence of the institutional players in the policy process by maximizing the number and impact of detours around them. On this view, direct democracy is a construction kit for detours around policy intersections that have been clogged and polluted by parties and organized interests.[114]

For Laycock, this conception of democracy rests on the assumption that the common people are essentially in agreement on general political matters and that it is traditional political parties or other organized special interests that sow confusion and division among the public. Importantly, given the strong anti-state, pro-market stance taken by both Manning and the larger Reform Party, special interests in their case were defined as groups "that support the welfare state, oppose major tax cuts, and propose that social resources should be allocated on the basis on non-market principles."[115] The solution, therefore, was to construct direct connections between the "people" and the "results" they seek (ultimately "freedom" according to Manning's world view) by curtailing any potential distortion of the people's preferences by intermediary political institutions that placed non-market-based impediments between individuals and freedom. The result is a genuine emphasis on "direct democracy" mechanisms such as recall, initiative, and referendum, which attempt to ascertain the people's preferences and bring them to bear on national policy debates, but in a way that bypasses "the social processes and political institutions that serve to moderate individual interests in light of community needs" and instead treat citizens as "political consumers who simply need to register privately formed preferences on a pre-established set of choices."[116] This plebiscitarian democratic outcome is the logical result of the anti-statism inherent in Reform, a view Laycock summarizes as follows:

Fundamentally, politicians and public life deserve our disdain because it is wrong to seek public, political solutions to problems that are essentially private. Instead of encouraging meaningful participation in deliberative, educational, and pluralistic political encounters, therefore, the new right undermines such democratic activity on the grounds that it may lead to state involvement in the effort to address collective problems. In order to reduce the role of the state in such efforts, new right politicians must translate the collective problems that animate such public gatherings into private challenges that self-sufficient individuals can tackle with the assistance of family and, at most, voluntary charity.[117]

There is something insightful in Laycock's analysis, but like most commentators on Reform, he largely misses the religious argument that underlies the anti-statist and fiscally conservative stance of Manning. Thus, like his prior analysis of the particular styles of populist democracy advocated by both Henry Wise Wood and William Aberhart, Laycock misses the vital religious dimension that underlies certain aspects of each of these distinct approaches to political participation. Of course, the religious reasoning behind Preston Manning's antipathy towards an active state and the special interests that fed off it was not widely shared by contemporary advocates of new right economics in Alberta, but their shared aversion to state-led economic collectivism ensured that a plebiscitarian form of democracy was central to the platform of Reform, despite a very real effort by Manning to implement a variety of mechanisms aimed at increasing the number of avenues of meaningful participation open to ordinary citizens.

Interestingly, the Alberta PC party under Klein would follow Manning's lead in this regard and similarly commit itself to this somewhat paradoxical apolitical yet populist approach to politics one finds in both the Alberta Social Credit and the Alberta-based Reform Party. Largely responding to Manning's insistence that governments implement mechanisms capable of restoring "the common sense of the common people" to its rightful place atop political structures, Klein embarked on a campaign to ensure that the demands of "ordinary Albertans" were adhered to.[118] In fact, recall that one of the central reasons social conservatism erupted in the way it did within the PC caucus was due to Klein's decision to allow free votes by PC MLAs, many of whom felt compelled to take social conservative positions owing to pressure from their constituents. Yet, as Gordon Laxer has noted, the precise neoliberal or anti-statist principles that guided Reform's broader approach to policy similarly appeared in the PCs:

In Klein's Alberta ... the public sphere is discredited. It is viewed as bloated, inefficient, and staffed by public employees holding on to their vested interests. By contrast, the marketplace is portrayed as the purveyor of all that is good. It's efficient, competitive, and teaches people tough love: how to be self-reliant. The marketplace removes the "privileges" of "special interest groups" who (it is im-

Religion and Political Thought in Contemporary Alberta   207

plied) are parasitically living off those who are "doers" in the private sector. These assumptions underlie an attempt to reverse the 1960s and 1970s expansion of what constituted the public sphere.[119]

Of course, this attack on the public sphere was a direct result of the ideological orientation of many in the PC party, which has little to do with religious interpretation or their particular understanding of democracy. However, it is worth noting that the implication of this ideological orientation, as Laycock notes with regard to Manning and the Reform Party, is a commitment to a form of democracy that is suspicious of meaningful debate and deliberation in traditional associations within the public sphere. Indeed, this approach seems to fit nicely with the broader non-deliberative or apolitical form of plebiscitarian populism that has dominated Alberta since the days of Aberhart and the early Social Credit party. Although religious interpretation seems to have little to do with the contemporary PC party's adherence to this approach to democratic politics, it is important to recall that this version of populism replaced the more participatory style advocated by Wood and the UFA. Just as Wood's version of postmillennial Christianity demanded such participation on the part of citizens, Aberhart's premillennial Christianity sought to reduce the demands the state placed on citizens, including the demand to participate in a way that went beyond simply voting. As the above quote demonstrates, a strong suspicion of "the public sphere" still exists in Alberta and this sentiment can be partly traced back to the religious-based anti-statism of Aberhart that was carried into contemporary Alberta through the thought of Ernest, and then Preston, Manning.

More broadly, Preston Manning's intense commitment to both populism and an unregulated economic market spoke to his adherence to the same "populist conservative" sentiment that had been previously established in Alberta by the long rule of both the UFA and Social Credit, two parties that inherited the unique tensions between conservative and radical tendencies from the American evangelical Protestant tradition. Indeed, Reform's platform, which demanded increased mechanisms for direct democracy, an end to government interference in the market, and a return to "common sense" approaches to law and order (with a tinge of religious-based social conservatism at its foundation from Byfield and his followers), represented a blatant populist conservative message. At its base was Manning's radical, Christian-based belief in the supreme value of ordinary individuals, including their moral and intellectual capacity, and a subsequent commitment to ensuring that their liberty was protected. This sentiment, which went well beyond the parameters of Tory conservative thought, stood behind Manning's pro-market, anti-statist sentiment, which informed much of Reform's economic policy platform as well as his commitment to democracy in general. Yet Reform's promise to protect the personal liberty of citizens in the marketplace was accompanied by the simultaneous demand that citizens behave responsibly in both the market and their general private lives. An explicit demand was obviously made by Byfield and members of the socially conservative wing of the party, who insisted that individuals should follow the moral laws of God. A more implicit though probably more significant demand for individuals to "behave properly" was the by-product of Manning's desire to reduce the size and scope of the state. In calling for a significant cut to government services, Reform issued a largely unspoken call for individual citizens to embrace the principles of individual responsibility and self-help rather than continue to rely on the state.

It is here that the paradox inherent in the Christian-based populist commitment to individual freedom is made apparent. Wood, Aberhart, and both Ernest and Preston Manning had incredible faith in the mental and moral capacity of individuals, yet it is precisely because individuals possess such capacities that they are expected to utilize them and thus act in an intelligent, moral, and responsible way. Citizens should be permitted a reasonable amount of freedom to pursue their ends, but if they fail to act "properly," the state, given its reduced size and scope, will no longer be there to provide much in terms of support. There is, therefore, a unique tension here between a radical populist celebration of the capacities of individuals and their subsequent right to be free and the corresponding conservative demand that this freedom be utilized in a particular way, either explicitly by following the moral laws of God or implicitly by acting responsibly in the marketplace and thus avoiding poverty and destitution. Indeed, when thinking about this paradox in the Christian-based political thought of Manning, one is again reminded of Phillip Hammond's point that the long tradition of American evangelical Protestantism had "saturated America with the idea that people should be free to do pretty much as they like, as long as they look out for themselves ... and, of course, behave."[120] Given the strong influence this same evangelical Protestant tradition had on the elite strands of political thought within Alberta, it should come as no surprise that the province's dominant political par-

Religion and Political Thought in Contemporary Alberta

ties seem to be guided to a degree by this precise tension identified by Hammond as well.

In fact, the notion of enhancing the economic freedom of individuals while simultaneously demanding a certain type of behaviour from citizens was at the heart of the drastic cuts to government expenditures made by Klein's PCs in the early 1990s. As Claude Denis has argued, this embrace of new-right economic policy was accompanied in Alberta by a largely unspoken attempt to regulate the population morally by instilling the values of self-help and self-discipline in the population, "admonishing individuals and communities to become responsible and independent, [and] castigating as un-Albertan whoever is not inclined or able to join the crusade."[121] Of course, it was largely secular fiscal conservatives in the PC cabinet who directed the revival of this general anti-statist, pro-market sentiment. In fact, much has been made by academics and journalists with respect to Alberta's adoption of a secular "new right" approach to the size and scope of government in 1993 that mirrored the neo-liberal economic policies of Margaret Thatcher in Britain and Ronald Reagan in the United States.[122] However, the revival of this general anti-statist, pro-market sentiment in Alberta by the Klein PCs had stronger roots in the province's traditional aversion to economic collectivism in general and Preston Manning's well-received demands for fiscally conservative policies in particular. Indeed, as a number of scholars have observed, the sudden rise of the Reform party in the late 1980s and early 1990s did much to shape the public mood in the province in a fiscally conservative manner. And, as I have argued throughout this chapter, Manning's call for a fiscally conservative and democratically enhanced state was derived squarely from a religious perspective that he largely shared with his father and William Aberhart.

In fact, when thinking about the long-running emphasis on populist politics and the rejection of economic collectivism in Alberta, stretching all the way back to Henry Wise Wood and the UFA's initial refusal to embrace the socialism advocated by the radical Prairie "social gospel" crowd, it is quite significant to note that a certain religious interpretation has undergirded this populist, pro-market sentiment from Wood, through the thought of Aberhart and Ernest Manning, and into the thinking of Preston Manning in contemporary Alberta. This is a vital point of continuity that binds together the political thought of four influential politicians from distinct points in Alberta's political history and sheds significant new light on the long-standing commitment to populist democracy as well as its aversion to government regulation in the marketplace by the province's dominant political parties. Thus, it is here, in this unique religiously-based distaste for state-led economic collectivism found in the thought of Wood, Aberhart and the Mannings, rather than in the oft-mentioned social conservatism of the 1990s and early 2000s, that one finds religion's most important and longest running source of influence on the political trajectory of Alberta. Of course, this is not to suggest that Preston Manning's political legacy can be witnessed as having solely, or even primarily, influenced the path of Alberta politics. Rather, it is clear that he has had a significant impact on the federal stage, especially given the makeup, ideological orientation, and return to power of the federal Conservative Party of Canada in 2006. In fact, Manning's influence on the federal Conservatives represents an important and interesting link between a religiously based individualistic or populist conservatism that first emerged in Alberta by way of political thought of Wood, was amplified in the thought and action of Aberhart and Ernest Manning, and now to exists as one of the key pillars atop which the current incarnation of the federal Conservative party now sits. Yet, however interesting this connection is, we should not allow ourselves to overlook the manner by which is has shaped contemporary Alberta politics as well, despite the fact that it is one of Canada's most secular provinces.

6

Conclusion

In the midst of the 2012 Alberta provincial election campaign, a blog post authored by Wildrose Party candidate and rural Alberta Christian pastor Allan Hunsperger emerged suggesting that homosexuals would "suffer the rest of eternity in the lake of fire." Despite holding a reputation as socially conservative, the majority of Albertans seemed repulsed by such a sentiment, and it is now widely held that this reaction played a significant role in the eventual victory of the PCs. Trailing badly in the polls, the PCs made up ground in part by castigating both Hunsperger and Wildrose leader Danielle Smith, who refused to rebuke her candidate.[1] In fact, PC leader and then Alberta premier Alison Redford went on the attack, happy to stoke fears that the Wildrose was full of individuals who held such views: "The fact that there are people who think that's a legitimate perspective just absolutely blows my mind ... I think they're shocking and I think it goes back to Albertans are about to decide who is going to govern their province. They are going to have to decide who their premier is. They're going to have to decide who the cabinet is."[2]

Apparently Redford did not see the irony of such a statement coming from the leader of the same PC party that had, in the 1990s and 2000s, engaged in a lengthy battle against the advancement of homosexual rights in the province, egged on by a number of outspoken and religiously motivated caucus members (including cabinet ministers) who routinely demonized homosexuality in the legislature and press. Of course, as Hunsperger's comments make clear, religiously motivated social conservatism has not entirely evaporated from Alberta, but both Redford's reaction and the PCs' subsequent electoral victory seem to say something quite important about its overall prevalence. And, as mentioned in Chapter 5, public opinion polls now confirm that views towards homosexual rights in Alberta have essentially shifted 180 degrees, leaving only a small minority opposed, an outcome that seems to mirror the decline in religious adherence in Alberta, now one of the most secular provinces in Canada.

For commentators who equate religious influence on politics solely with such social conservatism, the resulting picture looks clear. Aside from some hesitation around the loosening of liquor regulations or Sunday shopping rules in the 1940s and 1950s and the relatively short-lived but intensely negative reaction to legalized abortion and the advancement of homosexual rights in 1980s, 1990s, and early 2000s, the influence of religion on Alberta's politics has been sparse and is unlikely to return. Yet, as this book has argued, the manner by which religion has influenced Alberta's political trajectory is far more complex, nuanced, and significant than this interpretation. Indeed, the religiously inspired political thought and action of certain formidable leaders within Alberta's history have played important roles in shaping the province's political development, most especially its dominant parties' penchant for populist politics and consistent aversion to redistributive economics. In fact, as mentioned in the introduction, these two particular characteristics are actually two sides to a single "individualist" coin, and are clearly related to the strong individualist ethos associated with the versions of American evangelical Protestantism that blossomed in Alberta, especially among the leaders explored within this study. Although Henry Wise Wood's postmillennial Christian interpretation helped to lay the initial populist and anti-socialist foundations in the province, the contours of Alberta politics have been shaped most decisively by a particular individualist premillennial Christian interpretation introduced by Social Credit in 1935 and reinforced by the thought of Preston Manning in the late 1980s and early 1990s. This argument is briefly recapped below.

As the UFA's chief philosopher and long-time president, Wood was guided by a liberal and postmillennial stream of religious-based political thought. This was centred around a particularly optimistic understanding of humanity's capacity with respect to ushering in the kingdom of God on earth. Wood was convinced that by following the model of Christ and adopting a co-operative way of being, individuals and the groups they form would induce a broad social regeneration wherein Christ's law of co-operation would overcome the destructiveness of competition within society. This newly formed democratic and co-operative society, which Wood equated with the kingdom of God, was the end goal of his political thought and action. Although this line

Conclusion   213

of thinking helped encourage a strong populist and co-operative ethic within the UFA, it is important to recall that Wood refused to renounce the existing market system and embrace the socialism inherent in the more mainstream social gospel message of Prairie preacher Salem Bland and his followers. Importantly, this refusal was largely rooted in the individualistic nature of Wood's religious interpretation derived from the broader American evangelical Protestant tradition. Wood insisted that societal improvement was dependent on individual spiritual regeneration, not the introduction of socialist economics. This vitally important point deserves pause given the revered status that nearly all subsequent streams of Alberta political thought have granted to the individual, as well as to his or her need to act responsibly. Working out of the populist evangelical tradition, Wood understood the common individual as one of superb mental and moral capacity and therefore encouraged an anti-hierarchical political structure that would allow for maximum grassroots control. This relatively radical demand for the political freedom of the common citizen was, however, dependent upon simultaneous individual responsibilities. Society could only regenerate if each individual did his or her part to embrace the message of Christ. Thus, a certain conservatism attached itself to Wood's populist leanings from the very beginning.

The broad populist conservatism that initially emerged from the American evangelical Protestant tradition and characterized much of Wood's political theory would largely reappear in the political thought of Aberhart and his protegé, Ernest, founders and long-time leaders of Alberta Social Credit. Like Wood, they understood the common individual to possess a high degree of moral and mental ability that had the potential to culminate in total spiritual renewal. Beyond their basic commitment to democracy, the logical conclusion of this understanding for Aberhart and Manning was a devotion to individual liberty and a corresponding anti-establishmentarianism uncommon in the Tory conservative tradition. For Aberhart, this meant attacking the "Fifty Big Shots," whom he understood to be withholding credit from the common people and thus causing "poverty in the midst of plenty." For Manning, this meant supporting the free market in the face of an emerging socialism that threatened to subdue the common individual to the collective. Yet, the actualization of the individual's God-given moral and mental capacity, which made personal freedom a political requirement, simultaneously demanded that the individual follow the moral laws of God, and thus a certain conservatism was appended to the radical individualism espoused by Aberhart and Manning. In other words, the populist conservatism inherent in the thought of Wood, which both celebrated the capacity of the common individual and demanded a stern personal responsibility, largely continued unabated, and perhaps even grew stronger, throughout the years of Social Credit rule in Alberta.

However, the defeat of the UFA at the hands of Aberhart and Social Credit represented a vitally important change in the direction of Alberta's politics. Because Aberhart and Manning abided by a premillennial Christian interpretation that understood the coming kingdom of God to exist outside the realm of human agency, the notion of encouraging citizens to co-operate in an effort to usher in the kingdom made little sense. Rather, it was the job of Christians to assist those not yet reborn to find Christ and experience a spiritual rebirth prior to the Rapture. Aberhart and Manning sought to accomplish this goal by way of their radio evangelism. However, the severe conditions of the Depression, which provided a clear impediment to the personal freedom required to experience conversion, drew them into politics, where they set out to enhance and protect the freedom of the individual by promoting social credit economics. It is at this point that a significant shift occurred in the direction of Alberta politics. No longer was the state understood to be the culmination of a co-operative effort of individuals. Instead, it was understood to be a potential impediment to the individual freedom God had granted humanity. Thus, the proper role of government became that of ensuring that restrictions were placed on the state's size and scope. Correspondingly, both the call for a co-operative economic system and the intense pressure on citizens to participate politically in a deliberative and time-consuming way that had been stressed by the UFA were abandoned and replaced by an absolute rejection of economic collectivism and a call for citizens to state their preferences and allow benevolent politicians and their experts to install programs that would ensure that individual freedom would be protected as much as possible. This shift, which grew out of the distinction between post- and premillennial religious interpretations, represented a heightened focus on individual freedom that subsequently encouraged both a blatant anti-statism and the end of more radical and deliberative politics in Alberta.

The influence of religion on the politics of contemporary Alberta – which is far more secular than during the days of the UFA or Social Credit – is more complicated. Clearly, the religious-based social conservatism initially associated with journalist and early Reform Party advocate Ted Byfield has played a noticeable role, especially within the contemporary PC caucus. However, it was in the political thought of Preston Manning that one finds a strand of religious-based thought both quite distinct

Conclusion

from the social conservatism of Byfield and his followers and more significant in terms of its influence in shaping the direction of contemporary Alberta's politics. Largely adhering to the premillennial Christian interpretation espoused by his father, Ernest, Preston Manning believed that the ills of contemporary society had grown because of our distance from God and that only an individual effort on the part of the citizen to re-establish a relationship with God could make things better. However, because a truly perfected society was beyond humanity's reach, the divine role of the state in this process was simply to guarantee the individual the personal freedom necessary to allow this relationship with God to flourish. As with his father, this focus on individual freedom encouraged in Preston both a clear commitment to democracy and a certain anti-statism that, in turn, generated an aversion to any state-led efforts to impose an economic collectivism on an unwilling public. Hence, the result was a clear preference for an unregulated market economy and a simultaneous reduction in the size and scope of the state in response to the demands of the common people. Importantly, it is in this point of agreement between Ernest and Preston Manning that we find a vital, religious-based continuity with respect to both the populist sentiment and pro-market leanings that have defined so much of Alberta's politics for decades.

Of course, religious-based political thought at the elite level is not the only factor to have pushed Alberta in this direction, but it has played a significant role, one that has largely been neglected by academics eager to explain the particular political development of the province. This is especially so with respect to the contours of contemporary Alberta politics, which seem, aside from pockets of noisy social conservatives, to be completely devoid of religious influence.[3] In fact, it has become fashionable to interpret contemporary Alberta as the host of a new secular fiscal conservatism, or neo-liberalism, modelled after the Thatcher and Reagan governments in Britain and the United States. Certainly, a number of political and intellectual elites in Alberta became enamoured with academic neo-liberal arguments in the 1990s, but highlighting the shared convictions of Ernest and Preston Manning goes some way towards unravelling the newness of the economic approach taken by the Klein government in the mid-1990s. No doubt it was the decline in the province's economic fortunes, rather than their religious faith, that convinced average Albertans to accept the need to drastically reduce the size of government. And, of course, the fiscally conservative scholars working to spread new right ideas beyond the halls of academia in the province were largely driven by the arguments of Hayek rather than those of the Apostle Paul. Yet, it is important to remember that Preston Manning, who for all intents and purposes put fiscal conservatism back on the public agenda in Alberta with the creation of the Reform Party in 1987, was motivated by the same religious concerns that had led his father, Ernest, to battle the socialism of the CCF decades earlier. Thus, despite the fuss over the adoption of new right economics by secular fiscal conservatives within the Alberta PC government in the early 1990s, the immediate stimulus for this course of action was the popularity of the Reform Party and the calls for a reduction in the size and scope of government from its religiously motivated leader Preston Manning, who simply extended many of Ernest Manning's beliefs into the contemporary period. That Manning's political ideals are also strongly associated with the contemporary federal Conservative Party of Canada speaks to the influence of this religiously infused (at least initially) line of individualist and anti-statist thinking beyond Alberta as well.

More generally, however, the influence of religion on contemporary Alberta politics goes beyond either Byfield's social conservatism or Preston Manning's particular fiscal conservatism. It is found, rather, in the continued persistence of the broader populist conservative sentiment within the dominant rhetoric of Alberta politics. It is this sentiment – which both celebrates the intellectual and moral capacities of the common individual and places clear limits on his or her behaviour – that helps to explain both the individualistic, anti-statist, and populist tendencies within the province as well as the conservative emphasis on individual responsibility within the rhetoric and action of the province's dominant political parties, at least until the election of May 2015. Indeed, the surprise victory of the New Democratic Party (NDP) has been heralded by many as a historic change of course for Alberta, a province that has been dominated electorally by conservative parties since at least 1935 (if not earlier, although the UFA's simultaneous encouragement of individualism and economic co-operation makes a traditional left-right placement somewhat complicated). Clearly, the emergence of the NDP says something about the shifting attitudes and demographics of the fast-growing and ever-urbanizing province. However, I would hesitate to accept the argument that a seismic shift in the province's political trajectory has actually taken place.

As noted in the introduction, the Alberta populace has never been monolithically conservative. Sizable segments of the population have consistently voted against the governing party in several elections, going back decades, although this vote tended to be dispersed among, rather

Conclusion

than concentrated in, a single opposition party. Similarly, the policies of William Aberhart, Peter Lougheed, and Alison Redford did, at times, swing to the centre, if not the centre-left, a fact that speaks to the general openness the population has shown over several decades to more radical state-centred approaches. With respect to the 2015 election, a host of particular circumstances seemed to conspire against the governing PCs, leading to the widely held belief that they were a tired and out-of-touch government. These included various spending scandals, the poor performance of the party's supposed saviour, Jim Prentice, the public's negative feelings towards a secret deal to essentially merge the PC and Wildrose parties, and the near total collapse of the Alberta Liberal Party, allowing almost all of the centre and centre-left vote to coalesce around a single party. Finally, and perhaps most telling, despite these factors, right-leaning parties still captured the majority of the vote in the province, although it was split between the PCs (27.8 per cent of the vote) and the Wildrose (24.2 per cent of the vote), allowing the NDP (40.6 per cent of the vote) to claim victory. Further complicating the feel-good narrative that suggests the province has finally shed its incessant conservatism is the fact that, in the October 2015 federal election, roughly 60 per cent of Albertans voted for the Conservative Party of Canada.[4]

Of course, it is too early in the NDP's mandate to say anything of a concrete nature about the electoral future of the province, but given the historical strength of the strand of individualistic and anti-statist rhetoric so central to the dominant parties of the right in Alberta, it is hard to imagine that perspective disappearing from the political scene any time soon. Indeed, the sudden emergence and continued strength of the Wildrose in particular – the party that currently embodies the purest version of this populist conservative sentiment – seems to indicate its continued importance on the provincial political scene. And, as I have argued throughout, this populist conservatism is largely rooted in the religious arguments that emerged out of the American evangelical tradition and were initially imported into Alberta provincial politics by Wood and Aberhart. Surely the majority of Alberta citizens, who today celebrate individual freedom and thus reject both participatory politics and collectivist or redistributive economics in favour of this non-participatory anti-socialistic sentiment, have managed to disassociate this line of thought from these religious moorings. In fact, Jared Wesley has shown how the use of secular "political codes" within party literature has, over time, helped to congeal these individualistic anti-socialist values within a largely secular public.[5] Yet to overlook one of the vital initial sources of this sentiment, namely the particular evangelical Christian outlook that sat at the foundation of the political thought and action of the formative leaders studied in this book, is to miss a key dimension of the province's political development. This is not to suggest that religion will and can explain everything that is significant about Alberta politics. Obviously, the historical conditions related to the province's quasi-colonial status within Confederation, its distinct immigration patterns, its economic dependence on particular resources, and its subsequent wealth are vitally important in any attempt to understand the province's development. However, it is only by revealing the role of religion that we approach a clearer picture of what it was that influential political leaders such as Wood, Aberhart, and the Mannings were trying to accomplish and how these religiously motivated goals have helped set Alberta on a particular political trajectory that remains unique in Canada.

APPENDIX

Interview Participants

Interview date	Name	Description
12 Oct. 2010	****	Alberta Reform MP, 1993–2000
20 Oct. 2010	Lyle Oberg	Alberta Progressive Conservative MLA, 1993–2008
25 Oct. 2010	****	Alberta Progressive Conservative MLA, 1989–2012
30 Oct. 2010	Myron Thompson	Alberta Reform MP, 1993–2000
10 Nov. 2010 and 9 Nov. 2011	Preston Manning	Alberta Reform MP, 1993–2000 Leader of Reform Party of Canada, 1987–2000
15 Nov. 2010	****	Alberta Progressive Conservative MLA, 1993–2008
29 Nov. 2010	****	Alberta Progressive Conservative MLA, 1997–2012
30 Nov. 2010	Ken Kowalski	Alberta Progressive Conservative MLA, 1979–2012
15 Dec. 2010	****	Alberta Progressive Conservative MLA, 1993–2004
18 Jan. 2011	****	Alberta Progressive Conservative MLA, 2004–2013
27 Jan. 2011	Leroy Johnson	Alberta Progressive Conservative MLA, 1997–2008
14 Feb. 2011	Dave Hancock	Alberta Progressive Conservative MLA, 1997–2014
15 Feb. 2011	Raymond Speaker	Alberta Social Credit MLA, 1963–1982 Alberta Reform MP, 1993–1997
22 Feb 2011	Ted Byfield	Long-time publisher of *Alberta Report*
1 March 2011	Deborah Grey	Alberta Reform MP, 1989–2000
7 March 2011	Lindsay Blackett	Alberta Progressive Conservative MLA, 2008–2012
10 March 2011	****	Alberta Reform MP, 1993–2000
11 March 2011	Broyce Jacobs	Alberta Progressive Conservative MLA, 2001–2004 and 2008–2012
11 March 2011	****	Alberta Progressive Conservative MLA, 1997–2008
12 March 2011	Grant Hill	Alberta Reform mp, 1993–2000

**** Requested anonymity.

Notes

CHAPTER ONE

1 See, for example, Sharp, *The Agrarian Revolt in Western Canada*; Lipset, *Agrarian Socialism*; Morton, *The Progressive Party in Canada*; Macpherson, *Democracy in Alberta*; Wiseman, "The Pattern of Prairie Politics"; Friesen, *The Canadian Prairies: A History*; Laycock, *Populism and Democratic Thought in the Canadian Prairies, 1910 to 1945*; Rennie, *The Rise of Agrarian Democracy: The United Farmers and Farm Women of Alberta, 1909–1921*; Laycock, *The New Right and Democracy in Canada*; Warnock, *Saskatchewan: The Roots of Discontent and Protest*; and Wesley, *Code Politics: Campaigns and Cultures on the Canadian Prairies*.
2 Francis, "In Search of a Prairie Myth: A Survey of the Intellectual and Cultural Historiography of Prairie Canada," 56.
3 Wiseman, *In Search of Canadian Political Culture*, 2.
4 Wesley, *Code Politics*, 33.
5 These arguments were explored initially, although less thoroughly, in Banack, "Evangelical Christianity and Political Thought in Alberta."
6 Preston Manning, conversation with author, 9 November 2011.
7 See especially Wiseman, "The Pattern of Prairie Politics"; and Sharp, *The Agrarian Revolt in Western Canada*. For an updated statistical overview of American migration into Alberta, see Palmer and Palmer, *Alberta: A New History*, 82. For a discussion on the role American immigrants played within the upper echelons of the UFA, see Morton, *The Progressive Party in Canada*, 37–8.
8 Noll, "The End of Canadian History?," 33–4.
9 See Kettell, "Has Political Science Ignored Religion?" However, some recent work on religion and politics in Canada has begun to emerge. See, for example, Rayside and Wilcox, eds, *Faith, Politics, and Sexual Diversity in Canada and the United States*; Farney, *Social Conservatives and Party Politics in Canada and*

222 Notes to pages 10–19

the United States; and Malloy, "The Relationship between the Conservative Party of Canada and Evangelicals and Social Conservatives."

10 Taylor, *A Secular Age*, 428–9.

11 Harding, "Representing Fundamentalism: The Problem of the Repugnant Cultural Other," 375.

12 Marsden, *Fundamentalism and American Culture*, 2nd ed., 3.

13 Geertz, "Religion as a Cultural System," 121.

14 Taylor, "Interpretation and the Sciences of Man," 24.

15 For a broader theoretical discussion on Taylor's thesis with respect to the nature of the human subject and the methods of study appropriate in the quest for understanding human action, see Taylor, "Interpretation and the Sciences of Man," 15–57; and Taylor, *Sources of the Self*.

16 Taylor, *Sources of the Self*, 35.

17 Taylor, "Interpretations and the Sciences of Man," 17.

18 Ibid., 18.

19 Skinner, "Meaning and Understanding in the History of Ideas," 63.

20 Davison, *Secularism and Revivalism in Turkey: A Hermeneutic Reconsideration*, 73–4.

21 Skinner, "Meaning and Understanding in the History of Ideas," 64.

22 Appleby, *The Ambivalence of the Sacred: Religion, Violence, and Reconciliation*, 56.

23 McCormick, "Voting Behaviour in Alberta: The Quasi-Party System Revisited," 88.

24 Smith, "Alberta: A Province Like Any Other?," 250.

25 Stewart and Sayers, "Albertans' Conservative Beliefs," 249–67. On the relatively high per capita expenditures on the part of Social Credit, see Smith, "Alberta: A Province Like Any Other?," 247–8. On the relatively high per capita expenditures on the part of the contemporary PC government, see Boessenkool, "Does Alberta Have a Spending Problem?," 1. For a recent survey of political attitudes in Alberta on moral questions, see Ellis, *Traditional or Progressive: Albertans' Opinion Structure on Six Policy Issues*.

26 "Popular Vote Results in Alberta Provincial Elections," in *Election Almanac*, March 2011, http://www.electionalmanac.com/ea/alberta-popular-vote-results/ (accessed 25 November 2012).

27 Wesley, *Code Politics*, 55–6.

28 Macpherson, *Democracy in Alberta*, 21. For an updated and more convincing version of this thesis, see Dacks, "From Consensus to Competition: Social Democracy and Political Culture in Alberta," 186–204.

29 Wiseman, "The Pattern of Prairie Politics."

30 See Clark, "The Religious Sect in Canadian Politics"; Mann, *Sect, Cult, and Church in Alberta*; Guenther, "Training for Service: The Bible School Move-

Notes to pages 19–25   223

ment in Western Canada, 1909–1960"; and Goa, "Pietism, a Prairie Story: Spiritual Transformation."

31 See Richards and Pratt, *Prairie Capitalism: Power and Influence in the New West*; and Tupper, Pratt, and Urquhart, "The Role of Government."

32 Finkel, *The Social Credit Phenomenon in Alberta*, 122–39.

33 Stewart and Sayers, "Leadership Change in a Dominant Party: The Alberta Progressive Conservatives, 2006."

34 Cairns, "The Governments and Societies of Canadian Federalism."

35 Pal, "Hands at the Helm? Leadership and Public Policy," 16–19.

36 Wiseman, "Foreword." See also Wiseman, "The Pattern of Prairie Leadership," 178–9.

37 Laycock, *Populism and Democratic Thought in the Canadian Prairies*, 7.

38 Masciulli, Molchanov, and Knight, "Political Leadership in Context," 10, 4.

39 Ibid., 7.

40 McCormick, "Voting Behaviour in Alberta," 93–6.

41 Rolph, *Henry Wise Wood of Alberta*, 192.

42 Irving, *The Social Credit Movement in Alberta*, 337.

43 Barr, *The Dynasty: The Rise and Fall of Social Credit in Alberta*, 149.

44 See Pal, "The Political Executive and Political Leadership in Alberta," 23; Bell, "The Rise of the Lougheed Conservatives and the Demise of Social Credit in Alberta: A Reconsideration"; and Stewart and Archer, *Quasi-Democracy? Parties and Leadership Selection in Alberta*, 172.

45 Wesley, *Code Politics*, 33.

46 Goa, "Pietism, a Prairie Story," 12.

47 For a discussion on the left-wing support enjoyed by the UFA, see Rennie, *The Rise of Agrarian Democracy*. For a discussion on the left-wing support enjoyed by Aberhart's Social Credit, see Finkel, *The Social Credit Phenomenon in Alberta*.

48 Johnson, "The Failure of the CCF in Alberta: An Accident of History."

49 The argument is made in Finkel, *The Social Credit Phenomenon in Alberta*, 4–5.

50 Archer and Gibbins, "What Do Albertans Think? The Klein Agenda on the Public Opinion Landscape."

51 L. Ian MacDonald, "The Best Premier of the Last 40 Years: Lougheed in a Landslide," 13–17.

52 The term *political culture* has obviously spurred extensive debate among academics eager to provide a definitive definition of a concept that is often applied rather loosely. For a recent overview of this discussion in the Canadian context, see Wiseman, *In Search of Canadian Political Culture*. Within this study I use the term *Alberta's political culture* to refer to an ongoing set of political ideas and values that persist across the political parties, modes of polit-

224   Notes to pages 28–38

ical discourse, and shifting economic circumstances that characterize Alberta more than any other Canadian province.

53 This connection is noted in Barrie, *The Other Alberta: Decoding a Political Enigma*, 48–9.

54 Taras and Tupper, "Politics and Deficits: Alberta's Challenge to the Canadian Political Agenda," 66–7. For poll results that suggest that a provincial Reform Party would have easily defeated the PCs, see Harrison, "The Reform-Ation of Alberta Politics," 53.

CHAPTER TWO

1 Lipset, *Continental Divide: The Values and Institutions of the United States and Canada*, 1.

2 See, for example, Dayton, "Some Doubts about the Usefulness of the Category 'Evangelical.'"

3 For an excellent recent commentary on the role of this strain of Christian religion within the contemporary American public sphere, see Phillips, *American Theocracy*.

4 Stackhouse Jr, *Canadian Evangelicalism in the Twentieth Century*, 7.

5 Two valuable collections that demonstrate this variation in both Canada and the US respectively are Rawlyk, ed., *Aspects of the Canadian Evangelical Experience*; and D. Dayton and R. Johnston, eds, *The Variety of American Evangelicalism*.

6 Stackhouse Jr, "Who Whom? Evangelicalism and Canadian Society," 56. See also Bebbington, *Evangelicalism in Modern Britain*.

7 Noll, "Revolution and the Rise of Evangelical Social Influence in North Atlantic Societies," 129.

8 For a comprehensive and influential treatment of fundamentalism as a subset of Protestant evangelicalism and its strong American character, see Marsden, *Fundamentalism and American Culture*, 2nd ed.

9 For a more in-depth discussion of this point, see Noll, *The Old Religion in a New World: The History of North American Christianity*, 12–14.

10 Marsden, *Religion and American Culture*, 45.

11 Lambert, *Religion in American Politics: A Short History*, 17.

12 Noll, *A History of Christianity in the United States and Canada*, 100–5.

13 Marsden, *Religion and American Culture*, 20, 29.

14 Ibid., 29–30. See also Bailyn, *The Ideological Origins of the American Revolution*.

15 Hatch, *The Democratization of American Christianity*, 6.

16 Ibid., 9

17 Matthews, "The Second Great Awakening as an Organizing Process, 1780–1830: An Hypothesis," 39.

Notes to pages 39–45

18 Marsden, *Religion and American Culture*, 52–4.

19 McLoughlin, "Revivalism," 138.

20 Noll, "Protestant Reasoning about Money and the Economy, 1790–1860: A Preliminary Probe," 265–94.

21 For a more in-depth consideration of the relationship between "common sense" philosophy and evangelicalism, see Noll, "Common Sense Traditions and American Evangelical Thought." For a more in-depth demonstration of this relationship "on the ground," see Creech, *Righteous Indignation: Religion and the Populist Revolution*, 22–7.

22 Hofstadter, *Anti-intellectualism in American Life*, 7 and chaps 3–5.

23 See, for example, Williams and Alexander, "Religious Rhetoric in American Populism: Civil Religion as Movement Ideology"; and Creech, *Righteous Indignation*.

24 Gauvreau, "The Empire of Evangelicalism: Varieties of Common Sense in Scotland, Canada, and the United States," 219.

25 de Tocqueville, *Democracy in America*, 286–95.

26 McLoughlin, "Revivalism," 125–30.

27 Taylor, *A Secular Age*, 451–2. For a more in-depth treatment of these characteristics of American Protestantism, see Weber, *The Protestant Ethic and the Spirit of Capitalism*.

28 Hammond, *The Protestant Presence in Twentieth-Century America: Religion and Political Culture*, 45.

29 Rawlyk, *Canada Fire: Radical Evangelicalism in British North America*.

30 Christie, "In These Times of Democratic Rage and Delusion: Popular Religion and the Challenge to the Established Order, 1760–1815," 22–4, 36.

31 For further discussion on this shift and the evolution of this more conservative "British" evangelicalism, see French, "The Evangelical Creed in Canada"; Westfall, *Two Worlds: The Protestant Culture of Nineteenth-Century Ontario*; Gauvreau, *The Evangelical Century*; Van Die, "The Double Vision: Evangelical Piety as Derivative and Indigenous in Victorian English Canada"; and Rawlyk, "Introduction," xiii–xxv.

32 Noll, *A History of Christianity in the United States and Canada*, 268, 275–6.

33 Niebuhr, *The Kingdom of God in America*, ix, xii.

34 Weber, *Living in the Shadow of the Second Coming: American Premillennialism, 1875–1982*, 9.

35 Sandeen, *The Roots of Fundamentalism: British and American Millenarianism 1800–1930*, 42.

36 Dayton, "Millennial Views and Social Reform in Nineteenth Century America," 134–5. For a much more comprehensive history of millennial thought in Britain and America, see Sandeen, *The Roots of Fundamentalism*.

37 Marsden, *Fundamentalism and American Culture*, 2nd ed., 49.

226   Notes to pages 45–53

38 Smith, *Revivalism and Social Reform: American Protestantism on the Eve of the Civil War*.

39 More detailed commentaries on the American social gospel movement are available in Hopkins, *The Rise of the Social Gospel in American Protestantism, 1865–1915*; May, *Protestant Churches and Industrial America*; Carter, *The Decline and Revival of the Social Gospel: Social and Political Liberalism in American Protestant Churches, 1920–1940*; and White Jr and Hopkins, eds, *The Social Gospel: Religion and Reform in Changing America*.

40 See Goode, "The Godly Insurrection in Limestone County: Social Gospel, Populism, and Southern Culture in the Late Nineteenth Century"; and Harvey, *Freedom's Coming: Religious Culture and the Shaping of the South from the Civil War through the Civil Rights Era*, 47–53.

41 Creech, *Righteous Indignation*, 30.

42 Szasz, *The Divided Mind of Protestant America, 1880–1930*, 1–15.

43 Marsden, *Fundamentalism and American Culture*, 49–51.

44 Dayton, "Millennial Views and Social Reform in Nineteenth Century America," 133, 139.

45 The most thorough academic treatment of dispensational theology and its popularity within American evangelical circles is found in Boyer, *When Time Shall Be No More: Prophecy Belief in Modern American Culture*. For a succinct overview of the thought of Darby, see pages 86–90.

46 For a more detailed overview of this understanding of history, see Ryrie, *Dispensationalism*, 27–51.

47 Boyer, *When Time Shall Be No More*, 90–100.

48 Reuben Torrey as quoted in Boyer, *When Time Shall Be No More*, 93.

49 Boyer, *When Time Shall Be No More*, 5–15.

50 Marsden, "Fundamentalism as an American Phenomenon, A Comparison with English Evangelicalism," 216. This argument is expanded further in Marsden, *Fundamentalism and American Culture*.

51 See Marsden, "Fundamentalism as an American Phenomenon"; and Marsden, *Fundamentalism and American Culture*. A similar argument is made in Noll, *The Scandal of the Evangelical Mind*.

52 Westfall, *Two Worlds*, 159–90.

53 Elliott and Miller, *Bible Bill: A Biography of William Aberhart*, 10–16.

54 Stackhouse Jr, *Canadian Evangelicalism in the Twentieth Century*, 131–7.

55 On this point with respect to Canadian evangelicalism, see ibid., 198; Gauvreau, *The Evangelical Century*, 11; Airhart, *Serving the Present Age: Revivalism, Progressivism, and the Methodist Tradition in Canada*, 132–5; and Simpson and MacLeod, "The Politics of Morality in Canada," 228. For this point with respect to Britain, see Bebbington, *Evangelicalism in Modern Britain*, 182, 224, 227.

56 On this point, see Hoover, Martinez, Reimer, and Wald, "Evangelicalism Meets the Continental Divide: Moral and Economic Conservatism in the United States and Canada," 351–74; Reimer, *Evangelicals and the Continental Divide: The Conservative Protestant Subculture in Canada and the United States*; and Patrick, "Political Neoconservatism: A Conundrum for Canadian Evangelicals."

57 Gauvreau, "Baconianism, Darwinism, Fundamentalism: A Transatlantic Crisis of Faith."

58 Ibid., 443.

59 Wiseman, "The Pattern of Prairie Politics"; and Wiseman, *In Search of Canadian Political Culture.*

60 Morton, *The Progressive Party in Canada*, 37.

61 For more on the popularity of American periodicals in Alberta, see Sharp, *The Agrarian Revolt in Western Canada*, 2nd ed., 44.

62 Noll, "Revolution and the Rise of Evangelical Social Influence in North Atlantic Societies," 113–36.

63 Dawson, *Pioneering in the Prairie Provinces: The Social Side of the Settlement Process*, 207, 214–15.

64 Grant, *The Church in the Canadian Era*, 2nd ed., 51–3.

65 Clark, *Church and Sect in Canada*. See also Clark, "The Religious Sect in Canadian Politics."

66 Clark, "The Religious Sect in Canadian Politics."

67 Laycock has labelled this particular type of anti-political populist political culture "plebiscitarian populism" and discusses its role within the Social Credit days of Alberta in *Populism and Democratic Thought in the Canadian Prairies*. Similar findings are discussed with reference to the structure and support of the Reform Party of Canada in Laycock, *The New Right and Democracy in Canada.*

68 Mann, *Sect, Cult, and Church in Alberta*, 3, 4, 30–1.

69 Ibid., 27–9.

70 For more on Protestant Bible schools in western Canada, see Guenther, "Training for Service."

71 Mann, *Sect, Cult, and Church in Alberta*, 47.

72 Ibid., 52–4.

73 Hiller, "A Critical Analysis of the Role of Religion in a Canadian Populist Movement: The Emergence and Domination of the Social Credit Party in Alberta," 140–70.

74 Goa, "Pietism, a Prairie Story." For a brief commentary on the popularity of Aberhart's radio program, see Wiseman, "An Historical Note on Religion and Parties on the Prairies," 111.

75 Masciulli, Molchanov, and Knight, "Political Leadership in Context," 7.

CHAPTER THREE

1 Aspects of the UFA are discussed in Morton, "The Social Philosophy of Henry Wise Wood, the Canadian Agrarian Leader"; Morton, *The Progressive Party in Canada*; Macpherson, *Democracy in Alberta*; Friesen, *The Canadian Prairies: A History*; Wiseman, "The Pattern of Prairie Politics"; Flanagan, "Political Geography and the United Farmers of Alberta"; and Laycock, *Populism and Democratic Thought in the Canadian Prairies, 1910 to 1945*.

2 "Editorial: U.F.A. Sunday," *Western Independent*, 12 May 1920, 1.

3 Prairie historian W.L. Morton has written about this utopian tendency on a few occasions. See Morton, "The Bias of Prairie Politics"; and Morton, "A Century of Plain and Parkland."

4 Rennie, *The Rise of Agrarian Democracy*, 20, 57.

5 See Partridge, "The New Religion," *Grain Growers Guide*, 28 August 1909, 4. In addition to the agrarian leader Partridge, prominent social gospel clergymen such as J.S. Woodsworth and Salem Bland also secured regular columns in the *Grain Growers' Guide*. For an in-depth discussion of their message, see Allen, "The Social Gospel as the Religion of the Agrarian Revolt."

6 James Bower, "The United Farmers of Alberta and Co-operation," *Grain Growers' Guide*, 16 February 1910, 10.

7 W.J. Tregillus, "What of the Future," *Grain Growers' Guide*, 18 January 1911, 11. See also W.J. Tregillus, "UFA President's Address," *Grain Growers' Guide*, 28 January 1914, 8, 19.

8 Rennie, *The Rise of Agrarian Democracy*, 81–4.

9 Ibid., 207, 213.

10 The diversity of the UFA is discussed in much detail in Rennie, *The Rise of Agrarian Democracy*.

11 Rolph, *Henry Wise Wood of Alberta*, 170–92.

12 Allan Burt, "H.W. Wood's Position in Alberta Politics," *Toronto Star*, 31 July 1921.

13 "Who's Who in the Farmers Movement: H.W. Wood," *Western Independent*, 21 January 1920, 7.

14 For brief discussions on Wood's religious background, see Morton, "The Social Philosophy of Henry Wise Wood," 114–23; Rolph, *Henry Wise Wood of Alberta*, 9–11; Rennie, *The Rise of Agrarian Democracy*, 212–13; Allen, *The Social Passion: Religion and Social Reform in Canada 1914–1928*; Allen, "The Social Gospel as the Religion of the Agrarian Revolt"; and Foster, *The 1921 Provincial Election: A Consideration of Factors Involved with Particular Attention to Overtones of Millennialism within the UFA and Other Reform Movements*.

15 Allen, *The Social Passion*, 206.

Notes to pages 67–71

16 At the time of his death, Wood was reportedly working on a book-length exposition of the social aspects of Christianity, but all efforts to find notes from the incomplete work have been unsuccessful. That Wood was working on such a book is noted in Wiseman, *In Search of Canadian Political Culture*, 246.

17 Wood discusses the practical value of the message of Christ in an undated address entitled "My Religion," Alberta Wheat Pool Fonds, Glenbow-Alberta Museum Archives, Calgary, AB, file M-2369-125. For his definition of his religious creed, see H.W. Wood, letter to R.W. Frayne, 17 August 1925.

18 H.W. Wood, "UFA Sunday," *Grain Growers' Guide*, 19 April 1916, 11. See also "UFA Sunday," *Grain Growers' Guide*, 7 June 1916, 11.

19 For a comprehensive account of Wood's life, see Rolph, *Henry Wise Wood of Alberta*.

20 Wood's brother J.S. Wood noted this in a short untitled and undated biography he wrote on H.W. Wood currently located in the Alberta Wheat Pool Fonds, Glenbow-Alberta Museum Archives, Calgary, AB, file M-2369-125.

21 The standard histories of the American populist movement include Hicks, *The Populist Revolt: A History of the Farmers' Alliance and the People's Party*; Pollack, *The Populist Response to Industrial America*; and Goodwyn, *The Populist Moment: A Short History of the Agrarian Revolt in America*.

22 Williams and Alexander, "Religious Rhetoric in American Populism."

23 Creech, *Righteous Indignation*, 22–8.

24 See Goode, "The Godly Insurrection in Limestone County," 155–69; and Harvey, *Freedom's Coming: Religious Culture and the Shaping of the South from the Civil War through the Civil Rights Era*, 47–53.

25 Creech, *Righteous Indignation*, 30.

26 Ibid., 80.

27 Wood's membership in the Disciples is often mentioned as an important influence but rarely developed beyond a few paragraphs. See Morton, "The Social Philosophy of Henry Wise Wood"; Rolph, *Henry Wise Wood of Alberta*, 9–11; and Rennie, *The Rise of Agrarian Democracy*, 212–13.

28 Garrison and DeGroot, *The Disciples of Christ: A History*.

29 Harrell Jr, *Sources of Division in the Disciples of Christ, 1865–1900: A Social History of the Disciples of Christ*, vol. 2, 34–47.

30 Hatch, *The Democratization of American Christianity*, 71.

31 King, "Disciples of Christ and the Agrarian Protest in Texas, 1870–1906," 82. Creech also notes the significant relationship, with respect to both theoretical positions and active participation, between the Disciples of Christ and the American populist movement in the American South and Midwest. See Creech, *Righteous Indignation*, 12–13.

230   Notes to pages 71–81

32 Harrell Jr, *Sources of Division in the Disciples of Christ, 1865–1900*, 85–95.
33 Marsden, *Religion and American Culture*, 58–9.
34 Hatch, *The Democratization of American Christianity*, 76.
35 See note 20 above.
36 Wood mentions the influence of the teachings of Christ in H.W. Wood, "My Religion," *Winnipeg Free Press*, n.d. For scholarly discussions of the intellectual influences of Wood, see Rolph, *Henry Wise Wood of Alberta*, 11–14, 62–6; and Rennie, *The Rise of Agrarian Democracy*, 208–13.
37 Wood, "7th Annual Address of President H. W. Wood," 4.
38 Wood, "U.F.A. Political Movement and the Alberta Wheat Pool Greatest Products of the United Farmers of Alberta, Declares President Wood in Annual Address," 12.
39 Wood, "The Significance of Democratic Group Organization – Part One," 5.
40 Wood, "The Significance of Democratic Group Organization – Part Four," 25, 27.
41 Wood, "U.F.A. Political Movement and the Alberta Wheat Pool Greatest Products of the United Farmers of Alberta, Declares President Wood in Annual Address," 12.
42 Wood, "My Religion."
43 Wood, "Social Regeneration," 11.
44 Wood, "UFA Sunday," *Grain Growers' Guide*, 19 April 1916, 11.
45 Wood, "President Wood Discusses UFA Sunday," 11.
46 Wood, "Social Regeneration," 6.
47 Wood, "The Significance of U.F.A. Sunday," 5.
48 Wood, "Social Regeneration," 3.
49 Wood, "My Religion."
50 Wood, "The Significance of U.F.A. Sunday," 5.
51 Ibid.
52 Wood, "My Religion."
53 Wood, "Social Regeneration," 8.
54 Ibid.
55 Ibid., 10.
56 Ibid.
57 Wood, "My Religion."
58 Wood, "The Significance of U.F.A. Sunday," 14.
59 Wood, "Social Regeneration."
60 Wood, "The Significance of U.F.A. Sunday," 14.
61 Wood, "The Significance of Democratic Group Organization – Part Three," 5.
62 Wood, "The Significance of Democratic Group Organization – Part Four," 5.
63 See Rennie, *The Rise of Agrarian Democracy*, 217. For two examples noted by Rennie wherein Wood urges citizens not to create a new party, but to vote

for the best candidate within existing parties and collectively lobby for favourable legislation, see Wood, "The Price of Democracy," 12–13; and P.P. Woodbridge, "Organized Farmers and Politics," *Grain Growers' Guide*, 19 September 1917, 10.

64 Wood, "The Significance of Democratic Group Organization – Part One," 5.
65 See Macpherson, *Democracy in Alberta*, chap. 2.
66 Wood, "The Significance of Democratic Group Organization – Part Four," 5.
67 Wood rehashes his arguments in favour of occupational organizations over political parties in "Shall We Go Forward or Turn Back?," 1, 9.
68 Laycock, *Populism and Democratic Thought in the Canadian Prairies*, 90–4.
69 Quoted in ibid., 80.
70 For a detailed account of the practical co-operative efforts of many of the locals, see Rennie, *The Rise of Agrarian Democracy*, 138–60.
71 Wood, "Political Action in Alberta," 7.
72 Wood, "Democratic Organization," 8.
73 Wood, "Is UFA Cooperation Constructive?," 12. Wood also discussed the vital role played by locals in Wood, "UFA Subunits and Their Relation to the Whole," 8.
74 H.W. Wood, in a speech to the Alberta Institute of Co-operation in September 1929, quoted in Laycock, *Populism and Democratic Thought in the Canadian Prairies*, 92.
75 Quoted in Rolph, *Henry Wise Wood of Alberta*, 66.
76 An excellent overview of the tension between the grassroots members and the political arm of the UFA is available in Betke, "The United Farmers of Alberta, 1921–1935: The Relationship between the Agricultural Organization and the Government of Alberta."
77 Wood discusses his theoretical opposition to mandatory wheat boards as well as to a number of practical realties related to a mandatory wheat board and a voluntary wheat pool in Wood, "Compulsory Pooling of Wheat"; Wood, "Can We Afford to Abolish the Wheat Board. Part I," 4; Wood, "Can We Afford to Abolish the Wheat Board. Part II," 4; and Wood, "Cooperative Wheat Marketing System Can and Will Be Established," 11.
78 Wood, "U.F.A. Political Movement and the Alberta Wheat Pool Greatest Products of the United Farmers of Alberta, Declares President Wood in Annual Address," 12.
79 Quoted in Morton, "The Social Philosophy of Henry Wise Wood," 116.
80 Macpherson, *Democracy in Alberta*, 34.
81 Wood, "The Significance of Democratic Group Organization – Part Two," 5.
82 Allen, *The View from Murney Tower: Salem Bland, the Late Victorian Controversies, and the Search for a New Christianity*, vol. 1, xxxiv, 385–91.
83 Quoted in ibid., 388.

232   Notes to pages 87–97

84 Quoted in Allen, "Profile: Salem Goldworth Bland, Part 2: 1903–1950: The New Christianity in a New, Distressful Canada," 45.
85 For an overview of Irvine's life and thought, see Mardiros, *William Irvine: The Life of a Prairie Radical*.
86 See Irvine, "Hope of the Church," *Nutcracker* 5; and Irvine, "Prophet of the 20th Century," 6. Similar themes are also discussed in Irvine, "UFA Sermon," 11.
87 Irvine, *The Farmers in Politics*, 231–2. This distinction between Irvine and Wood is also discussed in Rennie, *The Rise of Agrarian Democracy*, 220–2.
88 Irvine, *Can a Christian Vote for Capitalism?*
89 Laycock, *Populism and Democratic Thought in the Canadian Prairies*, 116.
90 Macpherson, *Democracy in Alberta*, 220–1.
91 Allen, "Salem Bland and the Spirituality of the Social Gospel," 227.
92 Allen, *The Social Passion*, 151–2. For an exploration of the political thought of J.S. Woodsworth, see Mills, *Fool for Christ: The Political Thought of J.S. Woodsworth*.
93 Wood, "The Significance of Democratic Group Organization – Part Two," 5.
94 Wood, "Observe U.F.A. Sunday, May 27," 12.
95 Wood, "The Significance of Democratic Group Organization – Part Four," 5.
96 Wood, "U.F.A. President's Address," *Grain Growers' Guide*, 7, 22.
97 Betke, "The United Farmers of Alberta, 1921–1935," 71–2, 93.
98 Rennie, *The Rise of Agrarian Democracy*, 224. See also Palmer and Palmer, *Alberta*, 194.
99 Rennie, *The Rise of Agrarian Democracy*, 223.
100 "Who's Who in the Farmers Movement: H.W. Wood," 7.
101 Wood, "Compulsory Pooling of Wheat."
102 Rennie, *The Rise of Agrarian Democracy*, 217–18.
103 Rolph, *Henry Wise Wood of Alberta*, 176.
104 For a discussion of the radical farmers' push for a compulsory wheat board in Saskatchewan, see Spafford, "The Left Wing, 1921–1931." For a discussion of the broader left-leaning tendencies within the Saskatchewan farmers' movement, see Wiseman, *In Search of Canadian Political Culture*, 225; and Laycock, *Populism and Democratic Thought in the Canadian Prairies*, 174–6.
105 See "Province Supports Lawsuit by Friends of the Canadian Wheat Board," *Government of Saskatchewan*, 13 June 2007, http://www.saskatchewan.ca /government/news-and-media/2007/june/13 /province-supports-lawsuit-by-friends-of-the-wheat-board; and Hanneke Brooymans, "Going by the Board," *Alberta Views*, January/February 2005, 24–8. The CWB was stripped of its single-desk authority by the federal Conservative government in 2012.
106 Betke, "The UFA: Visions of a Cooperative Commonwealth," 8.

Notes to pages 98–108   233

107 This chain of events is summarized nicely in Betke, "The UFA." See also Foster, "John E. Brownlee, 1925–1934." For a discussion on the role played by Irvine, Gardiner, and Priestly in the formation of the CCF, see Young, *The Anatomy of a Party: The National CCF, 1932–61*, 18–20.

108 Betke, "The United Farmers of Alberta, 1921–1935," 17.

109 This point is made in Rennie, *The Rise of Agrarian Democracy*, 227–8; Betke, "The UFA, 7; and Foster, "John E. Brownlee, 1925–1934," 96–8. The split within the UFA over affiliating with the CCF is also discussed in Epp, "'Their Own Emancipators': The Agrarian Movement in Alberta."

110 Foster, *John E. Brownlee: A Biography*, 265.

111 Quoted in Foster, "John E. Brownlee, 1925–1934," 97.

112 Wiseman, "The Pattern of Prairie Politics."

113 Rennie, *The Rise of Agrarian Democracy*, 96. See also Morton, *The Progressive Party in Canada*, 34.

114 Masciulli, Molchanov, and Knight, "Political Leadership in Context," 7.

115 Macpherson, *Democracy in Alberta*, 220–1.

116 The classic Canadian articulation and defence of this Tory conservative variant remains Grant, *Lament for a Nation*. I originally discussed the distinction between Tory and populist conservatism in Banack, "American Protestantism and the Roots of 'Populist Conservatism' in Alberta."

117 See Irene Parlby, "Mrs. Parlby's Address," *Grain Growers' Guide*, 29 January 1919, 8. Rennie has also commented on the strong evangelical commitment to personal responsibility and character development within the UFA; see Rennie, *The Rise of Agrarian Democracy*, 122.

118 See, for example, Stewart and Sayers, "Albertans' Conservative Beliefs."

CHAPTER FOUR

1 See, for example, Irving, *The Social Credit Movement in Alberta*; Hiller, "A Critical Analysis of the Role of Religion in a Canadian Populist Movement"; Flanagan, "Social Credit in Alberta: A Canadian 'Cargo Cult'?"; and Flanagan and Lee, "From Social Credit to Social Conservatism: The Evolution of an Ideology."

2 Wesley, *Code Politics*, 76–7.

3 Elliott and Miller, *Bible Bill*, 9–12.

4 Aberhart recounts this experience in Aberhart, "God's Great Divisions of the World's History," 27–8.

5 Ibid., 30.

6 Ryrie, *Dispensationalism*, 27–51.

7 Elliott and Miller, *Bible Bill*, 10–16.

234 Notes to pages 108–13

8 Quoted in ibid., 12. Original source: William Aberhart, "Bible Reading #10."
9 For varying listenership estimates, see Laycock, *Populism and Democratic Thought in the Canadian Prairies*, 216; Wiseman, "An Historical Note on Religion and Parties on the Prairies," 111; and Barrie, *The Other Alberta*, 49. The quote on the popularity of the program in small-town Alberta is taken from Barrie, *The Other Alberta*, 49.
10 Aberhart, "The Old and the New Theology," 5–6.
11 For an overview of the central course teachings at the institute, see Aberhart, *Systematic Theology*, Course A, Book 1; Aberhart, *Systematic Theology*, Course A, Book 2; Aberhart, *Systematic Theology*, Course A, Book 3; Aberhart, *Systematic Theology*, Course B; and Aberhart, *Systematic Theology*, Course C.
12 Aberhart, "The Second Coming of Christ, and Its Signs and Shadows," 7 –8.
13 This summary is drawn from Elliott and Miller's excellent overview of Aberhart's theology. See Elliott and Miller, *Bible Bill*, 37–40. For Aberhart's precise depictions of these events, see, especially, Aberhart, "The Zionist Movement, or the Restoration of the Hebrews"; Aberhart, "Sign-Posts on the Way to Millennium, or the period-Divisions of Daniel's Seventieth Week"; Aberhart, "The Anti-Christ: Individual or System"; Aberhart, "The Anti-Christ: Man or Demon?"; and Aberhart, "Armageddon: The Climax of Battles."
14 Aberhart, *Systematic Theology*, Course A, Book 3.
15 Elliott and Miller, *Bible Bill*, 37–40.
16 Elliott, "The Devil and William Aberhart: The Nature and Function of his Eschatology," 326.
17 Elliott, "Antithetical Elements in William Aberhart's Theology and Political Ideology." See also Elliott and Miller, *Bible Bill*.
18 Elliott, "Antithetical Elements in William Aberhart's Theology and Political Ideology," 41.
19 Cited ibid., 40.
20 Ibid.
21 Ibid., 55, 46.
22 Elliott and Miller, *Bible Bill*, 175, 319.
23 Elliott, "Antithetical Elements in William Aberhart's Theology and Political Ideology," 57.
24 Aberhart, Radio Address, 19 April 1935.
25 Aberhart, Radio Address, 3 May 1935.
26 Aberhart, Radio Address, 7 May 1935.
27 See, for example, Aberhart, Radio Address, 18 June 1935.
28 Kirk, "Social Credit and the Word of God," 1935. For Aberhart's dismissal that he has turned his back on dispensationalism, see Aberhart, Radio Address, 21 April 1935.

Notes to pages 113–23

29 For examples of his speeches that touch on social gospel–like themes, see Aberhart, Sunday Radio Address, 7 November 1937; and Aberhart, Sunday Radio Address, 10 July 1938. For a continued focus on themes related to the Rapture, Tribulation, and Battle of Armageddon, see Aberhart, Sunday Radio Address, 30 October 1938; Aberhart, Sunday Radio Address, 13 November 1938; Aberhart, Sunday Radio Address, 11 December 1938; and Aberhart, letter to William Bollen, 12 March 1943.

30 Weber, *Living in the Shadow of the Second Coming*, 66–8.

31 Ibid., 71.

32 Boyer, *When Time Shall Be No More*, 297–301.

33 Marsden, *Fundamentalism and American Culture*, 2nd ed., 91.

34 "Doctrinal Basis of the Institute," in *Bulletin of the Calgary Prophetic Bible Institute*, n.d., Calgary Prophetic Bible Institute Fonds, Glenbow-Alberta Museum Archives, Calgary, AB, file M-1357-1.

35 Aberhart and Manning, *The Branding Irons of the Antichrist*, 1931.

36 E. Manning, Radio Address, 26 March 1949.

37 E. Manning, letter to T.G. Irwin, 1 November 1946.

38 Aberhart, letter to J.H. Caldwell, 15 October 1932.

39 E. Manning, "Interview by Lydia Semotuk," Interview 19 (20 August 1980).

40 E. Manning, "Interview by Lydia Semotuk," Interview 39 (17 May 1982).

41 E. Manning, "Interview by Lydia Semotuk," Interview 16 (18 July 1980).

42 E. Manning, letter to G. Drexhage, 28 February 1967.

43 Marsden, *Fundamentalism and American Culture*, 63.

44 Aberhart, letter to J.H. Caldwell, 15 October 1932.

45 E. Manning, letter to Ronald S. Dinnick, 10 January 1961.

46 E. Manning, letter to G.M. Wilson, 18 April 1962.

47 E. Manning, letter to Ruth Bedford, 18 April 1962.

48 E. Manning, letter to Lester C. Frets, 24 July 1958.

49 Aberhart, letter to J.H. Caldwell, 2 February 1933.

50 Marsden, *Fundamentalism and American Culture*, 208.

51 Finkel, *The Social Credit Phenomenon in Alberta*, 41–61, 67–71.

52 For a more extensive discussion of Social Credit legislation in its early years, see ibid., 43–72; Barr, *The Dynasty*, 83–119; and Bell, *Social Classes and Social Credit in Alberta*, 107–28.

53 Aberhart, "Speech from the Throne," 1938; and Aberhart, "The Record of the Government," 1939.

54 Johnson, "The Failure of the CCF in Alberta: An Accident of History."

55 A more detailed description of this chain of events can be found in Irving, *The Social Credit Movement in Alberta*, 43–9; and Elliott and Miller, *Bible Bill*, 100–10.

236   Notes to pages 124–34

56 An insightful and detailed examination of the economic theories of Douglas and the interpretation of such by Aberhart is provided in Macpherson, *Democracy in Alberta*, chaps 4 and 5. See also Bell, *Social Classes and Social Credit in Alberta*, 37–85.
57 Aberhart, letter to J.H. Caldwell, 29 March 1933.
58 P. Manning, conversation with author, 10 November 2010.
59 Aberhart, Radio Address, 21 April 1935.
60 Aberhart, Radio Address, 28 April 1935.
61 Aberhart, letter to J.H. Caldwell, 29 March 1933.
62 Aberhart, Radio Address, 12 July 1935.
63 Aberhart, Radio Address, 18 June 1935. See also Aberhart, Radio Address, 30 April 1935.
64 Aberhart, Radio Address, 7 July 1935.
65 Aberhart, "Freedom of the Press."
66 E. Manning, letter to G.M. Wilson, 18 April 1962.
67 Quoted in Dabbs, *Preston Manning: The Roots of Reform*, 17.
68 Aberhart, "The Individualism of Destiny."
69 Aberhart, "The Collapse of Prehistoric Conditions."
70 E. Manning, "Economic Crises #2."
71 E. Manning, "Interview by Lydia Semotuk," Interview 2 (18 December 1978).
72 E. Manning, "Interview by Lydia Semotuk," Interview 38 (10 May 1982).
73 "Materialistic and Spiritual Blend in the Social Credit Faith," *Alberta Social Credit Chronicle*, 7 September 1934, 1.
74 Aberhart, Radio Address, 18 June 1935.
75 Aberhart, Sunday Radio Address, 5 June 1938.
76 Aberhart, Sunday Radio Address, 4 September 1938.
77 Aberhart, Sunday Radio Address, 19 March 1939.
78 Aberhart, Radio Address, 11 August 1935.
79 Biblical verses are taken from the King James Version, which Aberhart perceived to be the only authentic translation.
80 Aberhart, "Money in the Fish's Mouth: The Dilemma of Taxation."
81 Aberhart, untitled lecture, in Religious Notebooks, 1933-2.
82 Aberhart, "Buying without Money: An Economic Feature Not Found in Present Day Capitalism."
83 Aberhart, "Money in the Fish's Mouth."
84 Irving, *The Social Credit Movement in Alberta*, 259–69.
85 Aberhart, letter to J.H. Caldwell, 2 February 1933.
86 This argument is most prominent in Finkel, *The Social Credit Phenomenon in Alberta*, 136. See also Flanagan and Lee, "From Social Credit to Social Conservatism."
87 Wesley, *Code Politics*, 68–9.

Notes to pages 134–41

88 Dennis Groh has related Manning's political thought to his broader Christian-based belief that society should be organized in such a way that the individual's "search for the grace of God" is facilitated. Although the complete relationship between Manning's religious theology and his political ideology is a bit more complex, or at least a bit more detailed than Groh admits, overall his interpretation of Manning is sound and his thesis remains, in my opinion, the most accurate work yet with respect to the role played by religion in the dominant ideology of the Social Credit. See Groh, "The Political Thought of Ernest Manning."

89 E. Manning, letter to G.M. Wilson, 18 April 1962.

90 Marshall, "Premier E.C. Manning, *Back to the Bible Hour*, and Fundamentalism in Canada," 239–40.

91 E. Manning, Radio Address, 3 May 1953.

92 For examples of this commentary, see E. Manning, Radio Address, 2 January 1949; E. Manning, Radio Address, 20 February 1949; E. Manning, Radio Address, 6 March 1949; and E. Manning, Radio Address, 5 April 1953.

93 E. Manning, Radio Address, 2 January 1949.

94 E. Manning, Radio Address, 29 March 1953.

95 E. Manning, Radio Address, 10 May 1953.

96 E. Manning, Radio Address, 2 January 1949.

97 E. Manning, Radio Address, 5 December 1948.

98 E. Manning, Radio Address, 10 May 1953.

99 Further commentaries on this aspect of Manning's theology are available in Marshall, "Premier E.C. Manning, *Back to the Bible Hour*, and Fundamentalism in Canada"; and Hesketh, *Major Douglas and Alberta Social Credit*.

100 Mackey, *Like Father, Like Son: Ernest Manning and Preston Manning*, 61.

101 Manning made this point repeatedly in speeches, broadcasts, and letters. See, for example, E. Manning, *Education and the Problem of Human Relationships*, 14–17; E. Manning, "Watchman What of the Night"; and E. Manning, letter to R.K. Macpherson, 24 February 1965.

102 E. Manning, "Interview by Lydia Semotuk," Interview 19 (20 August 1980).

103 E. Manning, Radio Address, 6 March 1949.

104 E. Manning, Radio Address, 19 December 1948.

105 E. Manning, letter to Phibbs, 4 February 1949.

106 E. Manning, "The Road to Serfdom or the Welfare State Syndrome."

107 E. Manning, "Economic Crises #2."

108 E. Manning, letter to Robert Sheath, 5 April 1967.

109 E. Manning, "Financial Tyranny and the Dawn of a New Day." Manning makes the same point nearly thirty years later in E. Manning, *Some Ground Rules for a Free Society*, 3.

110 E. Manning, *Political Realignment: A Challenge to Thoughtful Canadians*, 59.

238   Notes to pages 141–52

111 Ibid., 61.

112 Ibid., 62.

113 Ibid.

114 Ibid., 67.

115 For further discussion on this point, see Finkel, *The Social Credit Phenomenon in Alberta*, 99–140. See also Emery and Kneebone, "Socialists, Populists, Resources, and the Divergent Development of Alberta and Saskatchewan"; and Richards and Pratt, *Prairie Capitalism*. Pratt and Richards make it clear that although Manning's ideology motivated him to a significant degree on this matter, pragmatic concerns with respect to Alberta's geography, lack of available venture capital, and even the political power of early American oil-producing companies active in the province were also factors in his approach to developing an appropriate regulatory structure; see ibid., 66–8, 82–4.

116 For recent work on Alberta's contemporary approach to the oil industry, see Chastko, *Developing Alberta's Oil Sands*; and Brownsey, "Alberta's Oil and Gas Industry in the Era of the Kyoto Protocol."

117 Finkel, *The Social Credit Phenomenon in Alberta*, 108, 117–20, 145–55. See also Brennan, *The Good Steward: The Ernest C. Manning Story*, 154–5.

118 E. Manning, *National Medicare: Let's Look before We Leap*.

119 Wesley, *Code Politics*, 76–7.

120 E. Manning, letter to G. Drexhage, 28 February 1967.

121 Ray Speaker, conversation with author, 15 February 2011.

122 E. Manning, "Interview by Lydia Semotuk," Interview 14 (4 July 1980).

123 Barr, *The Dynasty*, 152–3.

124 E. Manning, "Interview by Lydia Semotuk," Interview 14 (4 July 1980).

125 This connection between their faith and their reluctance to enforce a particular Christian education on students in Alberta's public education system is explored in detail in von Heyking, "Aberhart, Manning and Religion in the Public Schools of Alberta." For Ernest Manning's precise thoughts on the issue, see E. Manning, letter to Lee, 6 June 1944; E. Manning, letter to Ewers, 6 February 1948; and E. Manning, letter to Hollowes, 15 September 1952.

126 E. Manning, "Interview by Lydia Semotuk," Interview 19 (20 August 1980).

127 Elliott and Miller, *Bible Bill*, 15–16.

128 Stackhouse Jr, *Canadian Evangelicalism in the Twentieth Century: An Introduction to Its Character*, 39.

129 Finkel, *The Social Credit Phenomenon in Alberta*, xi, 4–5.

130 For more on this point, see McInnis and Urquhart, "Protecting Mother Earth or Business? Environmental Politics in Alberta"; Chastko, *Developing Alberta's Oil Sands*; Brownsey, "Alberta's Oil and Gas Industry in the Era of the Kyoto Protocol"; Urquhart, "Alberta's Land, Water, and Air: Any Reason not to Despair"; and Laird, "Spent Energy: Re-fueling the Alberta Advantage."

Notes to pages 152–61   239

131 See Denis, "The New Normal: Capitalist Discipline in Alberta in the 1990s"; Laxer, "The Privatization of Public Life"; Drugge, "The Alberta Tax Advantage: Myth and Reality"; Renouf, "Chipping Away at Medicare: 'Rome Wasn't Sacked in a Day'"; Steward, "Hips and Knees: The Politics of Private Health Care in Alberta"; Flanagan, "Not Just about Money: Provincial Budgets and Political Ideologies"; Horne, "From Manning to Mazankowski and Beyond: Alberta's Fight to Privatize Health Care"; and Black and Stanford, "When Martha and Henry Are Poor: The Poverty of Alberta's Social Assistance Programs."

132 On the relatively high per capita expenditures on the part of Social Credit, see Smith, "Alberta: A Province Like Any Other?," 247–8. On the relatively high per capita expenditures on the part of the contemporary PC government, see Boessenkool, "Does Alberta Have a Spending Problem?," 1.

133 Wesley, *Code Politics*, 56. See also Harrison, Johnston, and Krahn, "Language and Power: 'Special Interests' in Alberta's Political Discourse," 82–94.

134 E. Manning, "Economic Crises #2."

135 Wesley, *Code Politics*, 86.

136 Quoted in ibid., 90. For the original, see Gibbins, "Western Alienation and the Alberta Political Culture," 143.

137 Macpherson, *Democracy in Alberta*, chaps 6 and 7; and Laycock, *Populism and Democratic Thought in the Canadian Prairies*, chap. 5.

138 Laycock, *Populism and Democratic Thought in the Canadian Prairies*, 218.

139 Quoted in Macpherson, *Democracy in Alberta*, 152.

140 E. Manning, "Interview by Lydia Semotuk," Interview 1 (4 December 1978).

141 Macpherson, *Democracy in Alberta*, 169–73, 194–8.

142 Laycock, *Populism and Democratic Thought in the Canadian Prairies*, 258.

143 Ibid., 259. Roger Epp has also located the roots of contemporary Alberta's apolitical populist leanings in this aspect of Social Credit democratic discourse. See Epp, "The Political De-skilling of Rural Communities," 315–16.

CHAPTER FIVE

1 Paquin, "How the West Was Won."

2 Brent Wittmeier, "Link Byfield, Journalist and Wildrose Party Co-founder, Dead at Age 63," *Edmonton Journal*, 25 January 2015, http://www
.edmontonjournal.com/Link+Byfield+journalist+Wildrose+Party+founder+dead
/10759489/story.html

3 For additional commentary on Byfield's influence on the political mood in Alberta in general and on the formation and early success of the Reform Party in particular, see Frum, "Foreword," in *The Book of Ted: Epistles from an*

240   Notes to pages 161–6

Unrepentant Redneck; and Harrison, *Of Passionate Intensity: Right-Wing Populism and the Reform Party of Canada*, chaps 2 and 3.

4 Ted Byfield, conversation with author, 22 February 2011.

5 Byfield mentions Dewey in a number of articles in *Alberta Report*, but his
   most complete articulation of Dewey's role in the decline of traditional
   Christian morality in North America is encapsulated in a more recent essay;
   see Byfield, *Why History Matters*.

6 Although these themes were repeated often in Byfield's columns, they are
   spelled out clearly in Ted Byfield, "As If the Family Hasn't Enough Trouble,
   Now It's Being 'Helped' by the Lib-Left," *Alberta Report*, 24 January 1994, 44.
   See also Ted Byfield, "Why This Magazine Ran That 'Disgusting' Story on
   Gay Pride," *Alberta Report*, 30 August 1993, 44.

7 Byfield, conversation with author, 22 February 2011.

8 Byfield, "Why This Magazine Ran That 'Disgusting' Story on Gay Pride."

9 Byfield, conversation with author, 22 February 2011.

10 That religiously inspired social conservatives made up a part of Reform's
   support base is confirmed in a number of commentaries on the party, in-
   cluding Flanagan, *Waiting for the Wave: The Reform Party and Preston Manning*;
   Harrison, *Of Passionate Intensity*; Archer and Ellis, "Opinion Structure of
   Party Activists: The Reform Party of Canada"; Laycock, *The New Right and
   Democracy in Canada*; and Farney, *Social Conservatives and Party Politics in
   Canada and the United States*. For specific instances of religious-based anti-
   homosexual sentiment within the party, see Peter O'Neil, "Reform MPs Turn
   Attention to Family Issues," *Edmonton Journal*, 17 June 1994, A3; and Sheldon
   Alberts, "Gay 'Family' Not in Party Vocabulary; Day One," *Edmonton Journal*,
   14 October 1994, A3.

11 James Farney has done more detailed work on the role of social conservatism
   within the wider Reform Party. See Farney, *Social Conservatives and Party Politics in Canada and the United States*, 98–113.

12 Klein's professed attachment to aspects of Aboriginal spirituality and his dis-
   taste for much of the social conservatism in his own party are discussed
   briefly in Johnsrude, "Moral Compass or Political Antennae," 33–7. See also
   Rayside, Sabin, and Thomas, "Faith and Party Politics in Alberta OR
   'Danielle, this is Alberta, not Alabama"; and Marta Gold, "Group Upset with
   Klein's Comments on Abortion," *Edmonton Journal*, 2 April 1995.

13 For further discussions on the Alberta PC government's religious-based hesi-
   tation with respect to homosexual rights, see Rayside, *Queer Inclusions, Conti-
   nental Divisions: Public Recognition of Sexual Diversity in Canada and the
   United States*; Lloyd and Bonnett, "The Arrested Development of Queer
   Rights in Alberta"; and Banack, "Conservative Christianity, Anti-Statism and
   Alberta's Public Sphere: The Curious Case of Bill 44."

Notes to pages 166–70

14 See Marilyn Moysa, "MLA Sees No End to Abortion on Demand," *Edmonton Journal*, 25 September 1995, A7; and Tom Arnold, "Abortion Fight Over, MLAs say," *Edmonton Journal*, 7 October 1995, A1.

15 See, for example, Canadian Press, "Mirosh Wins Support for Stand," *Edmonton Journal*, 11 February 1993, B5; and Ashley Geddes, "Premier Defends Kowalski Views," *Calgary Herald*, 10 June 1993, A8.

16 See, for example, Diane Coulter and Adrienne Tanner, "Province to Appeal Gay Rights Ruling," *Edmonton Journal*, 5 May 1994, A7; and Marta Gold, "Anti-Gay Tories Cool to Rights Appeal," *Edmonton Journal*, 20 October 1994, A1.

17 Marta Gold, "Homosexuality a 'Lifestyle' – Klein," *Edmonton Journal*, 20 March 1996, A3.

18 Adrienne Tanner, "Day Wary of Letting Gays Adopt: Social Services Minister Prefers Placing Children in 'normative societal situations," *Edmonton Journal*, 16 August 1996, A8.

19 Larry Johnsrude, "'I Will Do What I Believe Is Right and Pay the Price': Day Defends Stand on Gay Study Grant," *Edmonton Journal*, 31 August 1997, F2. See also David Howell, "Furor over Gays Study Grant: Attempt to Pull Back $10,000 in Funding Deplored by Liberal," *Edmonton Journal*, 17 August 1997, A5.

20 Allyson Jeffs, "Common-Law Relationships to Exclude Gays," *Edmonton Journal*, 26 February 1999, A6.

21 Larry Johnsrude, "Private Bill Would Block Recognition of Gay Marriage: Minister Downplays Significance of Measure," *Edmonton Journal*, 24 February 2000.

22 See Paula Simons, "One Step Forward, Two Steps Back: Alberta's Human Rights Legislation Still Being Written by Social Conservatives," *Edmonton Journal*, 30 April 2009, A18; and Paula Simons, "Bill 44 an Evolutionary Dead End: Amendments Create Whole New Class of Potentially Aggrieved Parties," *Edmonton Journal*, 5 May 2009, A14.

23 Janet Steffenhagen, "Gay Guarantee for Provincial Curriculum," *Vancouver Sun*, 16 June 2006, http://www.canada.com/vancouversun/news/story .html?id=223d5fea-2e50-4b1d-9678-f37850ca50cb (accessed 7 March 2011).

24 That the BC curriculum decision was central to the argument for parental rights in Alberta made by socially conservative MLAs within caucus was confirmed by two separate PC cabinet ministers in one-on-one interviews conducted by author.

25 For a more in-depth discussion of this issue, see Banack, "Conservative Christianity, Anti-Statism and Alberta's Public Sphere."

26 Clark, "Pockets of Belief: Religious Attendance Patterns in Canada."

242 Notes to pages 171–8

27 This was hinted at in Mann, *Sect, Cult, and Church in Alberta*.

28 Bowen, *Christians in a Secular World: The Canadian Experience*, 54–5.

29 See "Report of the Ministerial Task Force," Alberta Justice, 3 March 1999, http://justice.alberta.ca/publications/Publications_Library /ReportoftheMinisterialTaskForce.aspx/DispForm.aspx?ID=36 (accessed 12 February 2001). A full slide presentation containing all the statistical evidence from this research report is available at http://justice.alberta.ca /publications/Documents/alberta_justice_issues_research/index.html

30 Barrie, *The Other Alberta*, 51–4.

31 Ted Morton, "A Preferential Option for the Family," speech delivered to the World Congress of Families, 1999. Available at http://www.worldcongress.org /wcf2_spkrs/wcf2_morton.htm?search=morton&opt=EXACT (accessed 9 August 2010).

32 Ted Morton, "Same-Sex Marriage: A Human Right?," *Edmonton Journal*, 5 September 2006, A19.

33 For a brief report on the relationship between Morton and certain conservative Christian organizations in Alberta, see Jason Markusoff, "Religious Lobby Rallies Faithful to Morton's Camp," *Edmonton Journal*, 29 November 2006, A7.

34 See Sheldon Alberts, "Klein Pulls Tory Party to the Right: The Right Stuff: Today's Alberta Tories Are Proud to Say They've Gone from Red to Redneck," *Calgary Herald*, 11 June 1994, A1.

35 For evidence that opposition to same-sex rights was stronger in rural areas, see "Report of the Ministerial Task Force," Alberta Justice, 3 March 1999, http://justice.alberta.ca/publications/Publications_Library /ReportoftheMinisterialTaskForce.aspx/DispForm.aspx?ID=36 (accessed 12 February 2011). A full slide presentation containing all the statistical evidence from this research report is available at http://justice.alberta.ca /publications/Documents/alberta_justice_issues_research/index.html. For evidence related to the difference in levels of religious service attendance between rural and urban locations in Alberta, see Clark, "Pockets of Belief," 3–4.

36 In a one-on-one semi-structured interview with the author, one former cabinet minister expressed regret that the gay rights issue was thrust upon the government and thereby largely distracted a sizable number of MLAs from the overarching goal of fiscal responsibility.

37 This was confirmed by a former cabinet minister and evangelical Christian in the Klein government in a one-on-one semi-structured interview with the author. A second evangelical Christian who also served in Klein's cabinet agreed with this contention in a separate interview with the author. This former MLA lamented the fact that the caucus's position on same-sex issues had more to do with political calculation than with Christian belief.

Notes to pages 179–83

38 See Ellis, *Traditional or Progressive*; and Chris Varcoe, "Is Alberta Shifting Left When It Comes to Hard-Line Issues Like Abortion, Same-Sex Marriage?" *Calgary Herald*, 6 November 2011, A6.

39 Carrie Tait and Josh Wingrove, "Smith Blames Controversial Remarks, Strategic Voting for Loss," *Globe and Mail*, 24 April 2012, http://www.theglobeandmail.com/news/politics /smith-blames-controversial-remarks-strategic-voting-for-alberta-loss /article4102158/#dashboard/follows/ (accessed 14 July 2013).

40 Jen Gerson, "Newest Alberta Education Act Cuts Reference to 'Honour' Charter of Rights," *National Post*, 24 October 2012, http://news.nationalpost.com/2012/10/24/latest-alberta-education-act-cuts-schools-requirement-to-honour-charter-of-rights/ (accessed 3 July 2013). See also Graham Thomson, "Tories Weaken Stronger Effort from Liberals on Gay-Straight Alliances," *Edmonton Journal*, 26 December 2014, http://www .edmontonjournal.com/opinion/Thomson+Bill+swap+exercise+cynicism /10431433/story.html (accessed 27 December 2014). For an academic assessment of the role social conservatives play within the education policy community in contemporary Alberta, see Banack, "Understanding the Influence of Faith-Based Organizations on Education Policy in Alberta."

41 See Dobbin, *Preston Manning and the Reform Party*; Douglas Todd, "God, Politics and the Reform Party: As a Fundamentalist Christian and Political Leader, Preston Manning Has His Beliefs under Public Scrutiny," *Vancouver Sun*, 21 December 1991, B3; and Sharpe and Braid, *Storming Babylon: Preston Manning and the Rise of the Reform Party*.

42 Flanagan bases this assertion on his reading of Manning's chapter on the "spiritual dimension" in *The New Canada* and his own interactions with Manning. See Flanagan, *Waiting for the Wave*, 7–8. Manning biographer Frank Dabbs also makes this point; see Dabbs, *Preston Manning*, 60–1, 85–6.

43 The religious foundations of Ernest Manning's social conservative ideology are unpacked in Chapter 4.

44 Flanagan, *Waiting for the Wave*, 8.

45 P. Manning, conversation with author, 9 November 2011.

46 P. Manning, "The Gospel and the Canadian Political/Cultural Context."

47 P. Manning, *The New Canada*, 97–8. Manning also explores this two-dimension understanding of Christianity in P. Manning, "Faith in Its Vertical and Horizontal Dimensions."

48 P. Manning, "Wise as Serpents; Harmless as Doves."

49 P. Manning, personal journals, 6 July 1998.

50 Manning, *The New Canada*, 97.

51 Preston Manning, conversation with author, 9 November 2011.

52 Mackey, *Like Father, Like Son*, 123–4, 153–8.

53 Preston Manning, conversation with author, 10 November 2010.
54 Mackey, *Like Father, Like Son*, 123–4, 153–8.
55 Preston Manning, conversation with author, 10 November 2010.
56 Ibid.
57 P. Manning, *The New Canada*, 99.
58 Ibid.
59 Preston Manning, conversation with author, 10 November 2010.
60 See P. Manning, "Christians and Politics."
61 P. Manning, personal journals, 20 June 1992.
62 P. Manning, "Christians and Politics," presentation to a Regent College Seminar, Vancouver, BC, January 1988. See also P. Manning, "Where Does God Fit in the World of Politics"; and P. Manning, "My Understanding of the Christian Faith."
63 Jim Farney has written at length about Manning's attempts to censor outspoken social conservatives in his own party. See Farney, *Social Conservatives and Party Politics in Canada and the United States*, 102–10.
64 Preston Manning, conversation with author, 9 November 2011.
65 Ibid.
66 P. Manning, "The Gospel and the Canadian Political/Cultural Context."
67 P. Manning, "Bringing Faith to Bear on Public Issues."
68 P. Manning, "Christians and Politics."
69 P. Manning, personal journals, 18 May 1998.
70 Preston Manning, conversation with author, 10 November 2010.
71 P. Manning, "Laying the Foundations for a New Western Political Party."
72 These arguments are reviewed in Harrison, Johnston, and Krahn, "Special Interests and/or New Right Economics? The Ideological Bases of Reform Party Support in Alberta in the 1993 Federal Election."
73 E. Manning, *Political Realignment*. Richard Sigurdson has argued that Manning's thought was not a continuation of his father's social credit ideas but rather represented a new wave of "postmodern" political thought in Canada that sought to respond to the failures of the secular modern state with a program of conservatism that transcended the "old" left-right divisions. There is certainly some truth to the suggestion that Manning articulated a "new" approach to politics, and Sigurdson correctly notes that some of Manning's particular policy prescriptions are quite distinct from those espoused by earlier western Canadian populist movements, yet he largely ignores the deeply rooted religious perspective of Manning that stood behind his broader political ideology and thus misses the very real points of continuity between Preston's and Ernest's thought that are anchored in their shared faith. See Sigurdson, "Preston Manning and the Politics of Postmodernism in Canada."

Notes to pages 189–95 245

74 P. Manning, personal journals, 20 June 1992.

75 Preston Manning, conversation with author, 10 November 2010.

76 Ibid.

77 P. Manning, personal journals, 20 June 1992.

78 Preston Manning, conversation with author, 10 November 2010.

79 Ernest Manning's beliefs in this regard are explored in Chapter 4. For Preston Manning's thoughts on the importance of "God's Love" for this world, see P. Manning, personal journals, 8 March 1998. For Preston's thoughts on the need for a broad spiritual renewal, see P. Manning, personal journals, 24/30 March 1997.

80 Preston Manning, conversation with author, 10 November 2010.

81 P. Manning, "The Next Canada."

82 See, for instance, P. Manning, "Getting Canada's Fiscal House in Order"; P. Manning, "Toward the New Economy"; and P. Manning, "A New and Better Home for Canadians."

83 Preston Manning, conversation with author, 10 November 2010.

84 Ibid. Manning initially drew upon this story in the Book of Acts in his radio commentary "Christians and Politics," *Canada's National Back to the Bible Hour*, n.d.

85 Preston Manning, conversation with author, 10 November 2010.

86 Flanagan, *Waiting for the Wave*, 12–16.

87 Manning indicated this in a conversation with author, 10 November 2010. For Manning's interest in environmental issues stretching back to the very early years of the Reform Party, see P. Manning, "Fresh Approaches to Environmental Conservation."

88 P. Manning, "Bringing Faith to Bear on Public Issues."

89 Ibid."

90 See P. Manning, "The Next Canada."

91 There is a tension here that was initially flagged by Flanagan. Despite Manning's contention that Reform policy represented the wishes of the party's members, many of the original party principles were authored by Manning prior to any membership consultation. Of course, subsequent research has shown than Manning's pro-market policies were strongly favoured by Reform supporters, but this does not change the fact that Manning most likely had more influence initially in setting the direction of Reform policy than he often admits. See Flanagan, *Waiting for the Wave*, 24.

92 See ibid., chaps 1 and 2. For an example of Manning's early dedication to democratic reforms of this nature, see P. Manning, "Democratic Populism."

93 P. Manning, *The New Canada*, 26.

94 P. Manning, personal journals, 19 January 1997.

246   Notes to pages 196–209

95 Preston Manning recounts this lesson in "Christians and Politics." Ernest
    Manning recounted the very same story in an interview after his retirement.
    See E. Manning, "Interview by Lydia Semotuk," Interview 14 (4 July 1980).
96 P. Manning, "Christians and Politics."
97 Preston Manning, conversation with author, 10 November 2010.
98 Manning's approach to such occurrences is documented in P. Manning, *The
    New Canada*, 107–8.
99 Preston Manning, conversation with author, 10 November 2010.
100 Ibid.
101 P. Manning, personal journals, 22 September and 20 October 1996.
102 Ibid.
103 Flanagan, *Waiting for the Wave*, 24.
104 For a detailed discussion on the state-led economic development program
    under Lougheed, see Richards and Pratt, *Prairie Capitalism: Power and
    Influence in the New West*, chaps 7 and 9; and Tupper, "Peter Lougheed, 1971–
    1985."
105 Detailed commentaries on the approach taken by the Klein government can
    be found in Laxer and Harrison, eds, *The Trojan Horse: Alberta and the Future
    of Canada*; Cooper, *The Klein Achievement*; Lisac, *The Klein Revolution*; and
    Bruce, Kneebone, and McKenzie, eds, *A Government Reinvented: A Study of Al-
    berta's Deficit Elimination Program*.
106 Archer and Gibbins, "What Do Albertans Think?"
107 Taras and Tupper, "Politics and Deficits," 66–7.
108 Wesley, *Code Politics*, 96–7.
109 For poll results suggesting that a provincial Reform Party would have easily
    defeated the PCs, see Harrison, "The Reform-Ation of Alberta Politics," 53.
110 Ibid., 56. See also Stewart, "Klein's Makeover of the Alberta Conservatives."
111 E. Manning, "Interview by Lydia Semotuk," Interview 1 (4 December 1978).
112 Preston Manning, conversation with author, 9 November 2011.
113 Ibid.
114 Laycock, *The New Right and Democracy in Canada*, 95.
115 Ibid., 10.
116 Ibid., 109.
117 Ibid., 93.
118 Harrison, "The Changing Face of Prairie Politics: Populism in Alberta."
119 Laxer, "The Privatization of Public Life," 101.
120 Hammond, *The Protestant Presence in Twentieth-Century America*, 45.
121 Denis, "'Government Can Do Whatever It Wants': Moral Regulation in Ralph
    Klein's Alberta," 374.
122 See Laxer and Harrison, eds, *The Trojan Horse*; Lisac, *The Klein Revolution*; and
    Jeffrey, *Hard Right Turn: The New Face of Neo-Conservatism in Canada*.

Notes to pages 211–17

CHAPTER SIX

1 Carrie Tait and Josh Wingrove, "Smith Blames Controversial Remarks, Strategic Voting for Loss," *Globe and Mail*, 24 April 2012, http://www.theglobeandmail.com/news/politics /smith-blames-controversial-remarks-strategic-voting-for-alberta-loss /article4102158/#dashboard/follows/ (accessed 14 July 2013).

2 David Staples, "Wildrose Candidate Allan Hunsperger on Gays: 'You will suffer the rest of eternity in the lake of fire, hell," *Edmonton Journal Blog*, 15 April 2012, http://blogs.edmontonjournal.com/2012/04/15 /wildrose-candidate-allan-hunsperger-on-gays-you-will-suffer-the-rest-of-eternity-in-the-lake-of-fire-hell/ (accessed 1 August 2013).

3 For an analysis of the influence possessed by religiously inspired social conservatives within the field of education policy in Alberta, see Banack, "Understanding the Influence of Faith-Based Organizations on Education Policy in Alberta."

4 See the official results of the 2015 federal election in Alberta published by *Elections Canada*: http://enr.elections.ca/Provinces.aspx?lang=e

5 Wesley, *Code Politics*, 55–113.

Bibliography

NEWSPAPERS AND PERIODICALS

Alberta Non-Partisan
Alberta Report
Alberta Views
Calgary Herald
Edmonton Journal
Globe and Mail
Grain Growers' Guide
Maclean's Magazine
National Post
The Nutcracker
Social Credit Chronicle
Toronto Star
The UFA
Vancouver Sun
Western Independent

ARCHIVES

The Aberhart Foundation (aberhartfoundation.ca)
Alberta Wheat Pool Fonds, Glenbow-Alberta Museum Archives, Calgary
Calgary Prophetic Bible Institute Fonds, Glenbow-Alberta Museum Archives,
    Calgary
Earl G. Cook Fonds, Glenbow-Alberta Museum Archives, Calgary
E. Preston Manning Fonds, University of Calgary Archives, Calgary
Ernest Manning Fonds, University of Alberta Archives, Edmonton
Foothills Christian College Fonds, Glenbow-Alberta Museum Archives,
    Calgary

250   Bibliography

Fred Kennedy Fonds, Glenbow-Alberta Museum Archives, Calgary
Political Papers Collection, University of Calgary Archives, Calgary
Prairie Manifesto Project, personal collection held by Jared Wesley,
     jared.wesley@gov.ab.ca
Prairie Provinces Collection, Peels Prairie Provinces, University of Alberta
     Library, Edmonton
Premier's Papers, 1969.289, Provincial Archives of Alberta, Edmonton
Walter Norman and Amelia Turner Smith Fonds, Glenbow-Alberta Museum
     Archives, Calgary
William Aberhart Fonds, University of Calgary Archives, Calgary

SOURCES

Aberhart, William. "God's Great Divisions of the World's History." In *God's
     Great Prophecies*, Lecture 2, 27–8, 1925. Accessed via the Aberhart Founda-
     tion: http://www.aberhartfoundation.ca/PDF%20Documents/Preacher
     %20Documents/God%27s%20Great%20Propheces%20Middle%20Series/
     GdGtPropBk1-%20Lect%201%20-%202.pdf.
– "The Second Coming of Christ, and Its Signs and Shadows." In *God's Great
     Prophecies*, Lecture 4, 7–8, 1925. Accessed via the Aberhart Foundation:
     http://www.aberhartfoundation.ca/PDF%20Documents/Preacher
     %20Documents/God%27s%20Great%20Propheces%20Middle%20Series
     /GdGtPropSectBk%202-%20Lect%204,5,6.pdf.
– "The Zionist Movement, or the Restoration of the Hebrews." In *God's
     Great Prophecies*, Lecture 5, 1925. Accessed via the Aberhart Foundation:
     http://www.aberhartfoundation.ca/PDF%20Documents/Preacher
     %20Documents/God%27s%20Great%20Propheces%20Middle%20Series
     /GdGtPropSectBk%202-%20Lect%204,5,6.pdf.
– "Sign-Posts on the Way to Millennium, or the Period-Divisions of Daniel's
     Seventieth Week." In *God's Great Prophecies*, Lecture 6, 1925. Accessed via
     the Aberhart Foundation: http://www.aberhartfoundation.ca/PDF
     %20Documents/Preacher%20Documents/God%27s%20Great
     %20Propheces%20Middle%20Series/GdGtPropSectBk%202-%20Lect
     %204,5,6.pdf.
– "The Anti-Christ: Individual or System." In *God's Great Prophecies*, Lecture
     7, 1925. Accessed via the Aberhart Foundation: http://www.aberhart
     foundation.ca/PDF%20Documents/Preacher%20Documents/God%27s
     %20Great%20Propheces%20Middle%20Series/GdGtPropSect3-%20Lect
     %207,8,9.pdf.
– "The Anti-Christ: Man or Demon?" In *God's Great Prophecies*, Lecture 8,
     1925. Accessed via the Aberhart Foundation: http://www.aberhart

Bibliography

foundation.ca/PDF%20Documents/Preacher%20Documents/God%27s
%20Great%20Propheces%20Middle%20Series/GdGtPropSect3-%20Lect
%207,8,9.pdf.

- "Armageddon: The Climax of Battles," In *God's Great Prophecies*, Lecture 9, 1925. Accessed via the Aberhart Foundation: http://www.aberhart foundation.ca/PDF%20Documents/Preacher%20Documents/God%27s %20Great%20Propheces%20Middle%20Series/GdGtPropSect3-%20Lect %207,8,9.pdf.
- "The Old and the New Theology." *Prophetic Voice*, December 1926, 5–6. The text of this writing is available in David R. Elliott, *Aberhart: Outpourings and Replies* (Calgary: Historical Society of Alberta, 1991), 38–41.
- Letter to J.H. Caldwell, 15 October 1932. Walter Norman and Amelia Turner Smith Fonds, file M-1157-30. Glenbow-Alberta Museum Archives, Calgary.
- Letter to J.H. Caldwell, 2 February 1933. Walter Norman and Amelia Turner Smith Fonds, file M-1157-30. Glenbow-Alberta Museum Archives, Calgary.
- "The Individualism of Destiny." Religious Notebooks, 1933-2. William Aberhart Fonds, 2005.075/02.02, 12 March 1933. University of Calgary Archives, Calgary.
- Letter to J.H. Caldwell, 29 March 1933. Walter Norman and Amelia Turner Smith Fonds, file M-1157-30. Glenbow-Alberta Museum Archives, Calgary.
- "The Collapse of Prehistoric Conditions," Religious Notebooks, 1933-2. William Aberhart Fonds, 2005.075/02.02, 12 March 1933. University of Calgary Archives, Calgary.
- "Money in the Fish's Mouth: The Dilemma of Taxation." Religious Notebooks, 1933-2. William Aberhart Fonds, 2005.075/02.02. University of Calgary Archives, Calgary.
- "Buying without Money: An Economic Feature Not Found in Present Day Capitalism." Religious Notebooks, 1933-2. William Aberhart Fonds, 2005.075/02.02. University of Calgary Archives, Calgary.
- Untitled lecture. Religious Notebooks, 1933-2. William Aberhart Fonds, 2005.075/02.02. University of Calgary Archives, Calgary.
- Radio Address, 19 April 1935. Walter Norman and Amelia Turner Smith Fonds, Glenbow-Alberta Museum Archives, file M-1157-82. Glenbow-Alberta Museum Archives, Calgary.
- Radio Address, 21 April 1935. Walter Norman and Amelia Turner Smith Fonds, file M-1157-82. Glenbow-Alberta Museum Archives, Calgary.
- Radio Address, 28 April 1935. Walter Norman and Amelia Turner Smith Fonds, file M-1157-82. Glenbow-Alberta Museum Archives, Calgary.

Bibliography

- Radio Address, 30 April 1935. Walter Norman and Amelia Turner Smith Fonds, file M-1157-80. Glenbow-Alberta Museum Archives, Calgary.
- Radio address, 3 May 1935. Walter Norman and Amelia Turner Smith Fonds, file M-1157-82. Glenbow-Alberta Museum Archives, Calgary.
- Radio address, 7 May 1935. Walter Norman and Amelia Turner Smith Fonds, file M-1157-82. Glenbow-Alberta Museum Archives, Calgary.
- Radio address, 18 June 1935. Walter Norman and Amelia Turner Smith Fonds, file M-1157-83. Glenbow-Alberta Museum Archives, Calgary.
- Radio address, 7 July 1935. Walter Norman and Amelia Turner Smith Fonds, file M-1157-83. Glenbow-Alberta Museum Archives, Calgary.
- Radio address, 12 July 1935. Walter Norman and Amelia Turner Smith Fonds, file M-1157-83. Glenbow-Alberta Museum Archives, Calgary.
- Radio address, 11 August 1935. Walter Norman and Amelia Turner Smith Fonds, file M-1157-83. Glenbow-Alberta Museum Archives, Calgary.
- Social Credit Manual. 1935. Prairie Manifesto Project. Compiled by Jared Wesley, jared.wesley@gov.ab.ca.
- "Freedom of the Press," 5 June 1937. Fred Kennedy Fonds, file M-1621-10. Glenbow-Alberta Museum Archives, Calgary.
- Sunday Radio Address, 7 November 1937. Fred Kennedy Fonds, file M-1621-6. Glenbow-Alberta Museum Archives, Calgary.
- "Speech from the Throne." *Journals of the Legislative Assembly of Alberta*, 1938. Provincial Archives of Alberta. Text also available in L.H. Thomas, ed., William Aberhart and Social Credit in Alberta (Toronto: Copp Clark Publishing, 1977), 133–4.
- Sunday Radio Address, 5 June 1938. Fred Kennedy Fonds, file M-1621-6. Glenbow-Alberta Museum Archives, Calgary.
- Sunday Radio Address, 10 July 1938. Fred Kennedy Fonds, file M-1621-6. Glenbow-Alberta Museum Archives, Calgary.
- Sunday Radio Address, 4 September 1938. Fred Kennedy Fonds, file M-1621-6. Glenbow-Alberta Museum Archives, Calgary.
- Sunday Radio Address, 30 October 1938. Fred Kennedy Fonds, file M-1621-6. Glenbow-Alberta Museum Archives, Calgary.
- Sunday Radio Address, 13 November 1938. Fred Kennedy Fonds, file M-1621-6. Glenbow-Alberta Museum Archives, Calgary.
- Sunday Radio Address, 11 December 1938. Fred Kennedy Fonds, file M-1621-6. Glenbow-Alberta Museum Archives, Calgary.
- "The Record of the Government," Speech to the Legislature of Alberta, 17 February 1939. The text of this writing is available in David R. Elliott, *Aberhart: Outpourings and Replies* (Calgary: Historical Society of Alberta, 1991), 187–202.

Bibliography 253

- Sunday Radio Address, 19 March 1939. Fred Kennedy Fonds, file M-1621-7. Glenbow-Alberta Museum Archives, Calgary.
- Letter to William Bollen, 12 March 1943. Premier's Papers, 1969.289, file 1179. Provincial Archives of Alberta, Edmonton.
- Letter to J.H. Caldwell, 29 March 1933. Walter Norman and Amelia Turner Smith Fonds, file M-1157-30. Glenbow-Alberta Museum Archives, Calgary.
- Systematic Theology, Course A, Book 1. Calgary Prophetic Bible Institute, n.d. Accessed via the Aberhart Foundation: http://www.aberhart foundation.ca/Pages/Prophetic.htm.
- Systematic Theology, Course A, Book 2. Calgary Prophetic Bible Institute, n.d. Accessed via the Aberhart Foundation: http://www.aberhart foundation.ca/Pages/Prophetic.htm.
- Systematic Theology, Course A, Book 3. Calgary Prophetic Bible Institute, n.d. Accessed via the Aberhart Foundation: http://www.aberhart foundation.ca/Pages/Prophetic.htm.
- Systematic Theology, Course B. Calgary Prophetic Bible Institute, n.d. Accessed via the Aberhart Foundation: http://www.aberhartfoundation.ca /Pages/Prophetic.htm.
- Systematic Theology, Course C. Calgary Prophetic Bible Institute, n.d. Accessed via the Aberhart Foundation: http://www.aberhartfoundation.ca /Pages/Prophetic.htm.
- Aberhart, William, and Ernest Manning. *The Branding Irons of the Antichrist*. 1931. The text of this play is available in L.P.V. Johnson and Ola J. Mac-Nutt, *Aberhart of Alberta* (Edmonton: Co-op Press, 1970), 231–9.
- Airhart, Phyllis D. "Ordering a New Nation and Reordering Protestantism, 1867–1914." In *The Canadian Protestant Experience, 1760–1990*, edited by G. Rawlyk, 98–138. Burlington: Welch Publishing Company, 1990.
- *Serving the Present Age: Revivalism, Progressivism, and the Methodist Tradition in Canada*. Montreal and Kingston: McGill-Queen's University Press, 1992.
- Allen, Richard. *The Social Passion: Religion and Social Reform in Canada 1914– 1928*. Toronto: University of Toronto Press, 1971.
- "Salem Bland and the Spirituality of the Social Gospel." In *Prairie Spirit: Perspectives on the Heritage of the United Church of Canada in the West*, edited by D.L. Butcher, C. MacDonald, M.E. McPherson, and R.R. Watts, 217–32. Winnipeg: University of Manitoba Press, 1985.
- "The Social Gospel as the Religion of the Agrarian Revolt." In *Riel to Reform: A History of Protest in Western Canada*, edited by George Melnyk, 138–47. Saskatoon: Fifth House, 1992.
- *The View from Murney Tower: Salem Bland, the Late Victorian Controversies,*

and the Search for a New Christianity. Vol. 1. Toronto: University of Toronto Press, 2008.

– "Profile: Salem Goldworth Bland, Part 2: 1903–1950: The New Christianity in a New, Distressful Canada." *Touchstone*, May 2010, 38–51.

Anderson, Leona, Bryan Hills, and Margaret Sanche. "Religion." In *The Encyclopedia of Saskatchewan*, http://esask.uregina.ca/entry/religion.html. Accessed 17 November 2014.

Appleby, R. Scott. *The Ambivalence of the Sacred: Religion, Violence, and Reconciliation*. New York: Rowman and Littlefield, 2000.

Archer, Keith, and Faron Ellis. "Opinion Structure of Party Activists: The Reform Party of Canada." *Canadian Journal of Political Science* 27, no. 2 (June 1994): 277–305.

Archer, Keith, and Roger Gibbins. "What Do Albertans Think? The Klein Agenda on the Public Opinion Landscape." In *A Government Reinvented: A Study of Alberta's Deficit Elimination Program*, edited by Christopher J. Bruce, Ronald D. Kneebone, and Kenneth J. McKenzie, 462–85. Toronto: Oxford University Press, 1997.

Bailyn, Bernard. *The Ideological Origins of the American Revolution*. Cambridge: Harvard University Press, 1967.

Banack, Clark. "American Protestantism and the Roots of 'Populist Conservatism' in Alberta." In *Conservatism in Canada*, edited by J. Farney and D. Rayside, 231–48. Toronto: University of Toronto Press, 2013.

– "Conservative Christianity, Anti-Statism and Alberta's Public Sphere: The Curious Case of Bill 44." In *Religion in the Public Sphere: Canadian Case Studies*, edited by S. Lefebvre and L. Beaman, 257–74. Toronto: University of Toronto Press, 2014.

– "Evangelical Christianity and Political Thought in Alberta." *Journal of Canadian Studies* 48, no. 2 (Spring 2014): 70–99.

– "Faith-based Organizations and Education Policy in Alberta." *Canadian Journal of Political Science*," forthcoming.

Barr, John J. *The Dynasty: The Rise and Fall of Social Credit in Alberta*. Toronto: McClelland and Stewart, 1974.

Barrie, Doreen. *The Other Alberta: Decoding a Political Enigma*. Regina: University of Regina, Canadian Plains Research Center, 2006.

Bebbington, David W. *Evangelicalism in Modern Britain*. London: Unwin Hyman, 1989.

Bell, Edward. "The Rise of the Lougheed Conservatives and the Demise of Social Credit in Alberta: A Reconsideration." *Canadian Journal of Political Science* 26, no. 3: 455–75.

– *Social Classes and Social Credit in Alberta*. Montreal and Kingston: McGill-Queen's University Press, 1993.

Bibliography 255

Betke, Carl Frederick. "The United Farmers of Alberta, 1921–1935: The Relationship between the Agricultural Organization and the Government of Alberta." MA thesis, University of Alberta, 1971.

– "The UFA: Visions of a Cooperative Commonwealth." In *Alberta History* 27, no. 3 (Summer 1979): 7–14.

– "The United Farmers of Alberta, 1921–1935." In *Society and Politics in Alberta*, edited by C. Caldarola, 14–32. Toronto: Methuen, 1979.

Bibby, Reginald W. *Restless Gods: The Renaissance of Religion in Canada*. Toronto: Stoddart, 2002.

– *Beyond the Gods and Back: Religion's Demise and Rise and Why It Matters*. Lethbridge: Project Canada Books, 2011.

Black, Julie, and Yvonne Stanford. "When Martha and Henry Are Poor: The Poverty of Alberta's Social Assistance Programs." In *The Return of the Trojan Horse: Alberta and the New World (Dis)Order*, edited by T. Harrison, 285–96. Montreal: Black Rose Books, 2005.

Boessenkool, Ken. "Does Alberta have a Spending Problem?" *The School of Public Policy, SPP Communiqué*. University of Calgary 2, no. 1 (February 2010): 1–16.

Bowen, Kurt. *Christians in a Secular World: The Canadian Experience*. Montreal and Kingston: McGill-Queen's University Press, 2004.

Boyer, Paul. *When Time Shall Be No More: Prophecy Belief in Modern American Culture*. Cambridge MA: Harvard University Press, 1992.

Brownsey, Keith. "Alberta's Oil and Gas Industry in the Era of the Kyoto Protocol." In *Canadian Energy Policy and the Struggle for Sustainable Development*, edited by G. Bruce Doern, 200–22. Toronto: University of Toronto Press, 2005.

Bruce, Christopher J., Ronald D. Kneebone, and Kenneth J. McKenzie, eds. *A Government Reinvented: A Study of Alberta's Deficit Elimination Program*. Toronto: Oxford University Press, 1997.

Byfield, Ted. *Why History Matters*. Edmonton: Society to Explore and Research Christian History, 2008.

Cairns, Alan C. "The Governments and Societies of Canadian Federalism." *Canadian Journal of Political Science* 10, no. 4 (December 1977): 695–725.

Carter, Paul A. *The Decline and Revival of the Social Gospel: Social and Political Liberalism in American Protestant Churches, 1920–1940*. Hamden: Shoe String Press, 1956.

Chastko, Paul. *Developing Alberta's Oil Sands: From Karl Clark to Kyoto*. Calgary: University of Calgary Press, 2004.

Christie, Nancy. "In These Times of Democratic Rage and Delusion: Popular Religion and the Challenge to the Established Order, 1760–1815." In *The*

Canadian Protestant Experience, 1760–1990, edited by G. Rawlyk, 9–47. Burlington: Welch Publishing Company, 1990.

Clark, S.D. "The Religious Sect in Canadian Politics." *American Journal of Sociology* 51, no. 3 (November 1945): 207–16.

– *Church and Sect in Canada*. Toronto: University of Toronto Press, 1948.

Clark, Warren. "Pockets of Belief: Religious Attendance Patterns in Canada." *Canadian Social Trends* 68 (Spring 2003): 2–5.

Coats, R.H., and M.C. Maclean. *The American-Born in Canada: A Statistical Interpretation*. Toronto: Ryerson Press, 1943.

Cooper, Barry. *The Klein Achievement*. Toronto: University of Toronto Centre for Public Management, 1995.

Creech, Joe. *Righteous Indignation: Religion and the Populist Revolution*. Chicago: University of Illinois Press, 2006.

Dabbs, Frank. *Preston Manning: The Roots of Reform*. Vancouver: Greystone Books, 1997.

Dacks, Gurston. "From Consensus to Competition: Social Democracy and Political Culture in Alberta." In *Essays in Honour of Grant Notley: Socialism and Democracy in Alberta*, edited by Larry Pratt, 186–204. Edmonton: NeWest, 1986.

Davison, Andrew. *Secularism and Revivalism in Turkey: A Hermeneutic Reconsideration*. New Haven: Yale University Press, 1998.

Dawson, C.A. *Pioneering in the Prairie Provinces: The Social Side of the Settlement Process*. Toronto: Macmillan, 1940.

Dayton, Donald W. "Millennial Views and Social Reform in Nineteenth Century America." In *The Coming Kingdom: Essays in American Millennialism and Eschatology*, edited by M. Darrol Bryant and Donald W. Dayton, 131–47. New York: New Era Books, 1983.

– "Some Doubts about the Usefulness of the Category 'Evangelical.'" In *The Variety of American Evangelicalism*, edited by Donald W. Dayton and R. Johnston, 245–51. Knoxville: University of Tennessee Press, 1991.

Dayton, Donald W., and R. Johnston, eds. *The Variety of American Evangelicalism*. Knoxville: University of Tennessee Press, 1991.

Denis, Claude. "'Government Can Do Whatever It Wants': Moral Regulation in Ralph Klein's Alberta." *Canadian Review of Sociology and Anthropology* 32, no. 3 (August 1995): 365–83.

– "The New Normal: Capitalist Discipline in Alberta in the 1990s." In *The Trojan Horse: Alberta and the Future of Canada*, edited by T. Harrison and G. Laxer, 86–100. Montreal: Black Rose Books, 1995.

Dobbin, Murray. *Preston Manning and the Reform Party*. Toronto: James Lorimer, 1991.

Drugge, Sten. "The Alberta Tax Advantage: Myth and Reality." In *The Trojan*

Bibliography 257

Horse: Alberta and the Future of Canada, edited by T. Harrison and G. Laxer,
182-192. Montreal: Black Rose Books, 1995.

Elliott, David R. "Antithetical Elements in William Aberhart's Theology and
Political Ideology." *Canadian Historical Review* 59, no. 1 (1978): 38–58.

– "The Devil and William Aberhart: The Nature and Function of His Eschatology." *Studies in Religion* 9, no. 3 (Summer 1980): 325–37.

– *Aberhart: Outpourings and Replies.* Calgary: Historical Society of Alberta,
1991.

Elliott, David R., and Iris Miller. *Bible Bill: A Biography of William Aberhart.*
Edmonton: Reidmore Books, 1987.

Ellis, Faron. *Traditional or Progressive: Albertans' Opinion Structure on Six Policy
Issues.* Citizen Society Research Lab, Lethbridge, AB, November 2011,
research-lab/alberta-opinion-studies. Accessed 7 November 2011.

Emery, J.C. Herbert, and Ronald D. Kneebone. "Socialists, Populists, Resources, and the Divergent Development of Alberta and Saskatchewan."
Canadian Public Policy 34, no. 4 (2008): 419–40

Epp, Roger. "The Political De-skilling of Rural Communities." In *Writing Off
the Rural West: Globalization, Governments, and the Transformation of Rural
Communities*, edited by Roger Epp and Dave Whitson, 301–24. Edmonton:
University of Alberta Press, 2001.

– "'Their Own Emancipators': The Agrarian Movement in Alberta." In *We
Are All Treaty People: Prairie Essays*, 59–72. Edmonton: University of Alberta
Press, 2008.

Farney, James. *Social Conservatives and Party Politics in Canada and the United
States.* Toronto: University of Toronto Press, 2012.

Finkel, Alvin. *The Social Credit Phenomenon in Alberta.* Toronto: University of
Toronto Press, 1989.

Flanagan, Greg. "Not Just About Money: Provincial Budgets and Political
Ideologies." In *The Return of the Trojan Horse: Alberta and the New World
(Dis)Order*, edited by T. Harrison, 115–35. Montreal: Black Rose Books,
2005.

Flanagan, Thomas. "Political Geography and the United Farmers of Alberta."
In *The Twenties in Western Canada*, edited by S.M. Trofimenkoff, 138–69.
Ottawa: National Museum of Canada, 1972.

– "Social Credit in Alberta: A Canadian 'Cargo Cult'?" *Archives de sociologie
des religions* 34 (1972): 39–48.

Flanagan, Thomas, and Martha Lee. "From Social Credit to Social Conservatism: The Evolution of an Ideology." *Prairie Forum* 16, no. 2 (Fall 1991):
205–23.

Flanagan, Tom. *Waiting for the Wave: The Reform Party and Preston Manning.*
Toronto: Stoddart, 1995.

Foster, Franklin Lloyd. "The 1921 Provincial Election: A Consideration of Factors Involved with Particular Attention to Overtones of Millennialism within the UFA and Other Reform Movements." MA thesis, Queen's University, 1978.

– *John E. Brownlee: A Biography*. Lloydminster: Foster Learning Inc., 1996.

– "John E. Brownlee, 1925–1934." In *Alberta Premiers of the Twentieth Century*, edited by B.J. Rennie ed., 77–106. Regina: Canadian Plains Research Center, 2004.

Francis, R. Douglas. "In Search of a Prairie Myth: A Survey of the Intellectual and Cultural Historiography of Prairie Canada." *Journal of Canadian Studies* 24, no. 3 (Fall 1989): 44–69.

French, Goldwin. "The Evangelical Creed in Canada." In *The Shield of Achilles*, edited by W.L. Morton, 15–35. Toronto: McClelland and Stewart, 1968.

Friesen, Gerald. *The Canadian Prairies: A History*. Toronto: University of Toronto Press, 1987.

Frum, "Foreword." In *The Book of Ted: Epistles from an Unrepentant Redneck*. Edmonton: Keystone Press, 1998.

Garrison, Wilfred Ernest, and Alfred T. DeGroot. *The Disciples of Christ: A History*. St Louis: Bethany Press, 1948.

Gauvreau, Michael. "Baconianism, Darwinism, Fundamentalism: A Transatlantic Crisis of Faith." In Journal of *Religious History* 13, no. 4 (December 1985): 434–68.

– *The Evangelical Century*. Montreal and Kingston: McGill-Queen's University Press, 1991.

– "The Empire of Evangelicalism: Varieties of Common Sense in Scotland, Canada, and the United States." In *Evangelicalism: Comparative Studies of Popular Protestantism in North America, the British Isles, and Beyond*, edited by M. Noll, D. Bebbington, and G. Rawlyk, 219–52. New York: Oxford University Press, 1994.

Geertz, Clifford. "Religion as a Cultural System." In *The Interpretation of Cultures: Selected Essays by Clifford Geertz*, 87–125. New York: Basic Books, 1973.

Gibbins, Roger. "Western Alienation and the Alberta Political Culture." In *Society and Politics in Alberta*, edited by C. Caldarola, 143–67. Toronto: Methuen, 1979.

Goa, David. "Pietism, a Prairie Story: Spiritual Transformation." In *Pietism and the Challenges of Modernity*, 1–14. Edmonton: Occasional Papers of the Chester Ronning Centre, 2001.

Goode, Richard C. "The Godly Insurrection in Limestone County: Social Gospel, Populism, and Southern Culture in the Late Nineteenth Century." *Religion and American Culture* 3, no. 2 (Summer 1993): 155–69.

Bibliography

Goodwyn, Lawrence. *The Populist Moment: A Short History of the Agrarian Revolt in America*. New York: Oxford University Press, 1978.

Grant, George. *Lament for a Nation*. Toronto: McClelland and Stewart, 1965.

Grant, John Webster. *The Church in the* Canadian Era. 2nd ed. Burlington, ON: Welch Publishing Company, 1988.

Groh, Dennis G. "The Political Thought of Ernest Manning." MA thesis, University of Calgary, 1970.

Guenther, Bruce L. "Training for Service: The Bible School Movement in Western Canada, 1909–1960." PhD diss., McGill University, 2001.

Hammond, Phillip E. *The Protestant Presence in Twentieth-Century America: Religion and Political Culture*. Albany: State University of New York Press, 1992.

Harding, Susan. "Representing Fundamentalism: The Problem of the Repugnant Cultural Other." *Social Research* 58, no. 2 (Summer 1991): 373–93.

Harrell Jr, David Edwin. *Sources of Division in the Disciples of Christ, 1865–1900: A Social History of the Disciples of* Christ. Vol. 2. Tuscaloosa and London: University of Alabama Press, 2003.

Harrison, Trevor. *Of Passionate Intensity: Right-Wing Populism and the Reform Party of Canada*. Toronto: University of Toronto Press, 1995.

– "The Reform-Ation of Alberta Politics." In *The Trojan Horse: Alberta and the Future of Canada*, edited by Gordon Laxer and Trevor Harrison, 47–60. Montreal: Black Rose Books, 1997.

– "The Changing Face of Prairie Politics: Populism in Alberta." *Prairie Forum* 25, no. 1 (Spring 2000): 107–21.

– ed. *The Return of the Trojan Horse: Alberta and the New World (Dis)Order*. Montreal: Black Rose Books, 2005.

Harrison, Trevor, Bill Johnston, and Harvey Krahn. "Special Interests and/or New Right Economics? The Ideological Bases of Reform Party Support in Alberta in the 1993 Federal Election." *Canadian Review of Sociology* 33, no. 2 (May 1996): 159–97.

Harrison, Trevor W., William Johnston, and Harvey Krahn. "Language and Power: 'Special Interests' in Alberta's Political Discourse." In *The Return of the Trojan Horse: Alberta and the New World (Dis)Order*, edited by T. Harrison, 82–94. Montreal: Black Rose Books, 2005.

Harvey, Paul. *Freedom's Coming: Religious Culture and the Shaping of the South from the Civil War through the Civil Rights Era*. Chapel Hill and London: University of North Carolina Press, 2005.

Hatch, Nathan O. *The Democratization of American Christianity*. New Haven, CT: Yale University Press, 1989.

Hesketh, Bob. *Major Douglas and Alberta Social Credit*. Toronto: University of Toronto Press, 1997.

Bibliography

Hicks, John D. *The Populist Revolt: A History of the Farmers' Alliance and the People's Party*. Minneapolis: University of Minnesota Press, 1931.

Hiller, Harry H. "A Critical Analysis of the Role of Religion in a Canadian Populist Movement: The Emergence and Domination of the Social Credit Party in Alberta." PhD diss., McMaster University, 1972.

Hofstadter, Richard. *Anti-intellectualism in American Life*. New York: Alfred A. Knopf, 1962.

Hoover, Dennis R., Michael D. Martinez, Samuel H. Reimer, and Kenneth D. Wald. "Evangelicalism Meets the Continental Divide: Moral and Economic Conservatism in the United States and Canada." *Political Research Quarterly* 55, no. 2 (June 2002): 351–74.

Hopkins, Charles Howard. *The Rise of the Social Gospel in American Protestantism, 1865–1915*. New Haven, CT: Yale University Press, 1940.

Horne, Tammy. "From Manning to Mazankowski and Beyond: Alberta's Fight to Privatize Health Care." In *The Return of the Trojan Horse: Alberta and the New World (Dis)Order*, edited by T. Harrison, 215–35. Montreal: Black Rose Books, 2005.

Horowitz, Gad. "Conservatism, Liberalism, and Socialism in Canada: An Interpretation." *Canadian Journal of Economics and Political Science* 32, no. 1 (1966): 143–71.

Irvine, William. "Hope of the Church." *The Nutcracker*, 30 March 1917, 5.
– "Prophet of the 20th Century." *The Nutcracker*, 27 April 1917, 6.
– "UFA Sermon." *Western Independent*, 9 June 1920, 11.
– *Can a Christian Vote for Capitalism?* Ottawa: Labour Publishing Company, 1935.
– *The Farmers in Politics*. Toronto: McClelland and Stewart, 1976 [1920].

Irving, John. *The Social Credit Movement in Alberta*. Toronto: University of Toronto Press, 1959.

Jeffrey, Brooke. *Hard Right Turn: The New Face of Neo-Conservatism in Canada*. Toronto: HarperCollins, 1999.

Johnson, L.P.V., and Ola J. MacNutt. *Aberhart of Alberta*. Edmonton: Co-op Press, 1970.

Johnson, Myron. "The Failure of the CCF in Alberta: An Accident of History." In *Society and Politics in Alberta: Research Papers*, edited by C. Caldarola, 87–107. Agincourt: Methuen Publications, 1979.

Johnsrude, Larry. "Moral Compass or Political Antennas." *Alberta Views*, January/February 2003, 33–7.

Kettell, Steve. "Has Political Science Ignored Religion?" *PS: Political Science and Politics*, January 2012, 93–100.

King, Keith L. "Disciples of Christ and the Agrarian Protest in Texas, 1870–1906." *Restoration Quarterly* 35 (1993): 81–91.

Bibliography

Kirk, J. Fergus. "Social Credit and the Word of God," 1935. The text of this writing is available in David R. Elliott, *Aberhart: Outpourings and Replies* (Calgary: Historical Society of Alberta, 1991), 109–22.

Laird, Gordon. "Spent Energy: Re-fueling the Alberta Advantage." In *The Return of the Trojan Horse: Alberta and the New World (Dis)Order*, edited by T. Harrison, 156–72. Montreal: Black Rose Books, 2005.

Lambert, Frank. *Religion in American Politics: A Short History*. Princeton, NJ: Princeton University Press, 2008.

Laxer, Gordon. "The Privatization of Public Life." In *The Trojan Horse: Alberta and the Future of Canada*, edited by Gordon Laxer and Trevor Harrison, 101–17. Montreal: Black Rose Books, 1997.

Laxer, Gordon, and Trevor Harrison, eds. *The Trojan Horse: Alberta and the Future of Canada*. Montreal: Black Rose Books, 1995.

Laycock, David. *Populism and Democratic Thought in the Canadian Prairies, 1910 to 1945*. Toronto: University of Toronto Press, 1990.

– *The New Right and Democracy in Canada*. Toronto: Oxford University Press, 2002.

Lipset, Seymour Martin. *Agrarian Socialism*. Toronto: Oxford University Press, 1950.

– *Continental Divide: The Values and Institutions of the United States and Canada*. New York: Routledge, 1990.

Lisac, Mark. *The Klein Revolution*. Edmonton: NeWest Press, 1995.

Lloyd, Julia, and Laura Bonnett. "The Arrested Development of Queer Rights in Alberta." In *The Return of the Trojan Horse: Alberta and the New World (Dis)Order*, edited by Trevor Harrison, 328–41. Montreal: Black Rose Books, 2005.

MacDonald, L. Ian. "The Best Premier of the Last 40 Years: Lougheed in a Landslide." *Policy Options*, June-July 2012, 13–17.

Mackey, Lloyd. *Like Father, Like Son: Ernest Manning and Preston Manning*. Toronto: ECW Press, 1997.

Macpherson, C.B. *Democracy in Alberta*. Toronto: University of Toronto Press, 1953.

Malloy, Jonathan. "The Relationship between the Conservative Party of Canada and Evangelicals and Social Conservatives." In *Conservatism in Canada*, edited by J. Farney and D. Rayside, 184–206. Toronto: University of Toronto Press, 2013.

Mann, W.E. *Sect, Cult, and Church in Alberta*. Toronto: University of Toronto Press, 1955.

Manning, E.C. *Political Realignment: A Challenge to Thoughtful Canadians*. Toronto and Montreal: McClelland and Stewart, 1967.

Manning, Ernest. "Financial Tyranny and the Dawn of a New Day." Address to the Alberta Legislature, 6 March 1939. Political Papers, University of Calgary Archives, Calgary. Accessed via http://contentdm.ucalgary.ca/cdm4/document.php?CISOROOT=/reform&CISOPTR=10030&REC=7.

- Letter to Lee, 6 June 1944. Premier's Papers, 69.289, file 1179. Provincial Archives of Alberta, Edmonton.
- Letter to T.G. Irwin, 1 November 1946. Premier's Papers, 69.289, file 1179. Provincial Archives of Alberta, Edmonton.
- *Education and the Problem of Human Relationships*. Edmonton: King's Printer, 1946.
- Letter to Ewers, 6 February 1948. Premier's Papers, 69.289, file 1158. Provincial Archives of Alberta, Edmonton.
- Radio Address, 5 December 1948. Political Papers, Sunday Afternoon Radio Broadcasts 1948, University of Calgary Archives, Calgary. Accessed via http://contentdm.ucalgary.ca/cdm4/document.php?CISOROOT=/reform&CISOPTR=11484&REC=9.
- Radio Address, 19 December 1948. Political Papers, Sunday Afternoon Radio Broadcasts 1948, University of Calgary Archives, Calgary. Accessed via http://contentdm.ucalgary.ca/cdm4/document.php?CISOROOT=/reform&CISOPTR=11484&REC=9.
- Radio Address, 2 January 1949. Political Papers, Sunday Afternoon Radio Broadcasts 1949, University of Calgary Archives, Calgary. Accessed via http://contentdm.ucalgary.ca/cdm4/document.php?CISOROOT=/reform&CISOPTR=11726&REC=8.
- Letter to Phibbs, 4 February 1949. Premier's Papers, 1977.173, file 1860a. Provincial Archives of Alberta, Edmonton.
- Radio Address, 20 February 1949. Political Papers, Sunday Afternoon Radio Broadcasts 1949, University of Calgary Archives, Calgary. Accessed via http://contentdm.ucalgary.ca/cdm4/document.php?CISOROOT=/reform&CISOPTR=11726&REC=8.
- Radio Address, 6 March 1949. Political Papers, Sunday Afternoon Radio Broadcasts 1949, University of Calgary Archives, Calgary. Accessed via http://contentdm.ucalgary.ca/cdm4/document.php?CISOROOT=/reform&CISOPTR=11726&REC=8.
- Radio Address, 26 March 1949. Political Papers, Sunday Afternoon Radio Broadcasts 1949, University of Calgary Archives, Calgary. Accessed via http://contentdm.ucalgary.ca/cdm4/document.php?CISOROOT=/reform&CISOPTR=11726&REC=8.
- Letter to Hollowes, 15 September 1952. Premier's Papers, 69.289, file 1578. Provincial Archives of Alberta, Edmonton.
- Radio Address, 29 March 1953. Political Papers, Sunday Afternoon Radio Broadcasts 1953, University of Calgary Archives, Calgary. Accessed via

Bibliography

http://contentdm.ucalgary.ca/cdm4/document.php?CISOROOT=/reform
&CISOPTR=12925&REC=1.

- Radio Address, 5 April 1953. Political Papers, Sunday Afternoon Radio
Broadcasts 1953, University of Calgary Archives, Calgary. Accessed via
http://contentdm.ucalgary.ca/cdm4/document.php?CISOROOT=/reform
&CISOPTR=12925&REC=1.
- Radio Address, 3 May 1953. Political Papers, Sunday Afternoon Radio
Broadcasts 1953, University of Calgary Archives, Calgary. Accessed via
http://contentdm.ucalgary.ca/cdm4/document.php?CISOROOT=/reform
&CISOPTR=12925&REC=1.
- Radio Address, 10 May 1953. Political Papers, Sunday Afternoon Radio
Broadcasts 1953, University of Calgary Archives, Calgary. Accessed via
http://contentdm.ucalgary.ca/cdm4/document.php?CISOROOT=/reform
&CISOPTR=12925&REC=1.
- Letter to Lester C. Frets, 24 July 1958. Premier's Papers, 69.289, file 2187.
Provincial Archives of Alberta, Edmonton.
- Letter to Ronald S. Dinnick, 10 January 1961. Premier's Papers, 1977.173
file 394a. Provincial Archives of Alberta, Edmonton.
- Letter to G.M. Wilson, 18 April 1962. Premier's Papers, 1977.173 file 394b.
Provincial Archives of Alberta, Edmonton.
- Letter to Ruth Bedford, 18 April 1962. Premier's Papers, 1977.173 file
394b. Provincial Archives of Alberta, Edmonton.
- Letter to R.K. Macpherson, 24 February 1965. Premier's Papers, 1977.173,
file 800. Provincial Archives of Alberta, Edmonton.
- *National Medicare: Let's Look before We Leap.* 1965. Prairie Manifesto Project.
Compiled by Jared Wesley, jared.wesley@gov.ab.ca.
- *Some Ground Rules for a Free Society.* Edmonton: Alberta Social Credit
League, 1966.
- Letter to G. Drexhage, 28 February 1967. Premier's Papers, 1977.173 file
800. Provincial Archives of Alberta, Edmonton.
- Letter to Robert Sheath, 5 April 1967. Premier's Papers, 1977.173, file 800.
Provincial Archives of Alberta, Edmonton.
- "Interview by Lydia Semotuk." Interview 1, Edmonton, 4 December 1978.
Transcript located in Ernest Manning Fonds, University of Alberta
Archives, Edmonton.
- "Interview by Lydia Semotuk." Interview 2, Edmonton, 18 December
1978. Transcript located in Ernest Manning Fonds, University of Alberta
Archives, Edmonton.
- "Interview by Lydia Semotuk." Interview 14, Edmonton, 4 July 1980. Tran-
script located in Ernest Manning Fonds, University of Alberta Archives,
Edmonton.

264   Bibliography

- "Interview by Lydia Semotuk." Interview 16, Edmonton, 18 July 1980.
  Transcript located in Ernest Manning Fonds, University of Alberta
  Archives, Edmonton.
- "Interview by Lydia Semotuk." Interview 19, Edmonton, 20 August 1980.
  Transcript located in Ernest Manning Fonds, University of Alberta
  Archives, Edmonton.
- "Interview by Lydia Semotuk." Interview 38, Edmonton, 10 May 1982.
  Transcript located in Ernest Manning Fonds, University of Alberta
  Archives, Edmonton.
- "Interview by Lydia Semotuk." Interview 39, Edmonton, 17 May 1982.
  Transcript located in Ernest Manning Fonds, University of Alberta
  Archives, Edmonton.
- "Economic Crises #2." Radio Address, n.d. The Aberhart Foundation. Ac-
  cessed via http://www.aberhartfoundation.ca/PDF%20Documents/Preacher
  %20Documents/Radio%20Add_Economic%20Security_Manning.pdf.
- "Watchman What of the Night." Radio Address, n.d. Foothills Christian
  College Fonds, file M 7481-203. Glenbow-Alberta Museum Archives,
  Calgary.
- "The Road to Serfdom or the Welfare State Syndrome." Radio Address,
  n.d., Foothills Christian College Fonds, file M 7481-203. Glenbow-Alberta
  Museum Archives, Calgary.
Manning, Preston. "Laying the Foundations for a New Western Political
  Party." Presentation to a Public Information Meeting, Calgary, 10 August
  1987. Political Papers, University of Calgary Archives, Calgary.
- "Christians and Politics." Presentation to a Regent College Seminar, Van-
  couver, January 1988. Political Papers, University of Calgary Archives, Cal-
  gary. Accessed via http://contentdm.ucalgary.ca/cdm4/document.php
  ?CISOROOT=/reform&CISOPTR=3948&REC=8.
- "The Next Canada." Speech, 1 July 1988. Political Papers, Preston Manning
  Speeches, 1988, University of Calgary Archives, Calgary. Accessed via
  http://contentdm.ucalgary.ca/cdm4/document.php?CISOROOT=/reform
  &CISOPTR=3952&REC=9.
- "Where Does God Fit in the World of Politics." Address to Regent College,
  22 April 1989. Political Papers, University of Calgary Archives, Calgary.
  Accessed via http://contentdm.ucalgary.ca/cdm4/document.php
  ?CISOOOT=/reform&CISOPTR=4012&REC=13.
- "Fresh Approaches to Environmental Conservation." Speech, Swan Hills,
  AB, 21 June 1989. Political Papers, Preston Manning Speeches, 1989, Uni-
  versity of Calgary Archives, Calgary. Accessed via http://contentdm
  .ucalgary.ca/cdm4/document.php?CISOROOT=/reform&CISOPTR=3961
  &REC=10.

Bibliography

- "My Understanding of the Christian Faith." Address to Christian and Missionary Alliance Churches of Calgary, Calgary, 1 June 1991. Political Papers Collection, University of Calgary Archives, Calgary. Accessed via http://contentdm.ucalgary.ca/cdm4/document.php?CISOROOT=/reform &CISOPTR=4233&REC=13.
- *The New Canada*. Toronto: Macmillan Canada, 1992.
- "Getting Canada's Fiscal House in Order." Address, 19 January 1992. Political Papers, University of Calgary Archives, Calgary. Accessed via http://contentdm.ucalgary.ca/cdm4/document.php?CISOROOT=/reform &CISOPTR=4602&REC=6.
- Personal Journal, 20 June 1992. E. Preston Manning Fonds, 2003.054/14.04. University of Calgary Archives, Calgary.
- "Toward the New Economy." Address to Trinity Western University, Langley, BC, 8 October 1993. Political Papers, University of Calgary Archives, Calgary. Accessed via http://contentdm.ucalgary.ca/cdm4/document .php?CISOROOT=/reform&CISOPTR=4981&REC=15.
- "A New and Better Home for Canadians." Address to Reform Party Assembly, Ottawa, 15 October 1994. Political Papers, University of Calgary Archives, Calgary. Accessed via http://contentdm.ucalgary.ca/cdm4 /document.php?CISOROOT=/reform&CISOPTR=5467&REC=20.
- "Democratic Populism." Address, 23 June 1995. Political Papers, University of Calgary Archives, Calgary. Accessed via http://contentdm.ucalgary.ca /cdm4/document.php?CISOROOT=/reform&CISOPTR=5726&REC=10.
- Personal Journal, 22 September 1996. E. Preston Manning Fonds, 2003.054/14.07. University of Calgary Archives, Calgary.
- Personal Journal, 20 October 1996. E. Preston Manning Fonds, 2003.054/14.07. University of Calgary Archives, Calgary.
- Personal Journal, 19 January 1997. E. Preston Manning Fonds, 2003.054/14.07. University of Calgary Archives, Calgary.
- Personal Journal, 24/30 March 1997. E. Preston Manning Fonds, 2003.054/14.07. University of Calgary Archives, Calgary.
- Personal Journals, 8 March 1998. E. Manning Fonds, 2003.054/14.07. University of Calgary Archives, Calgary.
- Personal Journal, 18 May 1998. E. Preston Manning Fonds, 2003.054/14.10. University of Calgary Archives, Calgary.
- Personal Journal, 6 July 1998. E. Preston Manning Fonds, 2003.054/14.10. University of Calgary Archives, Calgary.
- *Think Big*. Toronto: McClelland and Stewart, 2003.
- "Wise as Serpents; Harmless as Doves." Address to the Calgary Police Chief's Prayer Breakfast, Calgary, 6 May 2004. Text provided to author by Preston Manning.

- "Faith in Its Vertical and Horizontal Dimensions." Address to the Ontario Prayer Breakfast, Toronto, 4 May 2005. Text provided to author by Preston Manning.
- "The Gospel and the Canadian Political/Cultural Context." Address to the Refocus Canada Conference, Burnaby, BC, 8 April 2010. Text provided to author by Preston Manning.
- "Bringing Faith to Bear on Public Issues." Address to Regent College Marketplace Institute, Vancouver, 26 January 2012. Text provided to author by Preston Manning.
- "Christians and Politics." In *Canada's National Back to the Bible Hour*, n.d. Prairie Provinces Collection, University of Alberta Library, Edmonton.
Mardiros, Anthony. *William Irvine: The Life of a Prairie Radical*. Halifax: James Lorimer, 1979.
Marsden, George M. "Fundamentalism as an American Phenomenon, A Comparison with English Evangelicalism." *Church History* 46 (1977): 215–32.
- *Religion and American Culture*. Orlando, FL: Harcourt Brace Jonavich, 1990.
- *Fundamentalism and American Culture*. 2nd ed. New York: Oxford University Press, 2006.
Marshall, David. "Premier E.C. Manning, *Back to the Bible Hour*, and Fundamentalism in Canada." In *Religion and Public Life in Canada*, edited by Marguerite Van Die, 237–54. Toronto: University of Toronto Press, 2001.
Masciulli, Joseph, Mikhail A. Molchanov, and W. Andy Knight. "Political Leadership in Context." In *The Ashgate Research Companion to Political Leadership*, edited by J. Masciulli, M.A. Molchanov, and W.A. Knight, 3–27. Farnam and Burlington: Ashgate Publishing, 2009.
Matthews, Donald G. "The Second Great Awakening as an Organizing Process, 1780–1830: An Hypothesis." *American Quarterly* 21, no. 1 (Spring 1969): 23–43.
May, Henry F. *Protestant Churches and Industrial America*. New York: Harper and Row, 1949.
McCormick, Peter. "Voting Behaviour in Alberta: The Quasi-Party System Revisited." *Journal of Canadian Studies* 15, no. 3 (Fall 1980): 85–98.
McInnis, John, and Urquhart, Ian. "Protecting Mother Earth or Business? Environmental Politics in Alberta." In *The Trojan Horse: Alberta and the Future of Canada*, edited by T. Harrison and G. Laxer, 239–53. Montreal: Black Rose Books, 1995.
McLoughlin, William G. "Revivalism." In *The Rise of Adventism*, edited by Edwin S. Gaustad, 119–53. New York: Harper and Row, 1974.
Mills, Allen. *Fool for Christ: The Political Thought of J.S. Woodsworth*. Toronto: University of Toronto Press, 1991.

Bibliography 267

Morton, W.L. "The Social Philosophy of Henry Wise Wood, the Canadian Agrarian Leader." *Agricultural History* 22, no. 2 (April 1948): 114–23.

– *The Progressive Party in Canada*. Toronto: University of Toronto Press, 1950.

– "The Bias of Prairie Politics." *Transactions of the Royal Society of Canada* 49, no. 3 (June 1955): 57–66.

– "A Century of Plain and Parkland." In *The Prairie West: Historical Readings*, edited by R. Douglas Francis and Howard Palmer, 27–42. Edmonton: Pica Press, 1992.

Neuhaus, Richard John, and Michael Cromartie, eds. *Piety and Politics: Evangelicals and Fundamentalists Confront the World*. Lanham, MD: University Press of America, 1987.

Niebuhr, Richard. *The Kingdom of God in America*. New York: Harper and Row, 1937.

Noll, Mark A. "Common Sense Traditions and American Evangelical Thought." *American Quarterly* 37, no. 2 (Summer 1985): 216–38.

– "Christianity in Canada: Good Books at Last." *Fides et Historia* 23, no. 2 (1991): 80–104.

– *A History of Christianity in the United States and Canada*. Grand Rapids, MI: Wm B. Eerdmans, 1992.

– "The End of Canadian History?" *First Things*, April 1992, 33–4.

– *The Scandal of the Evangelical Mind*. Grand Rapids, MI: Wm B. Eerdmans, 1994.

– "Revolution and the Rise of Evangelical Social Influence in North Atlantic Societies." In *Evangelicalism: Comparative Studies of Popular Protestantism in North America, the British Isles, and Beyond, 1700–1990*, edited by M. Noll, D. Bebbington, and G. Rawlyk, 113–36. New York: Oxford University Press, 1994.

– "Protestant Reasoning about Money and the Economy, 1790–1860: A Preliminary Probe." In *God and Mammon: Protestants, Money and the Market, 1790–1860*, edited by Mark A. Noll, 265–94. New York: Oxford University Press, 2001.

– *The Old Religion in a New World: The History of North American Christianity*. Grand Rapids, MI: Wm B. Eerdmans, 2002.

Pal, Leslie A. "Hands at the Helm? Leadership and Public Policy." In *Prime Ministers and Premiers: Political Leadership and Public Policy in Canada*, edited by Leslie A. Pal and David Taras, 16–26. Scarborough, ON: Prentice Hall, 1988.

– "The Political Executive and Political Leadership in Alberta." In *Government and Politics in Alberta*, edited by Allan Tupper and Roger Gibbins, 1–29. Edmonton: University of Alberta Press, 1992.

Palmer, Howard, and Tamara Palmer. *Alberta: A New History*. Edmonton: Hurtig, 1990.

Paquin, Carole. "How the West Was Won." *Ryerson Review of Journalism*, Spring 1991. Accessed 25 January 2011 via http://www.rrj.ca/m3663/.

Patrick, Margie. "Political Neoconservatism: A Conundrum for Canadian Evangelicals." *Studies in Religion* 38: 3–4, 481–506.

Phillips, Kevin. *American Theocracy*. New York: Viking, 2006.

Pollack, Norman. *The Populist Response to Industrial America*. Cambridge: Harvard University Press, 1962.

Rawlyk, G.A. *Canada Fire: Radical Evangelicalism in British North America*. Montreal and Kingston: McGill-Queen's University Press, 1994.

– *Is Jesus Your Personal Saviour? In Search of Canadian Evangelicalism in the 1990's*. Montreal and Kingston: McGill-Queen's University Press, 1996.

– "Introduction." In *Aspects of the Canadian Evangelical Experience*, edited by G.A. Rawlyk, xiii–xxxv. Montreal and Kingston: McGill-Queen's University Press, 1997.

– ed. *Aspects of the Canadian Evangelical Experience*. Montreal and Kingston: McGill-Queen's University Press, 1997.

Rayside, David. *Queer Inclusions, Continental Divisions: Public Recognition of Sexual Diversity in Canada and the United States*. Toronto: University of Toronto Press, 2008.

Rayside, David, Jerald Sabin, and Paul Thomas. "Faith and Party Politics in Alberta OR 'Danielle, This Is Alberta, not Alabama.'" Paper presented at the Canadian Political Science Association Annual Conference, Edmonton, 12 June 2012. Accessed via http://www.cpsa-acsp.ca/papers-2012/Rayside-Sabin-Thomas.pdf.

Rayside, David, and Clyde Wilcox, eds. *Faith, Politics, and Sexual Diversity in Canada and the United States*. Vancouver: University of British Columbia Press, 2011.

Reimer, Sam. *Evangelicals and the Continental Divide: The Conservative Protestant Subculture in Canada and the United States*. Montreal and Kingston: McGill-Queen's University Press, 2003.

Rennie, Bradford James. *The Rise of Agrarian Democracy: The United Farmers and Farm Women of Alberta, 1909–1921*. Toronto: University of Toronto Press, 2000.

Renouf, Simon. "Chipping Away at Medicare: 'Rome Wasn't Sacked in a Day.'" In *The Trojan Horse: Alberta and the Future of Canada*, edited by T. Harrison and G. Laxer, 223–38. Montreal: Black Rose Books, 1995.

Richards, John, and Larry Pratt. *Prairie Capitalism: Power and Influence in the New West*. Toronto: McClelland and Stewart, 1979.

Rolph, William Kirby. *Henry Wise Wood of Alberta*. Toronto: University of Toronto Press, 1950.

Ryrie, Charles C. *Dispensationalism*. Chicago: Moody Publishers, 2007.

Sandeen, Ernest R. *The Roots of Fundamentalism: British and American Millenarianism 1800–1930*. Chicago: University of Chicago Press, 1970.

Sharp, Paul F. *The Agrarian Revolt in Western Canada*. 2nd ed. Regina: Canada Plains Research Centre, 1997.

Sharpe, Sydney, and Don Braid. *Storming Babylon: Preston Manning and the Rise of the Reform Party*. Toronto: Key Porter Books, 1992.

Sigurdson, Richard. "Preston Manning and the Politics of Postmodernism in Canada." *Canadian Journal of Political Science* 27, no. 2 (June 1994): 249–76.

Simpson, John, and Henry MacLeod. "The Politics of Morality in Canada." In *Religious Movements: Genesis, Exodus, Numbers*, edited by R. Stark, 221–41. New York: Paragon, 1985.

Skinner, Quentin. "Meaning and Understanding in the History of Ideas." In *Meaning and Context: Quentin Skinner and His Critics*, edited by James Tully, 29–67. Princeton, NJ: Princeton University Press, 1988.

Smith, Christian. *Christian America? What Evangelicals Really Want*. Berkeley and Los Angeles: University of California Press, 2000.

Smith, Peter J. "Alberta: A Province Like Any Other?" In *The Provincial State: Politics in Canada's Provinces and Territories*, edited by Keith Brownsey and Michael Howlett, 243–64. Mississauga, ON: Copp Clark Pitman, 1992.

Smith, Timothy L. *Revivalism and Social Reform: American Protestantism on the Eve of the Civil War*. Baltimore, MD: Johns Hopkins University Press, 1980.

Spafford, Duff. "The Left Wing, 1921–1931." In *Politics in Saskatchewan*, edited by N. Ward and D. Spafford, 44–58. Don Mills, ON: Longmans, 1968.

Stackhouse Jr, John G. *Canadian Evangelicalism in the Twentieth Century*. Toronto: University of Toronto Press, 1993.

– "Who Whom? Evangelicalism and Canadian Society." In *Aspects of the Canadian Evangelical Experience*, edited by G.A. Rawlyk, 55–71. Montreal and Kingston: McGill-Queen's University Press, 1997.

Steward, Gillian. "Hips and Knees: The Politics of Private Health Care in Alberta." In *The Return of the Trojan Horse: Alberta and the New World (Dis)Order*, edited by T. Harrison, 52–64. Montreal: Black Rose Books, 2005.

Stewart, David. "Klein's Makeover of the Alberta Conservatives." In *The Trojan Horse: Alberta and the Future of Canada*, edited by Gordon Laxer and Trevor Harrison, 34–46. Montreal: Black Rose Books, 1997.

Stewart, David K., and Keith Archer. *Quasi-Democracy? Parties and Leadership Selection in Alberta*. Vancouver: University of British Columbia Press, 2000.

Stewart, David K., and Anthony M. Sayers. "Leadership Change in a Dominant Party: The Alberta Progressive Conservatives, 2006." *Canadian Political Science Review* 3, no. 4 (December 2009): 85–107.

Stewart, David K., and Anthony M. Sayers. "Albertans' Conservative Beliefs." In *Conservatism in Canada*, edited by J. Farney and D. Rayside, 249–67. Toronto: University of Toronto Press, 2013.

Szasz, Ferenc Morton. *The Divided Mind of Protestant America, 1880–1930.* Tuscaloosa: University of Alabama Press, 1982.

Taras, David, and Allan Tupper. "Politics and Deficits: Alberta's Challenge to the Canadian Political Agenda." In *Canada: The State of the Federation, 1994*, edited by Douglas M. Brown and Janet Hiebert, 61–83. Kingston, ON: Institute of Intergovernmental Relations, 1994.

Taylor, Charles. "Interpretation and the Sciences of Man." In *Philosophy and the Human Science: Philosophical Papers* 2: 15–57. Cambridge: Cambridge University Press, 1985.

– *Sources of the Self.* Cambridge: Harvard University Press, 1989.

– *A Secular Age.* Cambridge: Belknap Press of Harvard University Press, 2007.

Tocqueville, Alexis de. *Democracy in America.* Translated by G. Lawrence and edited by J.P. Mayer. New York: Perennial Classics, 2000.

Tupper, Allan. "Peter Lougheed, 1971–1985." In *Alberta Premiers of the Twentieth Century*, edited by Bradford J. Rennie, 203–28. Regina: Canadian Plains Research Center, 2004.

Tupper, Allan, Larry Pratt, and Ian Urquhart. "The Role of Government." In *Government and Politics in Alberta*, edited by Allan Tupper and Roger Gibbins, 31–66. Edmonton: University of Alberta Press, 1992.

Urquhart, Ian. "Alberta's Land, Water, and Air: Any Reason Not to Despair." In *The Return of the Trojan Horse: Alberta and the New World (Dis)Order*, edited by T. Harrison, 136–55. Montreal: Black Rose Books, 2005.

Van Die, Marguerite. "The Double Vision: Evangelical Piety as Derivative and Indigenous in Victorian English Canada." In *Evangelicalism: Comparative Studies of Popular Protestantism in North America, the British Isles, and Beyond, 1700–1990*, edited by M. Noll, D. Bebbington, and G. Rawlyk, 253–74. New York: Oxford University Press, 1994.

von Heyking, Amy. "Aberhart, Manning and Religion in the Public Schools of Alberta." *Alberta History*, Autumn 2013, 2–11.

Warnock, John W. *Saskatchewan: The Roots of Discontent and Protest.* Montreal: Black Rose Books, 2004.

Weber, Max. *The Protestant Ethic and the Spirit of Capitalism.* Oxford: Oxford University Press, 2010.

Weber, Timothy P. *Living in the Shadow of the Second Coming: American Premillennialism, 1875–1982.* New York: Oxford University Press, 1979.

Bibliography 271

Wesley, Jared J. *Code Politics: Campaigns and Cultures on the Canadian Prairies*. Vancouver: University of British Columbia Press, 2011.

Westfall, William. *Two Worlds: The Protestant Culture of Nineteenth-Century Ontario*. Kingston and Montreal: McGill-Queen's University Press, 1989.

White Jr, R.C., and C.H. Hopkins, eds. *The Social Gospel: Religion and Reform in Changing America*. Philadelphia: Temple University Press, 1976.

Williams, Rhys H., and Susan M. Alexander. "Religious Rhetoric in American Populism: Civil Religion as Movement Ideology." *Journal for the Scientific Study of Religion* 33, no. 1 (1994): 1–15.

Wiseman, Nelson. "An Historical Note on Religion and Parties on the Prairies." *Journal of Canadian Studies* 16, no. 2 (Summer 1981): 109–12.

– "The Pattern of Prairie Politics." *Queen's Quarterly* 88, no. 2 (Summer 1981): 298–315.

– "The Pattern of Prairie Leadership." In *Prime Ministers and Premiers: Political Leadership and Public Policy in Canada*, edited by Leslie A. Pal and David Tara, 178–91. Scarborough: Prentice Hall, 1988.

– *In Search of Canadian Political Culture*. Vancouver: University of British Columbia Press, 2007.

– "Foreword." In *Code Politics: Campaigns and Cultures on the Canadian Prairies*, by Jared J. Wesley. Vancouver: University of British Columbia Press, 2011.

Wood, H.W. "UFA Sunday." *Grain Growers' Guide*, 19 April 1916, 11.

– "U.F.A. President's Address." *Grain Growers' Guide*, 31 January 1917, 7.

– "Observe U.F.A. Sunday, May 27." *Grain Growers' Guide*, 18 April 1917, 12.

– "President Wood Discusses UFA Sunday." *Grain Growers' Guide*, 25 April 1917, 11.

– "The Price of Democracy." *Grain Growers' Guide*, 20 June 1917, 12–13.

– "Political Action in Alberta." *Grain Growers' Guide*, 7 May 1919, 7, 42.

– "Democratic Organization." *Western Independent*, 1 October 1919, 8.

– "The Significance of Democratic Group Organization – Part One." *The UFA*, 1 March 1922, 5.

– "The Significance of Democratic Group Organization – Part Two." *The UFA*, 15 March 1922, 5.

– "The Significance of Democratic Group Organization – Part Three." *The UFA*, 1 April 1922, 5.

– "The Significance of Democratic Group Organization – Part Four." *The UFA*, 15 April 1922, 25.

– "Social Regeneration." Speech given to the Calgary Labour Church, 30 April 1922. Walter Norman and Amelia Turner Smith Fonds, file M-1157-102. Glenbow-Alberta Museum Archives, Calgary.

– "Shall We Go Forward or Turn Back?" *The UFA*, 1 September 1922, 1, 9.

- "Is UFA Cooperation Constructive?" *The UFA*, 15 November 1922, 1, 12.
- "Can We Afford to Abolish the Wheat Board. Part I." *The UFA*, 15 December 1922, 4.
- "Can We Afford to Abolish the Wheat Board. Part II." *The UFA*, 15 January 1923, 4.
- "7th Annual Address of President Wood." *The UFA*, 1 February 1923, 4, 5, 18.
- "The Significance of UFA Sunday." *The UFA*, 15 May 1923, 5.
- "Cooperative Wheat Marketing System Can and Will Be Established." *The UFA*, 3 July 1923, 1, 11.
- "UFA Subunits and Their Relation to the Whole." *The UFA*, 15 August 1924, 8.
- Letter to R.W. Frayne, 17 August 1925. Alberta Wheat Pool Fonds, file M-2369-125. Glenbow-Alberta Museum Archives, Calgary.
- "U.F.A. Political Movement and the Alberta Wheat Pool Greatest Products of the United Farmers of Alberta, Declares President Wood in Annual Address." *The UFA*, 1 February 1927, 12.
- "Compulsory Pooling of Wheat," n.d. Alberta Wheat Pool Fonds, file M-2369-125. Glenbow-Alberta Museum Archives, Calgary.
- "My Religion," n.d. Alberta Wheat Pool Fonds, file M-2369-125. Glenbow-Alberta Museum Archives, Calgary.
- "My Religion." *Winnipeg Free Press*, n.d. Earl G. Cook Fonds, file M-255-47. Glenbow-Alberta Museum Archives, Calgary.
Young, Walter D. *The Anatomy of a Party: The National CCF, 1932–61*. Toronto: University of Toronto Press, 1969.

Index

Aberhart, William: adoption of social credit, 103, 121–33; being thy brother's keeper, 125–7; death of, 63, 104, 113, 123, 133; and dispensationalism, 106–11, 116, 120, 148; electoral success, 60, 64, 93, 98–9; entrance into politics, 61, 103, 121–33; *God's Great Prophecies*, 109–11; on individual freedom, 128–30; on poverty, 126, 129–30; on progressive social polices, 121–3; on purpose of the state, 105; radio program, 60–1, 104, 108; relationship with American evangelicalism, 47, 53, 55; social credit as God's plan, 131–2; on socialism, 124, 127–31; theology, 115–21. *See also* Alberta Social Credit; Christian fundamentalism; dispensationalism; premillennialism
Acts, Book of, 185, 189, 192–3
Adult Interdependent Relationships Act, 168
age of grace, 48, 107, 109, 117, 120, 130, 135. *See also* dispensationalism
Alberta Liberal Party, 177, 200–1, 217. *See also* Decore, Laurence
Alberta New Democratic Party (NDP): support from electorate, 18;

2015 electoral victory, 8, 17–18, 30, 216–17. *See also* Co-operative Commonwealth Federation (CCF)
Alberta Progressive Conservative Party (PC): general electoral success in Alberta, 17–19, 22, 153,158; make-up of caucus, 177–9; populism, 101, 206–9; pro-market rhetoric, 153; spending cuts and economic development, 24, 29, 200–2, 206, 216; social conservatism, 6, 17, 27–8, 159, 165–70, 174–6; 2012 election, 211; 2015 election, 217. *See also* Klein, Ralph; Lougheed, Peter
Alberta Report, 161–4, 178. *See also* Byfield, Ted
Alberta Social Credit: academic work on Social Credit, 15, 103; Christianity, relationship to, 112, 127–30, 132, 149; democracy, approach to, 27, 95, 154–5, 204; electoral success, 17, 22–3, 64, 99, 103, 133; ideology, 18–19, 112, 121–2, 127–30; influence on Alberta political culture, 151–7; Manning's leadership of Social Credit, 133, 142–8; Social Credit populism, 154–7, 213–14; vilification of so-

cialism, 9, 27, 100. *See also* Aberhart, William; Manning, Ernest; social credit economics

Alberta Wheat Pool, 84–6, 93–6. *See also* Wood, Henry Wise

Alberta Wildrose Party, 17, 179, 211, 217. *See also* Hunsperger, Alan; Smith, Danielle

Alline, Henry, 41–2

American Civil War, 44, 46–9, 54–5

American evangelicalism, 33, 36, 40–7, 54–5, 91–2, 105. *See also* Christian fundamentalism

American Great Awakenings: First Great Awakening, 36, 38, 42, 44; Second Great Awakening, 38–40, 44, 92, 120. *See also* revivalism

American immigration (to Alberta), 56–7

American Revolution, 31–5, 38–44, 56, 101

anti-intellectualism, 39, 51

Back to the Bible Hour, 60–1, 108, 136, 161. *See also* Aberhart, William; Calgary Prophetic Bible Institute; Manning, Ernest

Baconianism, 53

Battle of Armageddon, 48–50, 55, 109–10, 135, 183. *See also* dispensationalism

biblical literalism, 35, 46–8, 50–1, 149. *See also* Christian fundamentalism

Bill 44, 169–70, 176. *See also* Human Rights, Citizenship and Multiculturalism Amendment Act

Bland, Salem, 7, 64–7, 86–91, 100, 213. *See also* social gospel; Wesley College

Brownlee, John, 63–4, 98, 104

Byfield, Ted: on abortion, 162; on John Dewey, 162; on ills of contemporary society, 161–2; influence on Alberta politics, 27, 159–61, 164–5, 170, 174, 178–9, 207–8, 214–16; Preston Manning on, 185–6, 203; on same-sex relations, 162–3; on schooling, 162. *See also Alberta Report*; social conservatism

Calgary Prophetic Bible Institute, 15, 109, 115, 133, 148. *See also* Aberhart, William

Calvin, John, 36–7

Calvinist, 36–9, 120

Canadian Alliance, 187. *See also* Reform Party

Canadian Charter of Rights and Freedoms, 160, 165, 167

Carlyle, Thomas, 20

Christian fundamentalism: Aberhart's fundamentalism, 131, 143, 149, 183; academic treatment of fundamentalism, 10, 14–15; origins, 106; premillennialism, 104; relationship to American Protestantism, 39, 50, 53–4, 57, 114, 148. *See also* Aberhart, William; American evangelicalism; dispensationalism

Clark, S.D., 58–61

collectivism, 9, 18, 23, 28–9, 137, 142–52, 188, 202, 206, 209–10, 214–15. *See also* social gospel; socialism

Co-operative Commonwealth Federation (CCF), 3, 18, 23–4, 63, 67–8. *See also* Alberta New Democratic Party; collectivism; Douglas, Tommy; social gospel; socialism

Daniel, Book of, 48, 135. *See also* dispensationalism

Darby, John Nelson, 49–52, 107, 110. *See also* dispensationalism

Darwin, Charles, 46, 51, 54, 67, 92, 106. *See also* evolution

Day, Stockwell, 4, 167–8. *See also* Alberta Progressive Conservative Party

Decore, Laurence, 200–1. *See also* Alberta Liberal Party

Disciples of Christ, 70–2, 92. *See also* Wood, Henry Wise

dispensationalism: of Aberhart, 106–11, 116, 120, 148; American Liberal interpretation, 113–15; definition of, 47–9, 114–15; of Ernest Manning, 134–7, 148; of Preston Manning, 183, 202; in Ontario, 52–5; relationship to American evangelical Protestantism, 47–52, 55. *See also* Aberhart, William; Darby, John Nelson; Manning, Ernest; premillennialism

Doerksen, Victor, 166–8, 174. *See also* Alberta Progressive Conservative Party

Domestic Relations Act, 168

Douglas, Major C.H., 103–4, 112, 122–4, 128, 133, 154–6. *See also* Aberhart, William; social credit economics

Douglas, Tommy, 5, 97, 140, 144. *See also* Co-operative Commonwealth Federation; social gospel; socialism

Edwards, Jonathan, 44

evolution, theory of, 46, 106. *See also* Darwin, Charles

Ezekiel, Book of, 48, 135. *See also* dispensationalism

Farmers Unity League, 97

Finney, Charles, 38. *See also* revivalism

Flanagan, Tom, 64, 180–1, 186–7, 193, 195, 199

Gardiner, Robert, 66, 93, 97–8

Geertz, Clifford, 11

Gladden, Washington, 49, 65, 71–2. *See also* social gospel

Grain Growers' Guide, 64–5, 87

higher criticism, 46, 54, 67, 106

homosexual rights, 17, 27, 159, 165–8, 173–9, 211–12. *See also* social conservatism

Human Rights, Citizenship and Multiculturalism Amendment Act, 169. *See also* Bill 44

Hunsperger, Allan, 211

Irvine, William, 7, 64, 66, 81, 86–91, 96–100. *See also* social gospel; socialism

John, Book of, 114, 117, 182, 198

Klein, Ralph, 18, 22, 24, 29, 101, 143, 152–3, 158–9, 165–8, 176–81, 200–2, 206, 209, 215. *See also* Alberta Progressive Conservative Party

Lipset, S.M., 31–5, 41–3, 56–61

Lougheed, Peter, 18, 22–5, 152–3, 158, 177, 181, 200–2, 217. *See also* Alberta Progressive Conservative Party

Luther, Martin, 35–6

M vs H decision, 168

Macpherson, C.B., 64, 82, 86, 88, 100, 154–5

Mann, W.E., 58–61, 172

Manning, Ernest: dispensationalism of, 134–7, 148; on the free market, 133–45, 149–54; impact on Alberta politics, 151–7; on individual freedom, 128–31, 141–5; on moral responsibility, 146–7; on the National Medicare program, 143–4; premillennialism of, 134–8, 142, 147–8; relationship to Aberhart, 120–3, 133–5; and social conservative philosophy, 105, 141–5; on socialism, 19, 24, 27, 119, 139–42, 149, 151, 213, 216; on Soviet Union/Russia, 135–9. *See also* Aberhart, William; Alberta Social Credit; dispensationalism; premillennialism

Manning, Preston: on Ted Byfield, 185–6, 203; on charity, 192–3; on Christians in politics, 184–5; on Christ's Second Coming, 183; dispensationalism of, 183, 202; on the environment, 194; on God's purpose for a nation, 184–5, 189; on horizontal and vertical dimensions of Christianity, 181–2; impact on Alberta politics, 200–10; on individual freedom, 189–93; leadership of Reform, 4–5, 24, 28, 101, 159, 181,186–8; on MPs voting, 196–7; on Old and New Testaments, 183–4; on populism, 197–208; on populist ministry of Jesus, 198–9; premillennialism, 160, 183, 202; on socialism, 191–3. *See also* populism; Reform Party

Marriage Act, 168

Matthew, Book of, 48, 75–6, 198

Millennium, the, 7, 43–9, 54, 105–19, 131–4, 148. *See also* dispensationalism

Miller, William, 44, 52

Moody, Dwight L., 49, 110, 148

Moody Bible Institute, 53, 108, 148

Morton, Ted, 161, 168, 176–7. *See also* Alberta Progressive Conservative Party

National Energy Program, 161, 200. *See also* western alienation

neo-conservatism, 193

neo-liberalism, 215

Niebuhr, Richard, 43

Noll, Mark, 10, 34, 39, 42, 56

Non-Partisan League (NPL), 63, 81

Notwithstanding Clause, 168

populism: Alberta's populist political culture, 3–8, 18–26, 29, 56, 58, 61, 160, 171, 209–10, 212, 215–17; in America, 44–9, 92; American populist movements, 31, 39, 45, 68–70; Canadian prairie populism, 3, 21, 58; of Henry Wise Wood, 95, 100–1, 105, 213; plebiscitarian populism, 154–5, 207; populist conservatism, 8, 29–30, 100, 105, 210; populist religion, 31, 33, 38–9, 42, 50–1, 54–5, 60–1, 70–2; Preston Manning on, 197–208; Social Credit populism, 154–7, 213–14

postmillennialism: Aberhart's opposition to, 107–8, 119–20, 127, 157; definition of, 44; Henry Wise Wood's postmillennialism, 7, 23, 26–8, 67–8, 72, 78, 89, 93, 101, 104, 112–15, 147, 150, 154, 156, 207, 212; in Ontario, 52–5. *See also* Wood, Henry Wise; social gospel

Prairie Bible Institute, 53, 61, 113, 120

premillennialism: of Aberhart, 7, 9, 23, 27–9, 104–15, 122–7, 131, 148, 150–7, 203, 207; in America, 44, 47–55; definition of, 44; of Ernest Manning, 134–8, 142, 147–8; impact on Alberta politics, 212–15; of Preston Manning, 160, 183, 202. *See also* Aberhart, William; dispensationalism; Manning, Ernest

Prentice, Jim, 217

Priestly, Norman, 97–8

Protestant Reformation, 34, 36

Puritans, 36–7, 40, 43–4, 54

Rapture, the, 33, 48–50, 55, 109–16, 120, 130, 134–8, 145–8, 183, 214. *See also* dispensationalism

Rauschenbusch, Walter, 45, 69. *See also* social gospel

Reagan, Ronald, 160, 201, 209, 215

Redford, Alison, 211, 217

Reform Party: ideology, 17, 191, 205–7; impact on Alberta politics, 201, 209, 216; Preston Manning's leadership of, 4–5, 24, 28, 101, 159, 181, 186–7; religious views of Reform MPs, 3, 158, 164–5; Ted Byfield's support of, 16, 214; views of Reform members, 163–5. *See also* Byfield, Ted; Manning, Preston; social conservatism

Revelation, Book of, 43, 48–9, 76–7, 93, 135

revivalism, 36–9, 42, 44, 51, 54, 92. *See also* American Great Awakenings

same-sex marriage, 163, 165, 168, 173–9, 186, 203. *See also* Alberta progressive Conservative Party; homosexual rights; social conservatism

Samuel, Book of, 146, 196–7

Saskatchewan Grain Growers, 87

School Act, 169

Scofield, Cyrus, 49, 107–10, 148

Scottish philosophy of common sense, 39, 51, 54

Second Coming, 33, 43–55, 59, 107, 116, 183. *See also* dispensationalism

secularization thesis, 10

Sermon on the Mount, 75, 78, 120, 186, 192

Shields, T.T., 53

Skinner, Quentin, 13–15

Smith, Danielle, 211

social conservatism: of Ted Byfield, 161–4, 181, 207, 215–16; contemporary social conservative beliefs in Alberta, 4, 158–60, 179; impact of, on Alberta politics, 28–9, 166, 170, 177–80, 206, 210–12; Ernest Manning's social conservative philosophy, 105, 141–5. *See also* Alberta Progressive Conservative Party; Byfield, Ted; Day, Stockwell; Doerksen, Victor; homosexual rights; Manning, Ernest; same-sex marriage; Taylor, Lorne

social credit economics: Aberhart's interpretation of, 98, 111–13, 118–19, 121–33, 154; Major Douglas's theory of, 103, 122–4; Manning and, 133–4, 140–1, 145, 149; relation of, to Christianity, 128; relation of, to plebiscitarian populism, 154–7. *See also* Aberhart, William; Douglas, Major C.H.; Manning, Ernest; populism: plebiscitarian populism social gospel: Aberhart on, 111–13, 117–22, 126–7, 130; in America, 45–6, 49, 69, 71–2; of Salem Bland, 64–6, 86–7; on Canadian prairies, 4, 7, 9, 27, 55, 64, 96–7; of William Irvine, 86–8; Ernest Manning on, 133, 140, 144, 150; Preston Manning on, 181–2; within United Farmers of Alberta, 66, 86–8, 91; Henry Wise Wood on, 86–8, 95–8. *See also* Bland, Salem; Co-operative Commonwealth Federation; Irvine, William

socialism: William Aberhart on, 124, 127–31; agrarian socialism, 88; Alberta's anti-socialism political culture, 18, 100, 152; Ernest Manning on, 19, 24, 27, 119, 139–42, 149, 151, 213, 216; Preston Manning on, 191–3; social gospel and, 45, 86–8; UFA and, 95, 98; Henry Wise Wood on, 88, 96–7, 151, 209, 213. *See also* Bland, Salem; collectivism; Irvine, William; social gospel

special interests, 205–6

Spencer, Herbert, 20, 46, 72–4, 93

Taylor, Charles: on interpretation and hermeneutics, 12–14; on studying religion, 10

Taylor, Lorne, 166–8, 174. *See also* Alberta Progressive Conservative Party; social conservatism

Thatcher, Margaret, 160, 201, 209, 215

Thessalonians, Book of, 48

Tory conservatism, 8, 100, 149

Tribulation, the, 48, 50, 109–16, 134–8. *See also* dispensationalism

United Farmers of Alberta (UFA):

democracy, 23, 63–5, 83–5, 93–5; divisions within, 9, 66, 97–8; electoral support, 23; entrance into politics, 81–2, 87; influence of religion, 64–6, 75; leadership of Henry Wise Wood, 22, 26–7, 64–8, 93–102; role of William Irvine, 64, 87–8. *See also* Irvine, William; Wood, Henry Wise

United Farmers of Canada (Saskatchewan Section), 96–7

Upper Canada, 42. *See also* Tory conservatism

Vriend, Delwin, 165–9, 175–9

Wesley, John, 39

Wesley College, 64, 86–7. *See also* Bland, Salem

western alienation, 18, 164. See also *Alberta Report*; National Energy Program

Wood, Henry Wise: background of, 68–72; on democracy vs plutocracy, 78–81; on group government, 81–4; impact of, on Alberta politics, 22–3, 90–102; on individual regeneration, 26, 76–8, 85, 89, 96; on natural laws, 72–6; on Parable of the Tares, 76–7; on political parties, 80–3; postmillennialism of, 7, 23, 26–8, 67–8, 72, 78, 89, 93, 101, 104, 112–15, 147, 150, 154, 156, 207, 212; on social gospel, 86–8, 95–8; on social regeneration, 26, 76–8, 82, 85, 90–1, 212; on socialism, 88, 96–7, 151, 209, 213; on wheat marketing, 84–5

Woodsworth, J.S., 7, 66, 86–91, 97. *See also* social gospel